Contents

Figures

Private Pensions versus Social Inclusion?

Non-State Provision for Citizens at Risk in Europe

Edited by

Traute Meyer and Paul Bridgen

University of Southampton, UK

Barbara Riedmüller

Freie Universität Berlin, Germany

Edward Elgar

Cheltenham, UK • Northampton, MA, USA

Published by
Edward Elgar Publishing Limited
Glensanda House
Montpellier Parade
Cheltenham
Glos GL50 1UA
UK

Edward Elgar Publishing, Inc.
William Pratt House
9 Dewey Court
Northampton
Massachusetts 01060
USA

A catalogue record for this book
is available from the British Library

Library of Congress Cataloguing in Publication Data

Private pensions versus social inclusion? : non-state provision for citizens
at risk in Europe / edited by Traute Meyer, Paul Bridgen, Barbara Riedmüller.
    p. cm.
  Includes bibliographical references and index.
  1. Old age pensions—Europe—Case studies. 2. Social
security—Europe—Case studies. 3. Pensions—Europe—Finance—Case studies.
4. Older people—Government policy—Europe— Case studies. 5.
Poor—Europe—Case studies. 6. Public welfare—Europe—Case studies. 7.
Privatization—Europe. I. Meyer, Traute. II. Bridgen, Paul. III.
Riedmüller, Barbara, 1945–
  HD7164.5.P69 2007
  331.25′2094–dc22
                                                                    2007016041

ISBN 978 1 84720 353 3

Printed and bound in Great Britain by MPG Books Ltd, Bodmin, Cornwall

Tables

Contributors

Duco Bannink, PhD, works as a lecturer at the University of Twente, School of Management and Governance, Department of Social Risks and Safety Studies. His teaching and research concerns the implementation and reform of social policies at the EU and national levels. He is currently involved in an EU Sixth Framework research project on Work Organisation and Restructuring in the Knowledge Society (WORKS). Recent publications are *Hidden Change* (with Marcel Hoogenboom 2007) and various articles on pension reform (with Bert de Vroom).

Marek Benio is a researcher and teacher at the Department of Public Economy and Administration, Cracow University of Economics, Poland. His PhD in economics (2002) was devoted to Employees Pension Schemes in Poland. His academic interests encompass social security, labour law and public administration. He has participated in a number of international research projects. Recent publications include: 'Invisible Privatisation of Social Insurance', ZNAE nr 714/2006, Cracow; 'Pension System Reforms in Central and Eastern Europe', in: D. Rosati (ed.): *New Europe*; 'Report on Transformation', Instytut Wschodni Sorry, Krynica (with Jerzy Hausner).

Fabio Bertozzi is scientific collaborator at the social policy unit of the Swiss Graduate School of Public Administration (IDHEAP) in Lausanne, Switzerland. He has taken part in several national and international research projects in the area of comparative welfare state analysis, with a special focus on pensions and labour market policies. His publications include 'Swiss worlds of welfare', *West European Politics*, 1(4) 2004, pp. 20–44 (with K. Armingeon and G. Bonoli) and 'The Swiss welfare state: a changing public–private mix?' (in D. Béland and B. Gran, eds, *Social Policy Puzzles*, Palgrave Macmillan, forthcoming, with F. Gilardi).

Giuliano Bonoli is Professor of Social Policy at the Swiss Graduate School for Public Administration (IDHEAP), Lausanne, Switzerland. He received his PhD at the University of Kent at Canterbury for a study on pension reform in Europe. He has been involved in several national and international research projects on the process of welfare state transformation. His recent key publications include: *The Politics of Pension Reform: Institutions* *and Policy Change in Western Europe*, Cambridge University Press, 2000 and *Ageing and Pension Reform around the World: Evidence from Eleven Countries*, Edward Elgar, 2005 (ed. with Toshimitsu Shinkawa).

Paul Bridgen is a senior lecturer in social policy at the University of Southampton. He was the joint academic coordinator (with Traute Meyer) of the EU 5th Framework project on which this book is based. He has several publications on developments in British pensions policy from the end of the Second World War to the present day. He has also published on ageing and health and social care policy. He is currently working (with Traute Meyer) on a project on occupational pensions in Britain and Germany as part of the Anglo-German Foundation's Creating Sustainable Growth in Europe research initiative.

Bert de Vroom is sociologist and head of the Social Risks and Safety Studies Department, at the University of Twente, the Netherlands. He is and has been involved in various international comparative and national research projects and has published widely on issues such as changing labour markets, welfare state policies, new risks, early retirement and pensions. He has co-ordinated the European COST A13 research group, Ageing and Work. At the moment he is involved in the OECD project on disabilities and transitions, and in the Cinefogo Network of Excellence on the making of European citizenship.

Traute Meyer is a senior lecturer in social policy at the University of Southampton. She has participated in international research projects in the area of pensions, informal and care work. She is the co-editor of the *European Journal of Social Policy*. Publications include: 'Gender arrangements and pension systems in Britain and Germany', *International Journal of Ageing and Later Life* (2006, with B. Pfau-Effinger); 'When do benevolent capitalists change their mind? Explaining the retrenchment of defined-benefit pensions in Britain', *Social Policy and Administration* (2005); and 'Class, gender and chance and the social division of welfare', forthcoming 2008, in *Ageing and Society* (both with P. Bridgen).

Michele Raitano obtained a PhD in economics from University of Rome La Sapienza in 2004. Currently he is a research fellow at Istituto Studi Analisi Economica and the University La Sapienza and collaborates with the Italian government about the pension reform process. His main research topics are welfare state systems, with a special focus on pensions, an area on which he has published many papers. He is a contributing author to the annual *Welfare State Report* (*Rapporto sullo Stato Sociale*) edited by

Professor F.R. Pizzuti and issued by the Department of Public Economy of the University of Rome (La Sapienza) and the Centro Interuniversitario sullo Stato Sociale.

Joanna Ratajczak-Tucholka is a teacher and research assistant at the Department of Labour and Social Policy at Poznan University of Economics in Poland, where she earned her PhD. Her research focuses on social policy and social security, and she is particularly interested in the gender-specific impact of pension systems. Her PhD concentrated on how pension insurance influenced the situation of German and Polish women in old age.

Barbara Riedmüller is professor at the Political Science Department of the Freie Universität Berlin. Her main research focus is the German welfare state, analysed in the context of change in European countries. She carried out research on social policy and social inclusion, and on pension reform in European countries. She has advised high-level German social policy-makers regarding the consequences of German pension reforms for social inclusion.

Michaela Willert received her diploma in sociology from the Freie Universität Berlin. She works as senior research assistant at the Political Science Department of the FU. Her research interest is in comparative welfare state research, particularly pension policy. Moreover she examines trends of Europeanization of social policy.

Abbreviations

AOW	Algemene Ouderdomswet (General Old Age Pensions Law, the Netherlands)
AVS/AHV	Assurance Vieillesse et Survivants – Alters und Hinterlassenenversicherung (old age and survivors' insurance, Switzerland)
BSP	Basic State Pension (UK)
CDU	Christlich Demokratische Union (Christian Democratic Party)
DGB	Deutscher Gewerkschaftsbund
FDC	funded defined contribution
GDP	gross domestic product
IKE	Indywidualne Konta Emerytalne (Individual Pension Accounts, Poland)
LPP/BVG	Prévoyance professionnelle/Berufliche Vorsorge (occupational pension, Switzerland)
NDC	notional defined contribution
NHS	National Health Service (UK)
OECD	Organisation for Economic Co-operation and Development
PAYG	pay-as-you-go
PC/EL	Préstations complémentaires/Ergänzungsleistungen (Supplementary benefits, Switzerland)
PIPs	*piani pensionistici individuali* (personal pensions, Italy)
PPE	Pracownicze Programy Emerytalne (Employees Pension Schemes, Poland)
TFR	*trattamento di fine rapporto* (deferred wages retained by firms, Italy)
WWB	Wet Werk en Bijstand (General Social Assistance)

Acknowledgements

This book is based on the research project Private Pensions and Social Inclusion. This project was funded under the 5th Framework of the European Union, and the authors gratefully acknowledge this support. Research started in January 2003 and the project officially finished in October 2005. During this period, the contributors to this study met regularly to ensure a common methodological framework and to compare results. The country chapters are the outcome of this process. We thank everyone involved for their unwavering commitment to our common aim, to make comparable the simulation results for six countries, despite complexities of the national backgrounds. Moreover, we are very grateful to Karen Anderson and Maria Evandrou for intellectual support during the final stages of this book.

For their contribution to the preparation of the book for publication we would also like to thank Graham Baxendale and Jenny Routledge.

Traute Meyer, Paul Bridgen, University of Southampton
Barbara Riedmüller, Free University of Berlin

PART I

Introduction

1. Private pensions versus social inclusion? Citizens at risk and the new pensions orthodoxy

Paul Bridgen and Traute Meyer

Societal ageing is one of the major challenges facing social policymakers today. For many European countries it is predicted that in the near future there will be more pensioners than people in employment. During the 1990s a consensus amongst Western social policymakers has emerged that welfare states need more private pension provision in order to master this trend (Haverland 2001, pp. 310–11; World Bank 1994). The policy shift that has followed is justified on the basis of concerns about the effect of demographic changes on the sustainability of existing pensions systems and arguments about economic efficiency. A multi-pillar system, many believe (European Commission 2003; World Bank 1994), is better able to cope with the problems created by population ageing, with pre-funded pensions also regarded as superior to pay-as-you-go pensions in terms of rates of return. The basis for this consensus, which some call the 'new pensions orthodoxy' (Müller 1999), has not gone unchallenged (Augusztinovics 2002; Barr 2000) but, nevertheless, a shift away from public provision and an increase in private forms has been the predominant development in the pensions systems of most, if not all, industrialized countries (Bonoli et al. 2000; OECD 2005a; Pedersen 2004; Zaidi et al. 2006).

What do these trends mean for the adequacy of citizens' pensions? Are we about to see pensioner poverty rise after many years in which it has fallen in most industrialized welfare states (Casey and Yamada 2003)? Most European governments believe we are not; they are confident that steps taken towards privatizing national pension regimes have not compromised their aim to maintain social inclusion. This view is bolstered by the European Council and Commission who expressed confidence that public–private regimes are capable of protecting the great majority of citizens from social exclusion:

> Pension systems, through public earnings-related schemes (first pillar), private occupational schemes (second pillar) and individual retirement provision (third

pillar), provide good opportunities for most Europeans to maintain their living standards after retirement – as a result, and in combination with other tax-benefit policies for pensioners, older people, in most Member States, generally achieved a fair, and in some Member States even relatively high, living standard. (European Commission 2003, p. 6; see also European Council 2006)

This position, however entrenched it may be at the present time, is not based on a systematic theoretical and empirical appraisal of the potential of private provision. Despite the almost universal shift towards non-public forms of pensions, and even though European societies seem to have reached a 'point of no return' as far as the likelihood of governmental support for stronger public sectors is concerned, there remain important gaps in our knowledge about the implications of recent policy developments. The view among policymakers and in academia that pension regimes must have private elements to make them financially sustainable is very strong, but it is not clear how successful the joint performance of the different pillars of current regimes actually is with regard to social inclusion, particularly for the protection of citizens without lifelong, full-time employment biographies. It follows from this that there is also a lack of knowledge about what type of 'public–private mixes' best ensure not only financial sustainability but also a retirement free from social exclusion for citizens at risk. It is the aim of this book to address these knowledge gaps.

In the academic realm empirical studies are rare on the distributive implications of the increased use of non-state provision in European pension systems and thus the potential of occupational pensions and private savings to supplement the first pillar (OECD 2005b, p. 9). This is not to say that the field is untouched. Especially in the three countries analysed here with a long legacy of public and private pension provision – the Netherlands, Switzerland and the United Kingdom – knowledge is well established about the general level of public and private sector performance. Research on the Netherlands and Switzerland has demonstrated the general inclusiveness of the public pillar in conjunction with occupational pensions (Chapters 3 and 4), while in Britain academic analyses of pensions have highlighted the high poverty risks generated by the insufficient level of the public pension and the selective nature of occupational schemes (Chapter 2). However given the role non-state provision plays in these three 'veteran' countries, there has been less interest than one might expect in the heterogeneity of non-state provision. Questions that ask what types of arrangements are more or less successful, or which sectors of the economy do better than others for citizens at risk and why, still remain to be answered. Moreover little work has so far been done on the distributive consequences of recent retrenchments in all three countries (Bridgen and Meyer 2005; OFS 2004; van Riel et al. 2003). For obvious reasons, we know even less about private sector performance in the three other countries of our study that have only recently undergone system changes: Germany, Italy and Poland.

Given this deficit regarding individual countries it is not surprising that comparative assessments are even rarer (OECD 2005b; Social Protection Committee 2006; Zaidi et al. 2006). Few cross-national studies analyse pension regimes in terms of their contribution to social inclusion. Instead a substantial proportion of recently published comparative research on pensions or welfare regimes has concentrated on policy transformation and pension politics with much less attention paid to the distributive consequences of these changes (Immergut et al. 2007; Bonoli and Shinkawa 2005; Clark and Whiteside 2003; Rein and Schmähl 2004; Shalev 1996). Where analyses include the impact of such policies on citizens they have tended not to differentiate between private and public pension elements (Johnson and Rake 1998), and are generally based on the use of macro-level data, such as labour market or income figures (Disney and Johnson 2001). The problem with the latter is that such data give no clear sense of the connection between policies and outcomes because they are a product not just of the policy regime in a country but also the economic and social context. Micro-level data are thus essential in the analysis of present policy because they allow a firm connection to be made between the regime and the pension outcomes of individual biographies, and on this basis make it possible to assess the comparative performance of different pension regimes for identical individuals (Johnson and Rake 1998). On this basis one can demonstrate which of the national regimes works best for various types of individual. So far comparative research that utilizes such data to study processes of social exclusion has not generally considered the role of pensions (Aposori and Millar 2005; Barnes et al. 2004; Berthoud and Iacovou 2004; Goodin et al. 1999).

However there are a few pioneering comparative evaluations of the outcomes of public–private pensions regimes based on this type of approach (OECD 2005b; Social Protection Committee 2006). Yet in terms of evaluating the risks of social exclusion they have two important limitations. Firstly they are based on overly simplified biographies of individuals. In particular, the life events encountered by many contemporary citizens and the potential social risks they constitute remain unexplored. Secondly the studies simulate the income of individuals only. The potentially considerable impacts of marriage and divorce on social inclusion after retirement, through divorce payments, derived rights through marriage and through the pooling of resources in one household, are not considered at all.

Put in broad terms, therefore, this book will explore to what extent the widespread confidence that multi-pillar arrangements pose no major problems for levels of social exclusion is justified. We start from the premise that if this confidence were warranted, current pension regimes – public, collective, employer-related and personal – should be able to offer protection not just to citizens with incomes on or above the average, but also to those with working lives characterized by the complexity of typical contemporary social risks. Taking this perspective we examine the performance of six current national pension regimes in Europe for these 'risk biographies', individuals and couples. More specifically, the six country chapters that follow will concentrate on three main questions:

- What is the nature of the public–private mix in each pension regime?
- What pension levels can hypothetical 'risk biographies' on incomes below the average but above the poverty line expect under current conditions,[1] and what is the contribution of the private and the public sector to their pension outcomes?
- How do the policymakers responsible for reform aim to address the main shortcomings of their regimes for 'risk biographies', given that generally a strengthening of the public sector is not considered a viable option?

CONCEPTUAL AND METHODOLOGICAL ISSUES

The research on which this book is based has sought to avoid the main limitations in existing work on this area. Firstly public and private types of insurance were systematically included in the assessment of each of the country regimes in relation to social inclusion. Secondly in establishing the outcomes of these regimes, the research builds on a more realistic range of 'biographies', whose life courses reflect the variety of social risks experienced by individuals in post-industrial societies. This approach raised a number of important conceptual and methodological issues that need to be addressed at this stage.

Public and Private Pensions

Any assessment of the respective role of different types of pension provision in preventing social exclusion in retirement has first to address the debate about the meaning of some basic concepts, such as 'private pensions' and 'privatization'. Despite their prominence in political and academic debates, these remain shrouded by a good deal of ambiguity with important implications for their operationalization in the analysis of social policy change. For many economists and the World Bank, 'private' equals 'pre-funded' systems, and they see a superiority of this form over pay-as-you-go programmes in terms of financial sustainability. In the broader academic debate, a dichotomous public–private typology has often been used to categorize pensions,[2] with debate hinging on where to draw the line between public and private (for example Behrendt 2000, p. 26; Esping-Andersen 1990, p. 91; Pedersen 2004). On the basis of this dichotomizing approach 'privatization' involves a simple shift from the public side to the private side.

While this approach has its merits, there is a growing recognition that restrictive sectoral definitions of pension type unnecessarily limit or simplify the meaning of 'privatization' and hinder our understanding of the distributive consequences of pension regime design (Drakeford 2000; Hyde et al. 2003, pp. 189–90; Rein and Wadensjö 1997; Shalev 1996). In all countries studied in this book, pension entitlements are the outcome of complex interaction regarding regulation, funding and administration, and therefore the arrangements on which they are based defy a clear-cut public–private labelling (Leisering 2003). It is misleading to speak for example of the success of the 'private' Swiss or Dutch second pillar in terms of social inclusion, if the substantial role the state as regulator played for such success is neglected. For this reason, this book heeds the call for a 'more sophisticated approach' (Burchardt 1997, p. 2; Hyde et al. 2003; van Gunsteren and Rein 1985, p. 230) to the categorization of public and private welfare provision; one that recognizes the existence of a wide variety of instruments that involve different forms of public–private interaction. Thus rather than categorizing pension regimes as either 'public' or 'private', we suggest there is a continuum of regimes all of which mix in various ways pensions with public and private aspects (see below).

This also means that we understand 'privatization' not merely as a shift from 'public' to 'private' or unfunded to funded schemes; rather privatization is any process whereby the state's role in pension provision and regulation is reduced and the responsibility of a variety of other societal actors – employers, insurers, trade unions and individual citizens – for retirement provision is either passively or actively increased (Bonoli et al. 2000). On this basis our aim is to determine not whether 'public' regimes 'work' better than 'private' regimes but rather which combinations of public and private engagement in pensions are most consistent with social inclusion.

Constructing 'Risk Biographies'

To help us make this assessment we microsimulated the pension outcomes of a range of 'risk biographies'. We suggested above that a problem with existing assessments of pension regime performance on this basis was the use of unrealistically simple, standardized biographies for establishing outcomes. Thus in its study, the OECD only examines the 'pension entitlements of a worker who enters the system today and retires after a full career' (OECD 2005b, p. 40). Similarly the European Commission's Social Protection Committee selects for calculation three full-time, lifelong workers and one variant of a broken career, defined as a person with an employment biography of 30 full-time years, split in two phases by ten years outside the labour market (Social Protection Committee 2006, pp. 7–10).[3] While the latter approach incorporates to some extent care responsibility as a risk, the full-time, lifelong worker remains the centre of attention for both studies. Thus they do not, or to a limited extent only, consider the complex rules which determine pension rights across all pillars in case of life events such as care responsibilities, divorce, disability, unemployment, training, early retirement, change of employer or migration. In contrast the hypothetical individuals presented in this book are modelled according to the complexity of real people's lives. This implies that their wages oscillate throughout their lives, that employment interruptions may happen more than once, and for reasons other than childcare alone, for example because of unemployment, further training, an industrial accident, or because a person migrates from another country or changes employers. Above all, life's complexity stems from the fact that people have relationships with each other. All of our constructed biographies, bar one, are married to each other and either live in one household with their spouse when they start drawing their pension, or they retire as divorcees, or both. The following chapters show that different marital matches, and rematches, have a significant impact on an individual's chances of escaping social exclusion.

More specifically all country studies simulate pension entitlements for nine identical, hypothetical men and women and for variations of these. We call our types 'risk biographies' because they were created on the basis that during their adult lives each individual would experience a range of the social risks just discussed. Because of these risks their wages oscillate (see Appendix 1.1 for details), and their average yearly lifetime incomes are generally not much below 40 per cent of the average wage, our social inclusion line, and not much above the average (Table 1.1). All of these individuals started their working lives in 2003 and will retire in 2049, unless they retire early. All country teams thus worked with an identical set of hypothetical men, women and couples on the same wages in relation to the national average.

The following overview of our typology illustrates our types in detail (see also Figure 1.1 and Appendix 1.1).

Our typology consists of three women and five men, who are married to each other. Some remain married until retirement, others divorce and remarry and some stay single after separation. This made it possible to include in the simulations derived rights through marriage and divorce payments, and to assess the effect of combined household income on social

Table 1.1   A typology of risk biographies

Type of biography and risks explored	Qualification level	Years of employment	Full-time years	Lifetime wage % of average	Type of employer	Marriage status	Husband/ wife	Number of children
1) The mother and unqualified part-time worker in the retail sector								
1a) divorces (23–32), remarries (35) and retires early	low	39	6	39%	2 large companies	twice married	bio 4a or 5b	2
1b) divorces (23–32), changes to full-time work after child-rearing at 40	low	42	31	47%	2 large companies	divorced	bio 4a or 5b	2
1c) stays married (from 23) and changes to full-time work at 40	low	42	31	47%	2 large companies	once married	bio 4/b or 5a/c	2
2) The mother and qualified part-time worker in the welfare sector								
2a) divorces (25–35), remarries (37) and retires early	medium	37	6	42%	1 large company	twice married	bio 8b	2
2b) divorces (25–35), changes to full-time work after child-rearing at 42	medium	41	29	54%	1 large company	once married	bio 8b	2

9

Table 1.1 (continued)

Type of biography and risks explored	Qualification level	Years of employment	Full-time years	Lifetime wage % of average	Type of employer	Marriage status	Husband/ wife	Number of children
2c) stays married (from 25), changes type of employer and retires early	medium	37	6	42%	1 large, 1 small company	once married	bio 8a	2
3) The married carer and informal worker								
3a) stays married (from 23) and is dependent on partner because of care obligations incl. elderly care	low	40	40	22%	1 small, 1 family business (< 5)	once married	bio 4b, 5a/c or 6a	3
3b) divorces (23–45), is dependent on partner because of care obligations incl. elderly care	low	38	27	37%	1 small, 1 family business (< 5), 1 large food manufacturer	once married, divorced	bio 5b or 6b	2
4) The unqualified worker in the car industry								
4a) divorces (23–32), remarries (35), short spell of unemployment	low	46	46	79%	2 large companies	twice married	bio 1a	2

4b) stays married (from 23), changes employer and retires early, after longer spell of unemployment	low	37	37	65%	2 large companies, 1 small business (<5)	once married	bio 1c or 3a	2

5) The intermittent worker in the construction industry

5a) stays married (from 23), employment gaps, change of employer type, further training	medium	41	41	89%	1 medium, 1 small (<5) company, self-employed	once married	bio 1c or 3a	2/3
5b) divorces (23–32), employment gaps, change of employer type, further training	medium	41	41	89%	1 medium, 1 small (<5) company, self-employed	divorced	bio 1a or 3b	2
5c) stays married (from 23), employment gaps, change of employer type, self-employment, disabled at the age of 55	medium	31	31	62%	1 medium, 1 small (<5) company, self-employed	once married	bio 1c or 3a	2/3

Table 1.1 (continued)

Type of biography and risks explored	Qualification level	Years of employment	Full-time years	Lifetime wage % of average	Type of employer	Marriage status	Husband/ wife	Number of children
6) The small business entrepreneur								
6a) stays married (from 23)	medium	46	46	84%	1 small (<5) business of which he becomes owner	once married	bio 3a	3
6b) divorces (23–45)	medium	46	46	84%	1 small (<5) business of which he becomes owner	divorced	bio 3b	3
7) The divorced provider in the chemical industry								
divorced (23–32; 35–52), needed to explore impact of divorce on men	medium	45	45	113%	2 large companies	divorced twice from 1a, once from 3b	bio 1a or 3b	2
8) The middle manager in financial services								
8a) stays married (from 25), retires early	medium	41	41	131%	2 large companies	married	bio 2c	2
8b) divorces (25–35), retires early	medium	41	41	131%	2 large companies	divorced	bio 2a/2b	2

| 9) The incomplete resident in the electrical industry | low | 29 | 29 | 49% | 2 large companies | Single | n/a | 0 |

Note: The individual pension for 7 is calculated using types 1a and 3b as the biographical template for his two marriages and divorces. However, as individual biographies 1a and 3b only divorce once. The individual pension for 8b is calculated on the basis that he is single. However bio 8b is also used as the biographical template for the second marriage of bio2a. Hence the couple 2a and 8b.

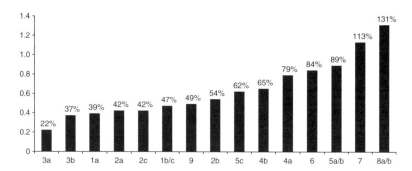

*Figure 1.1   Lifetime wage as percentage of average wages of risk
              biographies*

inclusion. In addition we included one individual who never married. Our
female types include one unqualified and one medium-qualified worker and
mother, and one traditional housewife and carer.

The mother and unqualified part-time worker in the retail sector (bio 1)
allows us to explore the impact of a combination of risks: the instability of
marriage, a fairly low lifetime income because of low qualifications and
part-time work, as well as employment gaps related to care responsibilities
for children. The variations in this category have different periods of part-
time and full-time work. They are married to an unqualified worker (bio 4)
or a worker with an intermittent career (bio 5). Two of these marriages end
in divorce.

The risk profile of our second type, the mother and qualified part-time
worker in the welfare sector (bio 2), also enables us to assess the role of an
employment career that changes to meet the needs of children; two of
our variants work full-time only for a few years, one much longer. All are
married, but one divorces and remarries. The main difference from the first
type is that the level of qualification of the women in this category is higher;
they therefore have higher wages. The same applies to their husbands,
middle managers in the financial services (bio 8).

The third type, the married carer and informal worker (bio 3), has an
independent income below 40 per cent of the average; for protection she
relies mostly on her husband, who for part of his working life owns a small
business (bio 5 or 6). Her level of formal qualification is low, and even
though she works no less than the first two types, she does so mainly as an
informal worker in a small family business. One variant has three children,
the other has only two. The latter divorces and for the last spell of her
working life she is single and employed by a large food manufacturer. Both
leave the labour force at the age of 57 to care for their elderly mother.

Our types 4 to 8 reflect male biographies. They too were chosen to represent low and medium levels of qualification, and where the women experience care-related employment gaps, some of the men are temporarily out of paid work because of unemployment, illness or training. Notwithstanding this gendered ascription, the results for our 'men' and 'women' are applicable to all individuals whose biographies have similar features, irrespective of their gender.

With our fourth type, the unqualified worker in the car industry (bio 4), we aimed to capture the lives of Fordist workers and breadwinners. His level of qualification is low, yet the first variant has a lifelong career as a manual worker in large companies, interrupted only by one year of unemployment between two employers. The second variant is more at risk. He was made redundant in his late thirties, and moved to a small company after that. In his late fifties he was redundant again and he retired early, after five years of unemployment. Both variants are married to retail workers (bio 1), and one has to share pension rights with his divorced spouse.

Our fifth type, the intermittent worker in the construction industry (bio 5), has a medium-level qualification and therefore his wage is higher than the previous type's. His main social risk stems from the fact that he works for three types of smaller company, including his own as a self-employed worker. Moreover, the third variant becomes disabled after an accident in his mid-fifties, which ends his employment career. All are married to either the unqualified worker (bio 1) or the carer (bio 3).

The small business entrepreneur is our sixth type (bio 6). This person like the previous one has a medium level of qualification, yet his lifetime income is lower because for most of his life he runs his own small business. He is married to the carer (bio 3).

Type 7, the divorced provider in the chemical industry (bio 7), was constructed with the main aim of exploring the extent to which pension-sharing obligations through divorce would increase his social exclusion risk. He is married to the unqualified worker (bio 1) or the carer (bio 3). His employment career is long and uninterrupted, and his income is above the average.

The middle manager in financial services has an even higher salary than the divorced provider and an uninterrupted employment career; we therefore did not expect him to be at risk. We included him as an eighth type for two reasons.

Firstly, this individual illustrates how the better-off do in the national regimes. Secondly, based on theories of social distance (Bottero 2004), we assumed that our qualified part-time worker and mother (bio 2) would marry a partner with a matching level of qualification. In order to calculate her household income, as a married and as a divorced pensioner, we had to include him.

Our final type is the incomplete resident. This individual has a full-time employment career on half the average lifetime wages, but this is shortened because she or he came to the respective country in their mid-thirties.

SIMULATING PENSION ENTITLEMENTS

This book assesses pension income from the public pillar, from occupational and from personal pension schemes (detailed assumptions in Appendix 1.2). To this end, the authors of each country study determined what type of public and collective private pension each individual would typically have access to under their national regime.

This was easiest for the public pillar because the conditions for rights accrual are transparent and systematic for all citizens, although it is important to note that we excluded means-tested benefits from the simulations, even those designed specifically for retired citizens. This was for two reasons. On philosophical grounds the group accepted Townsend's argument that means testing by itself can operate as an exclusionary process because it risks stigmatizing those it seeks to assist (Townsend 1979, pp. 879–82). Thus we wanted to focus on non-stigmatizing benefits because they are more consistent with social inclusion. The second reason is that where means testing has been applied it has in most cases encountered problems of take-up, such that significant proportions of those entitled to a particular income level do not actually receive it (see for example Evandrou and Falkingham 2005).

Decisions on non-state provision were more difficult, given that the degree of compulsion varies significantly. In Switzerland coverage by occupational schemes is compulsory and it is quasi-compulsory in the Netherlands. However in Britain, Germany, Italy and Poland occupational schemes are voluntary and coverage is patchier as a result. Given this difficulty we could have included the compulsory part of the pension regime exclusively, which was largely the approach taken by the authors of the study by the OECD (2005b) discussed above. The advantage of this perspective is that only pensions guaranteed to citizens are assessed. However this inevitably means the existing potential of private pensions in countries with voluntarist regimes to contribute to social inclusion would remain unexplored, despite their significance in many cases. Thus we would have had to exclude the very established British and the growing German occupational sector. Given that our study is focused precisely on the potential of the private sector to offer protection, we instead chose to include second pillar schemes in those cases where our individuals would have a prospect to have access to them, while making sure that we also explained what would happen if they did not. As a consequence of this methodological choice the reader will find simulations for second pillar coverage for Germany and Britain, but not for Italy, where occupational pensions are still very underdeveloped.

On this basis, country teams calculated for all risk biographies their individual projected gross pension level for 2050, at first only differentiated by public pensions and by collective plans offered through employers. Where individuals divorce, we calculated entitlements according to pension-sharing legislation in each country; in practice this often means that one of the ex-spouses receives entitlements from the other while the other has to share them.

To assess the social inclusiveness of these outcomes, we compare the hypothetical pension of every individual, irrespective of marriage status, with three gradually increasing social inclusion thresholds. The first one measures poverty only. It captures the amount of means-tested social assistance retired citizens with inadequate pension rights would be entitled to claim in each country. This amount also shows what each society has determined as necessary minimum threshold below which no person should fall. National generosity in this regard differs quite strongly between our countries, as the relationship of social assistance and national wage levels show. In four of our cases the poverty line is much lower than 40 per cent of the average wage, a measure that we use as the social inclusion line. Social assistance for the elderly is only near the social inclusion line in Switzerland and, to a slightly lesser extent, in the Netherlands. Finally we use 50 per cent of average wages as a comfortable social inclusion line (see Appendix 1.2 for further explanations). The results give an overview of the combined performance of public pensions and collective plans offered through employers in each country for individual citizens at risk.

Personal savings calculations are added for those individuals not protected sufficiently by public and employer-related schemes. This may be because entitlements are too low, or because citizens do not have access to public or occupational schemes in the first place, such as the self-employed and some carers.

The calculations just described evaluate the inclusiveness of each national regime for individuals at risk. To assess the position of the 11 retired couples we compare their joint pension income with the same gradually increasing inclusion thresholds, adjusted for couples (see Appendix 1.2).

A JUSTIFICATION OF OUR APPROACH

So far we have made an argument for simulating entitlements of complex rather than simplified biographies, because they are closer to the lives people lead, and they are more likely to show where the weaknesses of public and private pension regimes are with regard to social inclusion. This general justification does not however explain how exactly we arrived at the types summarized above. More specifically it needs to be explained why we did not develop types that closely represent 'real lives', and opted instead for a looser construction of hypothetical people.

The first answer to this question is that using risk profiles representative of 'real lives' would have been impossible. To evaluate the inclusiveness of present pension regimes, and thus of recent reforms – this study's main aim – can only be done by simulating future entitlements, and this involves making assumptions about how people's lives will develop. If we had wanted to measure the pension entitlements of real people, we would have had to conduct an analysis of the employment histories of individuals nearing retirement. Yet because pension systems undergo constant change, such an analysis would only partially show the impact of the present regime, and in addition 'echoes of decisions taken at the age of 18 as well as the influence of policies long since reformed' (Rake 1999, p. 223). Given this inevitable effect, the only way to avoid evaluating the impact of cumulative reforms is to freeze programmes and regulations at a set point in time, and to model the consequences (Johnson and Rake 1998, pp. 265–6; Moffit 1999; OECD 2005a, pp. 40–6).

However why did we not attempt to ground our types more firmly in detailed data about the life courses of younger citizens, to make the typology more representative, rather than illustrative? The development of biographies representative of a range of individuals is very difficult, even for one country, not least because of the 'data hunger' of sophisticated microsimulation (Johnson and Rake 1998, pp. 265–6). This appetite would have been voracious in a large comparative project. However even if this problem could have been overcome it would have left us with six national typologies. These would have been useful for national evaluations of the inclusiveness of each system from the perspective of typical British, Dutch, German, Italian, Polish and Swiss citizens, but the comparative aims of the project would have been undermined (Johnson and Rake 1998, pp. 265–6). To gauge the comparative performance of the six regimes it was vital to use a single typology of individuals for all countries.

Based on these considerations our types could not be too specifically grounded in national data. Instead the risks we selected for our individuals had to be typical for the broad social and economic trends in post-industrial societies: the transformation of the 'male breadwinner model', expressed by an increase in mothers' employment, mostly on a part-time basis, and particularly in the expanding service sector, which is apparent also through a destabilization of marriage as expressed by rising divorce rates and an increasing rate of births outside marriage and single parents. Moreover we observe a demise of the 'standard worker' with citizens experiencing greater flexibility in the workplace. This increases the need for further training, makes interrupted employment careers more likely and pushes increasing numbers of people towards self-employment. Last but not least, with more flexible borders citizens who move into countries from outside Europe may find themselves with incomplete social rights. These trends are taken from academic analyses (see Armingeon and Bonoli 2006; Castles 2003; Hantrais 1999; Pierson 2001). In addition they reflect many policymakers' expectations of the future, as the following quote from the European Commission's joint report on social protection and social inclusion illustrates:

> Demographic changes are compounded by wider changes in cultural values, social relationships, the organisation of families and the nature of work . . . The increased feminisation of the labour force is reflected in new social demands (for example, for care facilities for children, elderly and dependent people) and in a new basis for the division of responsibilities within the household. Notable changes in family structures have taken place, in terms both of a reduction of household sizes and increasing diversity – driven by lower rates of partnership formation and higher rates of dissolution. As a consequence family links are weakening and, in cases of need, more people have to rely on alternative forms of support. Finally the working environment has become far more volatile and heterogeneous. (European Commission 2005a, p. 4)

Some manifestation of these trends is evident in all six countries, yet they also differ. Thus each country has seen an 'increased feminisation of the labour force', although in 2005 employment rates varied substantially. Table 1.2 shows that at least 60 per cent of adult women are in paid work, mostly in the service sector, in Switzerland, the United Kingdom, the Netherlands and Germany. For Dutch and Swiss women this is normally part-time work, while the majority of British and German female employees work full-time. In contrast non-employment is the norm in Italy and Poland, where less than half of adult women have a job, and where self-employment is more important than in the other countries.

Full-time adult carers continue to play a role in all countries too, and high labour force participation of women in a country does not rule out their existence, just as low female economic activity does not automatically increase their number. It is true that the share of women between 25 and 54 who stay outside the labour force in order to look after their families is highest in Italy, where labour force participation is lowest, but it is not much lower in Switzerland where female employment is highest and rather low in Poland, despite high inactivity.

These figures thus show a diverse country spectrum, but at the same time they demonstrate that each of our female biographies has current relevance

Table 1.2   Employment and inactivity in the six countries

	UK	NL	CH	GER	IT	PL
Women						
Employment rates, 2005	65.9	66.4	70.4	59.6	45.3	46.8
Part-time (%) of female employment, 2005	43.1	75.3	58.8	44.3	25.7	14.2
Employment in services (%) of female employment, 2004	91.6	90.1	85.1	84.3	79.6	65.2*
Employment in industry (%) of female employment, 2004	7.9	7.8*	12.1	14.1	17	16.5*
Self-employment (%) of female employment, 2004	7.6	11.2	8	7.9	20	26.1
Average exit age from the labour force, 2005**	61	61	62	61	61	56
Inactivity rates (25–54 yrs) because of personal/family responsibilities, 2004	13	9	15	12	17	10
Men						
Employment rates, 2005	77.6	79.9	83.9	71.2	69.9	58.9
Part-time (%) of male employment, 2005	10.6	22.6	11.8	7.7	4.5	7.7
Employment in services (%) of male employment, 2004	72	68	62.7	60.2	58	44.2*
Employment in industry (%) of male employment, 2004	26.7	27.7*	32.7	37	36.9	35.7*
Self-employment (%) of male employment, 2004	17.2	16.4	10.6	13.3	28.6	31.4
Average exit age of men from the labour force, 2005**	63	61	64	61	61	60
Inactivity rates (25–54 yrs) because of personal/family responsibilities, 2004	0	0	0	0	0	0

Notes:
*   Figures for 2003
** Exit age for Italy, Switzerland: 2003

Sources: http://epp.eurostat.cec.eu.int; European Commission (2005b); CH: Swiss Federal Statistical Office (2005a)

for each of our countries. By the same token with regard to men despite some variation – a high rate of part-time work in the Netherlands and a very low rate in Italy, very low participation rates in Poland and very high in Switzerland, as well as very high levels of self-employment in Poland and Italy – the male norm, reflected by our typology, is still to be a full-time worker in either the service or the manufacturing sector who does not take time off to take on family responsibilities.

The majority of our hypothetical individuals retire at the age of 65; early retirement, at 60, is an exception. Those with lower qualification levels enter the labour market at 18, those with medium-level qualifications at 20. While these assumptions do not reflect the decisions of some governments to raise the pension age above 65, they are higher than the current real average exit age from the labour force in all our countries. The protracted nature of the process of raising the real retirement age is illustrated by the fact that the EU-wide target set by the Stockholm European Council in 2001 to raise employment rates of older citizens between 55 and 64 by at least 50 per cent by 2010 so far has only been met by Britain (56 per cent) and Switzerland (65 per cent) and that the Commission is concerned the target will not be reached by many unless countries increase their efforts (European Commission 2005a, pp. 10, 34; European Commission 2006, pp. 28–9; OECD 2005a).

The growing importance of more 'volatile' working environments is captured in our typology by periods of unemployment and further training, which several of our male types encounter. This reflects current trends; Table 1.3 shows that there is a chance either event will be experienced in any of our countries, yet the likelihood varies quite a lot. Lifelong education is significant in Switzerland, Britain and the Netherlands, while unemployment is low. Conversely unemployment is very high in Poland and substantial in Germany and Italy, while adults in these three countries have fewer opportunities to be in training programmes. It is noticeable that female unemployment rates are higher than those of men in all countries but Britain. This increased social risk that women bear is reflected in our typology by the greater employment gaps our hypothetical women are subjected to.

An indicator for the occurrence of our ninth type, the incomplete resident, is also included in Table 1.3. It shows that the highest share of non-nationals of the population by far live in Switzerland and the lowest in Poland. These figures include non-nationals from EU countries whose pension rights are protected by EU legislation, but more differentiated data is not available.

Finally divorce plays an important role for our hypothetical biographies. This is reflected by real current divorce figures shown in Table 1.4. Again they vary a lot; with marriage more stable in Italy and Poland and most

Table 1.3   Employment interruptions in the six countries

	UK	NL	CH	GER	IT	PL
Men						
% of 25–64-year-olds in education and training, 2004	24	17	30	8	6	5
% of 25-year-olds and over unemployed, 2005	3.5	3.8	3.2	7.8	4.8	13.8
Women						
% of 25–64-year-olds in education and training, 2004	34	18	27	7	7	6
% of 25-year-olds and over unemployed, 2005	3	4.4	4.5	9.6	8.4	16.6
Non-nationals of national population around 2004	4.7	4.3	20	8.9	3.4	1.8

Sources: http://epp.eurostat.cec.eu.int; CH: Swiss Federal Statistical Office (2005b)

Table 1.4   Divorce in the six countries

Divorces per 100 marriages	1985	1995	2002
United Kingdom	44.6	52.8	50.5
Netherlands	41.1	41.9	39.5
Switzerland	29.4	38.5	40.8
Germany	36.1	39.4	52.1
Italy	5.2	9.3	15.4
Poland	18.4	18.4	23.7

Source: Eurostat_ http://epp.eurostat.cec.eu, UK figures for 2002 are from 2000

fragile in Germany and the UK, but the figures show that in all countries, except for the Netherlands, divorce has been on the rise over the last 20 years.

The discussion above shows that all types resonate with the situation in the six countries. Complete mismatches do not exist, but it is important to keep in mind that certain life course events are currently less likely in some countries than in others. This issue will be further discussed as it arises in the individual country case-studies. With regard to the book's main questions the country characterizations indicate that, were the conditions of 2004/05 to continue into the future, Poland, Italy and Germany would probably face greater problems insuring their populations against social risks in retirement than Switzerland, the Netherlands and the United Kingdom, simply because a larger share of their populations – women and men – are economically inactive or unemployed. The country studies will show whether and to what extent this is the case and what type of systems are in place to deal with these trends.

WHY THESE SIX COUNTRIES?

Private Pension Veterans

The countries included in this book allow us to study the relationship between private pensions and social inclusion against diverse institutional backgrounds. They can be grouped according to either their 'Beveridgean' or 'Bismarckian' legacies, which determined whether they developed multi-pillar systems fairly early during the second half of the twentieth century or whether they were dominated by one public programme (Bonoli 2003, p. 400).

The Swiss, British and Dutch pension systems have historically been based on a first, revenue-funded part, paid as flat rate benefit, which covers at most basic needs (Bonoli 2003, pp. 400–402). However despite this structural similarity there are important differences between the first pillar arrangements in each country. In Switzerland a public pay-as-you-go (PAYG) pension to meet basic needs was introduced in 1946 and was moderately earnings-related, and universal. In contrast the Dutch public PAYG pension, introduced in 1959, is a basic flat rate benefit for all seniors based on residence. The British Basic State Pension, introduced in 1946, is different again: it is flat rate like the Dutch pension but like Swiss state provision is social insurance based. It has never risen above subsistence level (Hannah 1986, pp. 54, 59), although in 1975 a serious attempt was made to create a more inclusive state pension through the introduction of the State Earnings Related Pension Scheme.[4] In the changed political climate of the 1980s this system was cut down again before it could mature, but a new State Second Pension is still likely to provide an important supplementary income to future retirees.

Partly because of the relatively low level of state provision in each country, substantial occupational pension systems have developed, initially on a voluntary basis. Because the level of the first pillar was regarded as insufficient by higher earners, interest grew in pensions above this level. This voluntary development of occupational pension is also likely to have been the result of employers, particularly the larger and thus richer ones, using occupational provision as a tool to ensure the recruitment and retention of workers, particularly skilled ones, the early retirement of older surplus labour, and to manage the relationship with trade unions (Clark et al. 2007, p. 19; Green et al. 1984; Hannah 1986, pp. 18–30; Hart 1984, pp. 45, 50–51; Hawkesworth 1977; Mares 2001, pp. 195–6; Myles and Pierson 2001; Rein 1996, p. 40; Sass 1997, pp. 18–37; Whiteside 2003, p. 33, 2006). In each country government intervention has further encouraged occupational provision through fiscal incentives (Hannah 1986, p. 38; Sinfield 2000, p. 141; Titmuss 1958).[5]

However although the early development of occupational pension systems in all of our veteran countries was initially voluntary they now differ considerably regarding the degree of compulsion imposed on employers and employees. In Switzerland, in 1985, occupational pensions became compulsory for employees above a fixed earnings threshold, with a minimum standard set for benefits. This reform followed strong pressure from left-wing parties expressed through the Swiss federal referendum system. They wanted the income replacement benefits of occupational pensions to be distributed on a more universal basis (Bonoli 2004). However the system does not cover the self-employed and is less inclusive with regard to women, because they are more likely to fall below the earnings threshold (Bonoli 2007; Chapter 4).

In the Netherlands, moves towards more general coverage of occupational provision occurred much earlier as part of broader corporatist arrangements (Whiteside 2006). Legislation enacted in 1947 prescribed that, where the Ministry of Social Affairs adjudged it appropriate, collective agreements about pensions in one company had a binding effect for the respective sector as a whole. This became particularly relevant during the 1980s and 1990s when the second Dutch pillar expanded greatly, taking pressure off the public system (see also Clark and Whiteside 2003, p. 145; Haverland 2001, pp. 309, 314). Yet while the state sets the regulatory framework for occupational schemes, the specific conditions of sector-wide pension plans are negotiated between employers and trade unions (Anderson 2007; van Riel et al. 2003, p. 67). As in Switzerland the system generally does not cover the self-employed but it is more open for part-time workers than the Swiss and therefore more inclusive overall. In 2005 it covered more than 90 per cent of the workforce (OECD 2005a, p. 152).

The British system is the most voluntarist regime in this group (Pierson 1994, pp. 53–73). Coverage has always been selective because occupational pension provision is not compulsory (Clark 2000). It has been provided mainly, but not exclusively, for those with full-time earnings, stable employment careers, likely to work in private companies or the public sector (Baldwin 1990, pp. 239–40, 243; GAD 2003, p. 18; Ginn 2003, pp. 13–14; Meyer and Bridgen forthcoming 2008) and has traditionally excluded those in small businesses, or with less stable contracts. Until the 1990s part-time workers, too, were much more likely not to be members (Groves 1983, p. 40; Groves 1987, pp. 209, 211), but as in the Netherlands, this has begun to change through improved equal pay and sex discrimination legislation (Mazey 1998, pp. 139–44).

Thus Switzerland, the Netherlands and the United Kingdom all have a mature occupational pension system in addition to the first pillar, yet the differences are also significant. Firstly while the Swiss and the Dutch state pensions aimed to prevent poverty, the British has been below the poverty line, creating greater dependency on other sources of income, such as occupational or private provision or other means-tested benefits. Secondly coverage through occupational schemes in the Netherlands and Switzerland has been much higher than in Britain, because of a greater degree of compulsion in the former two countries which nevertheless allowed for both regimes to exclude the self-employed. Swiss and Dutch second pillars are enforced through legislation, with the difference that Swiss businesses have to meet minimum standards, which they can exceed if they wish, while Dutch employers and trade unions have greater scope to negotiate scheme details. Britain in contrast allows us to study the impact of an essentially voluntarist regime.

Private Pension Newcomers

Until the late 1990s Germany, Italy and Poland fitted into the classic Bismarckian mould. After extending their scope and generosity from the late 1950s, by the end of the 1960s state-regulated and compulsory pay-as-you-go pension systems existed for all employed citizens in the three countries. These were largely funded through social insurance contributions from employers and employees in Germany and Italy, and through taxes in Poland. Pension entitlements were dependent on length of employment career and were designed to preserve pre-retirement standards of life for full-time workers, although the link between earnings and benefits in Poland and Italy was not always transparent with some workers privileged over others, for example Polish miners and steelworkers. In the 1970s the Italian public pension replaced 80 per cent of final earnings for a full-time worker after 40 years, while this rate was 70 per cent in Germany and 51 per cent in Poland. In addition means-tested social assistance benefits had been introduced in order to protect those without sufficient insurance from poverty (Chapter 5, 6, 7 in this book; Ferrera and Jessoula 2007; GUS 2003, p. 447; Müller 1999; Stroinski 1998, p. 30). Funded systems as well as voluntary arrangements through companies or individuals only played a small role, if any. They were crowded out by the strong public sector (Bonoli 2003, p. 400; Haverland 2001, p. 312).

During the 1990s reform pressures mounted because all three countries suffered from chronic high unemployment and low activity rates, driving up the social insurance contribution for the economically active population and for employers (Table 1.3). It is fair to say that Poland's as well as Germany's economic problems were influenced too by the collapse of the Eastern Bloc, leading to a fundamental change in both societies, but particularly in Poland and the East German New Länder (Schulze and Jochem 2007). To make matters worse, Germany, Italy and Poland are affected particularly strongly by ageing populations; they are amongst the countries with the lowest fertility rates in Europe and thus their predicted dependency ratios for the elderly population were comparatively high too, increasing the need for pension reform. Against this background governments in all three countries felt compelled to implement fundamental changes during the 1990s. These are detailed in Chapters 5, 6 and 7. However, briefly put, they involved the sweeping away of the principle of the first pillar as guarantor of the customary standard of living for the long-term employed. They also led to a lowering of public pensions and to the strengthening of actuarial principles in the first pillar in Italy and Poland, which now grant relatively insignificant compensation for citizens with care responsibilities or for part-time workers. Thus German, Italian and Polish citizens are now expected to depend more strongly on the less redistributive second and third pillars in order to fill the gap that decreased public pension levels are likely to leave. So far in all countries reliance has been placed on the voluntarism of non-state actors. Incentives in the form of tax and subsidies have been created for citizens as well as for corporate actors to invest voluntarily in occupational or personal schemes in order to make up for the public shortfall.

This brief overview demonstrates that our three countries share a Bismarckian legacy and that all have recently made a sudden private turn. However it also became apparent that 'privatization' looks rather different for each of them. In moving away from predominantly statist systems they have each chosen a different mix of public and private provision. Our study will show how these different approaches affect the way these three countries fare in producing pension outcomes consistent with social inclusion.

In conclusion our group comprises three countries that already had substantial funded components, and therefore have been able to adjust to current circumstances by more incrementally reforming their existing programmes. The other three countries have recently implemented substantial changes to their pension systems, introducing funded elements into mature pay-as-you-go schemes. As a result of these developments comparing the six pension regimes as they exist today, the systematic public–private differences between the two groups disappear on the level of programmes and legislation, and a continuum of regimes takes their place which mix in various ways pensions with public and private aspects. Where different countries might lie on this continuum depends on the principle chosen to organize it. In this regard one important issue is the role of the state either as provider or regulator. At one end of a continuum organized on this basis, we would find Switzerland and the Netherlands where state provision is inclusive and redistributive and where the coverage of occupational schemes is broad in scope because of legislation, but where employers and trade unions still have some freedom to use occupational schemes to further their own interests. At the other end of this type of continuum are Germany and the United Kingdom. Here state provision is lower and the regulation of occupational and personal schemes is based on setting standards and offering incentives, leaving it to other societal actors to decide whether occupational provision is supplied. In the middle, we find Italy and Poland, which are similar in that the role of the state in pension provision remains dominant, but where differences exist in the state's engagement with non-state providers, Italy having moved more in this direction than Poland. However if we chose instead to organize our continuum in relation to the size and generosity of the state pay-as-you-go system, and thus the role left to non-state provision in preventing social exclusion, our order would be Italy, Switzerland, the Netherlands, Germany and the UK, followed by Poland as the country with the smallest pay-as-you-go pension in our group. In terms of assessing the combination(s) of public and private approaches most consistent with the aim of social inclusion in retirement, such distinctions are, as will be seen, extremely important.

We can therefore say that by selecting these six countries we have chosen examples from two distinct institutional legacies which today show a broad range of combinations of private and public elements. Our aim is to see which combinations are most consistent with social inclusion.

SPENDING PATTERNS AND AGE PROFILE

One would expect that Beveridgean and Bismarckian trajectories would also generate two distinct spending patterns, with higher public expenditure displayed by the newcomers and greater engagement in privately owned pension funds in the veteran group.

However as Table 1.5 indicates, countries with mature three pillar systems do not necessarily spend less money on public pensions than those with predominantly public pillars.[6] The differences between some of the 'veteran' and 'newcomer' group were small in 2003 but they become insignificant when we take dependency rates into account. Italy and Poland

Table 1.5   Public expenditure on pensions in the six countries

	UK	NL	CH	GER	IT	PL
Public expenditure on pensions, current prices (% of GDP), 2003	11.0	12.6	13.2	13.4	15.1	14.3
Old age dependency ratio, 2004	24.3	20.5	25	26.8	28.9	18.6

Sources: Expenditure: Eurostat_ http://epp.eurostat.cec.eu; Old Age Dependency Ratio (Population 65 and over as percentage of population 15–65): EPC (2006) Annex; Switzerland: figures for 2000 from Bundesamt für Sozialversicherungen (2006): T14.

are certainly top spenders, but the former also has the highest dependency rates in the group. German expenditure is almost the same as two veteran countries, the Netherlands and Switzerland, but on the basis of a higher dependency ratio than either of them. This suggests that the Dutch and Swiss public systems are more generous than the German system and almost equal in generosity to the Italian system, despite the fact that they also have large private pillars. Thus the only 'veteran' country that does indeed display low expenditure on public pensions is Britain, but even here the difference is not great. We therefore conclude that while a three pillar regime may be accompanied by low public spending on pensions under certain circumstances, there are no reliable systematic differences in public expenditure between the two groups.

When we consider the role of funded pensions in each country through the amount invested by pension funds and life insurance companies the anticipated difference between veterans and newcomers is confirmed more clearly (Figure 1.2).[7] Due to the mature funded systems of Switzerland, the Netherlands and the United Kingdom investments were worth more than these countries' GDP in 2004, and far above the OECD average (OECD 2005d, p. 3). In fact Switzerland and the Netherlands, together with Iceland, are the countries with the strongest-funded pension markets globally (OECD 2005d). Britain is somewhat less developed, probably because second pillar coverage is patchier, due to its voluntarist nature, and therefore less money is invested than in the quasi-compulsory occupational pensions sectors of Switzerland and the Netherlands (OECD 2005b). However the fact that British life insurance investment is higher than anywhere else suggests that individuals have taken the initiative to make up for the shortcomings of the public and occupational sectors; as we will argue in Chapter 2, these are unlikely to be citizens on lower incomes, though.

In summary it is true that the three countries with a long history of funded pensions invest large amounts of their national wealth in these systems; this is also true under the conditions of British voluntarism, albeit

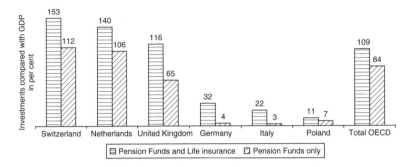

Notes: CH/NL 2003 data used for 2004; CH: 2003 data preliminary estimates, http//www.oecd.org/document/46/0,2340,en_2649_34853_36091822_1_1_1_1,00.html, accessed August 2006

Figure 1.2   *Total assets for pension funds and life insurance investments as a percentage of GDP in 2004 in the six countries*

to a lesser extent. Funded schemes are growing fast in the newcomer group, too (OECD 2005d), yet levels are still comparatively low.

Overview

As we have just shown, in spite of very different legacies, in 2006, the pension systems of the privatization veterans and the privatization new-comers look less different. This is because the latter group has followed the trend for multi-pillar systems so dominant in highly developed countries. Against this background the main aim of this study is to explore what risk of social exclusion public–private pension regimes pose for citizens who lead complex lives, which include risks typical for post-industrial society. In this introduction we have sought to explain the rationale behind this question and to justify to the reader why, to examine it, we use microsimulation of retirement income of illustrative individuals.

In the following, each of the case-studies is structured in the same way. First they characterize all pillars of their current pension regime, consider-ing in particular how occupational schemes and private savings programmes are regulated by the state and/or the trade unions and to what extent such non-state actors can engage in this area on a voluntary basis. In a second step each country study calculates how socially inclusive their national regimes are on the basis of the microsimulation methodology outlined above. Finally consideration is given to the extent to which the weaknesses in each country's performance are being addressed in the current policy debate. On the basis of the responses provided to these questions in the country chapters, the final chapter assesses whether it is possible to identify public–private pension mixes which successfully provide socially inclusive outcomes.

NOTES

1. This research generally relates to the pension systems in each country as they operated in 2003, when this research started. However in some countries (for example Germany and Italy) the impact of ongoing reform processes on system design was anticipated. This is detailed in the country chapters.
2. This has occurred notwithstanding a recognition of the difficulties involved in defining exactly 'what should be considered public or private'. See Esping-Andersen (1990) p. 91; see also Shalev (1996); an exception was van Gunsteren and Rein (1985).
3. The study by the OECD (2005a) simulates pension levels for individuals starting work in 2002 in all OECD countries by different income levels. Another big difference to our study is that only mandatory pension schemes and those with very broad coverage are included, paying less attention to the British second pillar for example. Secondly, the OECD focuses on replacement rates of pensions, and does not compare all pillar entitlements with social inclusion lines, as we do, this is also true for the Social Protection Committee Report commissioned by the EU on projected pension replacement rates. Thirdly, the OECD takes into account gross and net figures, that is it assesses the impact of tax and social insurance. We use this study to compare and discuss our results.
4. An earnings-related pension was introduced in 1961 but this was insubstantial and designed mainly to provide additional contributions to reduce the Exchequer cost of pensions (see Bridgen 2006).
5. However in recent years government regulation has also increased employers' costs and smothered their willingness to engage in occupational pensions (Clark 2003, p. 234; Cutler and Waine 2001, pp. 108–9; Quadango and Hardy 1996; Ross and Wills 2002; Sass 1997, pp. 233–8; Whiteside 2003, pp. 41–2).
6. These figures include as public expenditure on pensions the contracted-out national insurance rebate used in Britain to fund private alternatives to the State Second Pension.
7. To assess the approximate role of funded pensions in each of our countries, we use the OECD's figures on the sum of investments of pension funds and of life insurance companies. These figures comprise assets of most occupational and personal pensions savings in the public and private sectors of the countries we studied (OECD 2005c, 2005d). The caveat here is that these figures do not include book reserves, that is, 'sums entered in the balance sheet of the plan sponsor as reserves or provisions for occupational pension plan benefits' (OECD 2005b, p. 41). In our group book reserves are mainly used in Germany, where as a consequence real pension claims of households are higher than suggested by pension fund and life insurance investments (OECD 2005d; Chapter 5).

BIBLIOGRAPHY

Anderson, K.M. (2007), 'The Netherlands: political competition in proportional system', in E.M. Immergut, K.M. Anderson and I. Schulze (eds), *Handbook of West European Pension Politics* (pp. 713–57), Oxford: Oxford University Press.

Aposori, E. and Millar, J. (eds) (2005), *The Dynamics of Social Exclusion in Europe: Comparing Austria, Germany, Greece, Portugal and the UK*, Cheltenham, UK and Northampton, MA, USA: Edward Elgar.

Armingeon, K. and Bonoli, G. (eds) (2006), *The Politics of Post-Industrial Welfare States*, Oxford: Routledge.

Augusztinovics, M. (2002), 'Issues in pension system design', *International Social Security Review*, **55**(1), 21–35.

Baldwin, P. (1990), *The Politics of Social Solidarity: Class Bases of the European Welfare State 1875–1975*, Cambridge: Cambridge University Press.

Barnes, M., Heady, C., Middleton, S., Millar, J., Room, G., Papadopoulos, F. and Tsakloglou, P. (2004), *Poverty and Social Exclusion in Europe*, Cheltenham, UK and Northampton, MA, USA: Edward Elgar.

Barr, N. (2000), 'Reforming pensions: myths, truths and policy choices', IMF working paper WP/00/139, Washington, DC: IMF.

Behrendt, C. (2000), 'Private pensions: a viable alternative? Their distributive effects in comparative perspective', *International Social Security Review*, **53**(3), 3–26.

Berthoud, R. and Iacovou, M. (eds) (2004), *Social Europe: Living Standards and Welfare States*, Cheltenham, UK and Northampton, MA, USA: Edward Elgar.

Bonoli, G. (2003), 'Two worlds of pension reform in Western Europe', *Comparative Politics*, **35**(4), 399–416.

Bonoli, G. (2004), 'The institutionalisation of the Swiss multipillar pension system', in M. Rein and W. Schmähl (eds), *Rethinking the Welfare State: The Political Economy of Pension Reform* (pp. 102–21), Cheltenham, UK and Northampton, MA, USA: Edward Elgar.

Bonoli, G. (2007), 'Switzerland: development and crisis of a multipillar pension system', in E.M. Immergut, K.M. Anderson and I. Schulze (eds), *Handbook of West European Pension Politics* (pp. 203–47), Oxford: Oxford University Press.

Bonoli, G., George, V. and Taylor-Gooby, P. (2000), *Towards a Theory of Retrenchment*, Cambridge: Polity Press.

Bonoli, G. and Shinkawa, T. (eds) (2005), *Ageing and Pension Reform Around the World: Evidence from Eleven Countries*, Cheltenham, UK and Northampton, MA, USA: Edward Elgar.

Bottero, W. (2004), *Stratification: Social Division and Inequality*, London: Routledge.

Bridgen, P. (2006), 'A straitjacket with wriggle room: the Beveridge Report, the Treasury and the Exchequer's pension liability 1942–59', *Twentieth Century British History*, **17**(1), 1–25.

Bridgen, P. and Meyer, T. (2005), 'When do benevolent capitalists change their mind? Explaining the retrenchment of defined benefit pensions in Britain', *Social Policy and Administration*, **39**(4), 764–85.

Bundesamt für Sozialversicherungen (2006), *Statistiken zur Sozialen Sicherheit. AHV Statistik 2006 Tabellenteil*. Bern.

Burchardt, T. (1997), 'Boundaries between public and private welfare: a typology and map of services', London: CASE paper, CASE/2, LSE.

Casey, B. and Yamada, A. (2003), 'The public–private mix of retirement income in six OECD countries: some evidence from micro-data and an exploration of its implications', in M. Rein and W. Schmähl (eds), *Rethinking the Welfare State: The Political Economy of Pension Reform*, Cheltenham, UK and Northampton, MA, USA: Edward Elgar.

Castles, F.G. (2003), 'The world turned upside down: below replacement fertility, changing preferences and family-friendly public policy in 21 OECD countries', *Journal of European Social Policy*, **13**(3), 209–27.

Clark, G. (2000), *Pension Fund Capitalism*, Oxford: Oxford University Press.

Clark, G. (2003), *European Pensions and Global Finance*, Oxford: Oxford University Press.

Clark, G., Munnell, A. and Orszag, M. (2007), 'Pensions and retirement income in a global environment', in G. Clark, A. Munnell and M. Orszag (eds), *The Oxford Handbook of Pensions and Retirement Income* (pp. 10–28), Oxford: Oxford University Press.

Clark, G. and Whiteside, N. (eds) (2003), *Pension Security in the 21st Century*, Oxford: Oxford University Press.

Cutler, T. and Waine, B. (2001), 'Social insecurity and the retreat from social democracy: occupational welfare in the long boom and financialisation', *Review of International Political Economy*, **18**(1), 96–118.

Dimson, E., Marsh, P. and Staunton, M. (2002), *Triumph of the Optimists: 101 Years of Global Investment Returns*, New Jersey: Princeton University Press.

Disney, R. and Johnson, P. (eds) (2001), *Pension Systems and Retirement Incomes Across OECD Countries*, Cheltenham, UK and Northampton, MA, USA: Edward Elgar.

Drakeford, M. (2000), *Social Policy and Privatisation*, Harlow: Pearson Education.

DWP (Department of Work and Pensions) (2002), *Simplicity, Security and Choice: Working and Saving for Retirement*, London: HMSO.

Economic Policy Committee (EPC) (2006), *The Impact of Ageing on Public Expenditure: Projections for the EU25 Member States on Pensions, Health Care, Long-term Care, Education and Unemployment Transfers (2004–2050)*, Report prepared by the Economic Policy Committee and the European Commission (*DG ECFIN*), Brussels.

Esping-Andersen, G. (1990), *The Three Worlds of Welfare Capitalism*, Princeton, NJ: Princeton University Press.

European Central Bank (2004), Statistics Pocket Book, December, http://www.ecb.eu/pub/pdf/stapobo/spb200412en.pdf.

European Commission (2003), *Adequate and Sustainable Pensions. Joint report by the Commission and the Council.* DG Employment and Social Affairs, Brussels: European Communities.

European Commission (2005a), *Communication from the Commission to the Council, the European Parliament, the European Economic and Social Committee and the Committee of the Regions. Joint Report on Social Protection and Social Inclusion, COM(2005)14 final*, http://ec.europa.eu/employment_social/social_inclusion/docs/com_en.pdf, accessed August 2006.

European Commission (2005b), *Employment in Europe*, http://ec.europa.eu/employment_social/employment_analysis/employ_2005_en.htm, accessed August 2006.

European Commission (2006), *Employment in Europe 2006*, Brussels: European Commission.

European Council (2006), *New Common Objectives 2006*, http://ec.europa.eu/employment_social/social_protection/pensions_en.htm, accessed 17 Jan 2007.

Evandrou, M. and Falkingham, J. (2005), 'A secure retirement for all? Older people and New Labour', in J. Hills and K. Stewart (eds), *A More Equal Society? New Labour, Poverty, Inequality and Exclusion* (pp. 167–88), Bristol: Policy Press.

Ferrera, M. and Jessoula, M. (2007), 'Italy: a narrow gate for path-shift', in E.M. Immergut, K.M. Anderson and I. Schulze (eds), *Handbook of West European Pension Politics* (pp. 396–498), Oxford: Oxford University Press.

GAD (2003), *Occupational Pension Schemes 2000, Eleventh Survey by the Government Actuary*, London: Government Actuary's Department, www.gad. gov.uk/ Publications/docs/opss 2000_final_results_final_7april2003.pdf, accessed October 2005.

Ginn, J. (2003), *Gender, Pensions and the Life Course: How Pensions Need to Adapt to Changing Family Forms*, Bristol: Policy Press.

Goodin, R.E., Headey, B., Muffels, R. and Dirven, H-J. (1999), *The Real Worlds of Welfare Capitalism*, Cambridge: Cambridge University Press.

Green, F., Hadjimatheou, G. and Smail, R. (1984), 'Unequal fringes', Occasional Papers on Social Administration No. 75, London: NCVO.

Groves, D. (1983), 'Members and survivors: women and retirement-pension legislation', in J. Lewis (ed.), *Women's Welfare, Women's Rights* (pp. 18–63), London and Canberra: Croom Helm.

Groves, D. (1987), 'Occupational pension provision and women's poverty in old age', in C. Glendinning and J. Millar (eds), *Women and Poverty in Britain* (pp. 199–220), Brighton: Wheatsheaf.

GUS (2003), *Historia Polski w liczbach*, Warsaw: t.I – Panstwo i Spolecznenstwo.

Hannah, L. (1986), *Reinventing Retirement: The Development of Occupational Pensions in Britain*, Cambridge: Cambridge University Press.

Hantrais, L. (1999), 'Socio-demographic change, policy impacts and outcomes in social Europe', *Journal of European Social Policy*, **9**(4), 291–309.

Hart, R.A. (1984), *The Economics of Non-wage Labour Costs*, London: George Allen & Unwin.

Haverland, M. (2001), 'Another Dutch Miracle? Explaining Dutch and German pension trajectories', *Journal of European Social Policy*, **11**(4), 308–23.

Hawkesworth, R.I. (1977), 'Fringe benefits in British industry', *British Journal of Industrial Relations*, **15**(3), 396–402.

Hyde, M., Dixon, J. and Drover, G. (2003), 'Welfare retrenchment of collective responsibility? The privatisation of public pensions in Western Europe', *Social Policy and Society*, **2**(3), 189–90.

Immergut, E.M., Anderson, K.M. and Schulze, I. (eds) (2007), *Handbook of West European Pension Politics*, Oxford: Oxford University Press.

Johnson, P. and Rake, K. (1998), 'Comparative social policy research in Europe', *Social Policy Review*, **10**, 257–78.

Leisering, L. (2003), 'From redistribution to regulation: regulating private pension provision for old age as a new challenge for the welfare state in ageing societies', paper presented at the 4th International Research Conference on Social Security, Antwerp, 5–7 May, Regina Working Paper No. 3, University of Bielefeld.

Mares, I. (2001), 'Firms and the welfare state: when, why, and how does social policy matter to employers?', in P. Hall and D. Soskice (eds), *Varieties of Capitalism* (pp. 184–212), Oxford: Oxford University Press.

Mazey, S. (1998), 'The European Union and women's rights: from the Europeanization of national agendas to the nationalization of a European agenda?', *Journal of European Public Policy*, **5**(1), 131–52.

Meyer, T. and Bridgen, P. (forthcoming 2008), 'Class, gender and chance: the social division of welfare and British occupational pensions', *Ageing and Society*.

Moffit, R.A. (1999), 'Simulating transfer programmes and labour supply', in T. Callan (ed.), *Taxes, Transfers and Labour Market Responses: What can Microsimulation Tell Us?*, Dublin: Economic and Social Research Institute.

Müller, K. (1999), *The Political Economy of Pension Reform in Central-Eastern Europe*, Cheltenham, UK and Northampton, MA, USA: Edward Elgar.

Myles, J. and Pierson, P. (2001), 'The comparative political economy of pension reform', in P. Pierson (ed.), *The New Politics of Welfare* (pp. 305–33), Oxford: Oxford University Press.

OECD (2005a), *Employment Outlook 2005*, Paris.

OECD (2005b), *Pensions at a Glance, Public Policies across OECD Countries*, 2005 Edition, Paris.

OECD (2005c), *Pension Markets in Focus Newsletter*, June, Issue 1.

OECD (2005d), *Pension Markets in Focus Newsletter*, December, Issue 2.

OFS (2004), *La prévoyance professionnelle en Suisse*, Neuchâtel: OFS.

Pedersen, A.W. (2004), 'The privatization of retirement income? Variation and trends in the income packages of old age pensioners', *Journal of European Social Policy*, **14**(1), 5–23.

Pierson, P. (1994), *Dismantling the Welfare State?*, Cambridge: Cambridge University Press.

Pierson, P. (2001), 'Post-industrial pressures on mature welfare states', in P. Pierson (ed.), *The New Politics of the Welfare State* (pp. 80–104), Oxford: Oxford University Press.

Quadango, J. and Hardy, M. (1996), 'Private pensions, state regulation and income security for older workers: the US auto industry', in M. Shalev (ed.), *The Privatization of Social Policy? Occupational Welfare and the Welfare State in America, Scandinavia and Japan* (pp. 136–58), Basingstoke: Macmillan Press.

Rake, K. (1999), 'Accumulated disadvantage? Welfare state provision and the incomes of older women and men in Britain, France and Germany', in J. Clasen (ed.), *Comparative Social Policy: Concepts, Theories and Methods* (pp. 22–245), Oxford: Blackwell.

Rein, M. (1996), 'Is America exceptional? The role of occupational welfare in the United States and the European Community', in M. Shalev (ed.), *The Privatization of Social Policy? Occupational Welfare and the Welfare State in America, Scandinavia and Japan* (pp. 27–43), Basingstoke: Macmillan Press.

Rein, M. and Schmähl, W. (eds) (2004), *Rethinking the Welfare State: The Political Economy of Pension Reform*, Cheltenham, UK and Northampton, MA, USA: Edward Elgar.

Rein, M. and Wadensjö, U. (1997), 'The emerging role of enterprise in social policy', in M. Rein and E. Wadensjo (eds), *Enterprise and the Welfare State*, Cheltenham, UK and Lyme, USA: Edward Elgar.

Ross, D. and Wills, L. (2002), 'The shift from defined benefit to defined contribution retirement plans and the provision of retirement savings', Pensions Institute Discussion Paper PI-0210, London: Pensions Institute.

Sass, S. (1997), *The Promise of Private Pensions: The First Hundred Years*, Cambridge, MA: Harvard University Press.

Schulze, I. and Jochem, S. (2007), 'Germany: beyond policy gridlock', in E.M. Immergut, K.M. Anderson and I. Schulze (eds), *Handbook of West European Pension Politics* (pp. 660–711), Oxford: Oxford University Press.

Shalev, M. (ed.) (1996), *The Privatization of Social Policy? Occupational Welfare in America, Scandinavia and Japan*, Basingstoke: Macmillan.

Sinfield, A. (2000), 'Tax benefits in non-state pensions', *European Journal of Social Security*, **2**(2), 137–68.

Social Protection Committee (2006), 'Current and prospective theoretical pension replacement rates', Report by the Indicators Sub-Group (ISG) of the (SPC), 19 May 2006, http://ec.europa.eu/employment_social/social_protection/docs/isg_repl_rates_en.pdf, accessed 17 January 2007.

Stroinski, K. (1998), 'Poland: the reform of the pension system', *Agenda*, March, 29–33, http://agenda.anu.edu.au/, accessed 20 August 2006.

Swiss Federal Statistical Office (2005a), *Employment Statistics*, Neuchâtel: SFSO.

Swiss Federal Statistical Office (2005b), *Swiss Labour Force Survey 2005*, Neuchâtel: SFSO.

Titmuss, R. (1958), *Essays on the Welfare State*, London: Allen & Unwin.

Townsend, P. (1979), *Poverty in the United Kingdom: A Survey of Household Resources and Standards of Living*, Harmondsworth: Penguin.

van Gunsteren, H. and Rein, R. (1985), 'The dialectic of public and private pensions', *Journal of Social Policy*, **14**(2), 129–49.

van Riel, B., Hemerijck, A. and Visser, J. (2003), 'Is there a Dutch way to pension reform?', in G. Clark and N. Whiteside (eds), *Pension Security in the 21st Century* (pp. 64–91), Oxford: Oxford University Press.

Whiteside, N. (2003), 'Historical perspectives and the politics of pension reform', in G. Clark and N. Whiteside (eds), *Pension Security in the 21st Century* (pp. 21–43), Oxford: Oxford University Press.

Whiteside, N. (2006), 'Adapting private pensions to public purposes: historical perspectives on the politics of reform', *Journal of European Social Policy*, **16**(1), 43–54.

World Bank (1994), *Averting the Old Age Crisis*, Oxford: Oxford University Press.

Zaidi, A., Marin, B. and Fuchs, M. (2006), *Pension Policy in EU 25 and its Possible Impact on Elderly Poverty*, Vienna: European Centre for Social Welfare Policy and Research.

APPENDIX 1.1

Table A1.1   Assumptions for working time (w-t) and earnings in relation to average (e/a) per year, all biographies

Year in employment	Age	Bio 1 a		Bio 1b, c		Bio 2a, c		Bio 2b		Bio 3a		Bio 3b		Bio 4a	
		w-t	e/a	w-t	e/a	w-t	e/a	w-t	e/a	w-t	e/a	w-t	e/a	w-t	e/a
2003	18	1	0.5	1	0.5					1.0	0.60	1.0	0.60	1	0.65
2004	19	1	0.5	1	0.5					1.0	0.60	1.0	0.60	1	0.65
2005	20	1	0.6	1	0.6	1.0	0.60	1.0	0.60	1.0	0.60	1.0	0.70	1	0.7
2006	21	1	0.7	1	0.6	1.0	0.60	1.0	0.60	1.0	0.60	1.0	0.75	1	0.7
2007	22	1	0.7	1	0.6	1.0	0.65	1.0	0.65	1.0	0.60	1.0	0.75	1	0.75
2008	23	1	0.7	1	0.6	1.0	0.65	1.0	0.65	0.0	0.00	0.0	0.00	1	0.75
2009	24	0	0.0	0	0	1.0	0.70	1.0	0.70	0.0	0.00	0.0	0.00	1	0.75
2010	25	0	0.0	0	0	1.0	0.70	1.0	0.70	1.0	0.13	1.0	0.35	0	0.8
2011	26	0.5	0.35	0.5	0.3	0.0	0.00	0.0	0.00	1.0	0.13	1.0	0.32	1	0
2012	27	0	0.0	0	0	0.0	0.00	0.0	0.00	1.0	0.13	1.0	0.32	1	0.75
2013	28	0	0.0	0	0	0.6	0.42	0.6	0.42	1.0	0.13	1.0	0.32	1	0.75
2014	29	0	0.0	0	0	0.6	0.42	0.6	0.42	1.0	0.13	1.0	0.40	1	0.75
2015	30	0.5	0.35	0.5	0.3	0.0	0.00	0.0	0.00	1.0	0.13	1.0	0.38	1	0.8
2016	31	0.5	0.35	0.5	0.3	0.0	0.00	0.0	0.00	1.0	0.13	1.0	0.31	1	0.8
2017	32	0.5	0.35	0.5	0.3	0.5	0.38	0.5	0.38	1.0	0.13	1.0	0.32	1	0.8
2018	33	0.5	0.35	0.5	0.3	0.5	0.38	0.5	0.38	1.0	0.13	1.0	0.35	1	0.8
2019	34	0.5	0.35	0.5	0.3	0.5	0.38	0.5	0.38	1.0	0.13	1.0	0.36	1	0.8
2020	35	0.5	0.35	0.5	0.3	0.5	0.38	0.5	0.38	1.0	0.25	1.0	0.40	1	0.85
2021	36	0.5	0.35	0.5	0.3	0.5	0.38	0.5	0.38	1.0	0.25	1.0	0.40	1	0.85
2022	37	0.5	0.35	0.5	0.3	0.5	0.38	0.5	0.38	1.0	0.25	1.0	0.45	1	0.85
2023	38	0.5	0.35	0.5	0.3	0.5	0.38	0.5	0.38	1.0	0.25	1.0	0.50	1	0.85

Year	Age														
2024	39	0.5	0.35	0.5	0.3	0.5	0.38	0.5	0.38	1.0	0.25	1.0	0.50	1	0.85
2025	40	0.5	0.35	1	0.6	0.6	0.50	0.6	0.50	1.0	0.25	1.0	0.45	1	0.85
2026	41	0.6	0.45	1	0.6	0.6	0.50	0.6	0.50	1.0	0.25	1.0	0.50	1	0.85
2027	42	0.6	0.45	1	0.6	0.6	0.50	1.0	0.70	1.0	0.25	1.0	0.50	1	0.85
2028	43	0.6	0.45	1	0.6	0.6	0.50	1.0	0.70	1.0	0.25	1.0	0.50	1	0.85
2029	44	0.6	0.45	1	0.6	0.6	0.58	1.0	0.70	1.0	0.25	1.0	0.50	1	0.85
2030	45	0.65	0.5	1	0.6	0.6	0.58	1.0	0.72	1.0	0.25	1.0	0.40	1	0.85
2031	46	0.65	0.5	1	0.6	0.6	0.58	1.0	0.72	1.0	0.25	1.0	0.30	1	0.85
2032	47	0.65	0.5	1	0.6	0.6	0.58	1.0	0.72	1.0	0.25	1.0	0.45	1	0.85
2033	48	0.65	0.5	1	0.6	0.6	0.58	1.0	0.72	1.0	0.25	1.0	0.45	1	0.85
2034	49	0.65	0.5	1	0.6	0.6	0.58	1.0	0.72	1.0	0.25	1.0	0.45	1	0.85
2035	50	0.65	0.5	1	0.6	0.6	0.58	1.0	0.74	1.0	0.25	1.0	0.50	1	0.85
2036	51	0.65	0.5	1	0.6	0.6	0.58	1.0	0.74	1.0	0.25	1.0	0.50	1	0.85
2037	52	0.65	0.5	1	0.6	0.6	0.58	1.0	0.74	1.0	0.25	1.0	0.50	1	0.85
2038	53	0.65	0.5	1	0.6	0.6	0.58	1.0	0.74	1.0	0.25	1.0	0.50	1	0.85
2039	54	0.65	0.5	1	0.6	0.6	0.58	1.0	0.74	1.0	0.25	1.0	0.50	1	0.85
2040	55	0.65	0.5	1	0.6	0.6	0.58	1.0	0.74	1.0	0.00	0.6	0.50	1	0.8
2041	56	0.65	0.5	1	0.62			1.0	0.74	0.0	0.00			1	0.8
2042	57	0.65	0.5	1	0.62			1.0	0.74	0.0	0.00			1	0.8
2043	58	0.65	0.5	1	0.62			1.0	0.74	0.0	0.00			1	0.8
2044	59	0.65	0.5	1	0.62			1.0	0.74	0.0	0.00			1	0.8
2045	60	0.65	0.5	1	0.62			1.0	0.74	1.0	0.25			1	0.8
2046	61	0.7	0.5	1	0.62			1.0	0.74	1.0	0.25			1	0.8
2047	62			1	0.62			1.0	0.74	1.0	0.25			1	0.8
2048	63			1	0.62			1.0	0.74	1.0	0.25			1	0.8
2049	64			1	0.62			1.0	0.74	1.0	0.25			1	0.8

Table A1.1 (continued)

Year in employment	Age	Bio 4b		Bio 5a, b		Bio 5c		Bio 6a/b		Bio 7		Bio 8a, b		Bio 9	
		w-t	e/a	w-t	e/a	w-t	e/a	w-t	e/a	w-t	e/a	w-t	e/a	w-t	e/a
2003	18	1	0.65					1	0.5			0.0	0		
2004	19	1	0.65					1	0.5			0.0	0		
2005	20	1	0.7	1.0	0.8	1.0	0.8	1	0.5	1	0.8	1.0	0.9		
2006	21	1	0.7	1.0	0.8	1.0	0.8	1	0.5	1	0.85	1.0	0.9		
2007	22	1	0.75	1.0	0.85	1.0	0.8	1	0.5	1	0.85	1.0	1		
2008	23	1	0.75	1.0	0.85	1.0	0.85	1	0	1	0.9	1.0	1		
2009	24	1	0.75	1.0	0.85	1.0	0.85	1	0.75	1	0.9	1.0	1.1		
2010	25	1	0.8	1.0	0.9	1.0	0.85	1	0.75	1	0.9	1.0	1.1		
2011	26	0	0	1.0	0.9	1.0	0.9	1	0.75	1	1	1.0	1.1		
2012	27	1	0.75	1.0	0.9	1.0	0.9	1	0.75	1	1	1.0	1.4		
2013	28	1	0.75	0.0	0	0.0	0.9	1	0.75	1	1.1	1.0	1.4		
2014	29	1	0.75	1.0	0.85	1.0	0	1	0.75	1	1.1	1.0	1.4		
2015	30	1	0.8	1.0	0.85	1.0	0.85	1	0.8	1	1.2	1.0	1.5		
2016	31	1	0.8	1.0	0.9	1.0	0.85	1	0.8	1	1.2	1.0	1.5		
2017	32	1	0.8	1.0	0.9	1.0	0.9	1	0.9	1	1.2	1.0	1.5		
2018	33	1	0.8	1.0	0.9	1.0	0.9	1	0.8	1	1.2	1.0	1.5		
2019	34	1	0.8	0.0	0	0.0	0.9	1	0.8	1	1.2	1.0	1.5		
2020	35	1	0.85	0.0	0	0.0	0	1	0.9	1	1.2	1.0	1.55		
2021	36	1	0.85	0.0	0	0.0	0	1	1	1	1.2	1.0	1.55	1.0	0.65
2022	37	1	0.85	1.0	0.8	1.0	0	1	0.9	1	1.2	1.0	1.55	1.0	0.7
2023	38	1	0.85	1.0	0.8	1.0	0.8	1	0.9	1	1.2	1.0	1.55	1.0	0.7
2024	39	1	0.85	1.0	0.8	1.0	0.8	1	0.85	1	1.2	1.0	1.55	1.0	0.8
2025	40	1	0.85	1.0	0.9	1.0	0.8	1	1.1	1	1.25	1.0	1.6	1.0	0.8

Year														
2026	1	0.85	1.0	1	1.0	0.9	1	1	1	1.25	1.0	1.6	1.0	0.8
2027	1	0.85	1.0	1	1.0	1	1	1.1	1	1.25	1.0	1.6	1.0	0.85
2028	1	0.85	1.0	1.1	1.0	1	1	1.1	1	1.25	1.0	1.6	1.0	0.85
2029	1	0.85	1.0	1.1	1.0	1.1	1	0.9	1	1.25	1.0	1.6	1.0	0.85
2030	1	0.85	1.0	1.2	1.0	1.1	1	0.8	1	1.25	1.0	1.65	1.0	0.85
2031	1	0.85	1.0	1	1.0	1.2	1	0.8	1	1.25	1.0	1.65	1.0	0.68
2032	1	0.85	1.0	1.1	1.0	1	1	0.9	1	1.25	1.0	1.65	1.0	0.8
2033	1	0.85	1.0	1.1	1.0	1.1	1	1	1	1.25	1.0	1.65	1.0	0.8
2034	1	0.85	1.0	1	1.0	1.1	1	1	1	1.25	1.0	1.65	1.0	0.8
2035	1	0.85	1.0	1.2	1.0	1	1	1	1	1.25	1.0	1.65	1.0	0.8
2036	1	0.85	1.0	1	1.0	1.2	1	1.1	1	1.25	1.0	1.65	1.0	0.8
2037	1	0.85	1.0	1.1	1.0	1	1	1.1	1	1.25	1.0	1.65	1.0	0.8
2038	1	0.85	1.0	1.3	1.0	1.1	1	1.1	1	1.25	1.0	1.65	1.0	0.8
2039	1	0.85	1.0	1.2	1.0	1.1	1	1	1	1.25	1.0	1.65	1.0	0.8
2040	1	0.8	1.0	1			1	1	1	1.3	1.0	1.7	1.0	0.8
2041	1	0.8	1.0	0.9			1	1.1	1	1.3	1.0	1.7	1.0	0.8
2042	0	0	1.0	1.1			1	0.8	1	1.3	1.0	1.8	1.0	0.8
2043	0	0	1.0	1.3			1	0.8	1	1.3	1.0	1.8	1.0	0.8
2044	0	0	1.0	1.3			1	0.8	1	1.3	1.0	1.8	1.0	0.8
2045	0	0	1.0	1.3			1	0.8	1	1.3	1.0	1.8	1.0	0.8
2046	0	0	1.0	1.3			1	0.8	1	1.3				0.78
2047	0.0	0.00	1.0	1.3			1	0.8	1	1.3				0.78
2048			1.0	1.3			1	0.8	1	1.3				0.78
2049			1.0	1.4			1	0.8	1	1.3				0.78

Notes: Assumptions: Real earnings growth: 2% per year; comprises nominal wage growth of 3.9% and an inflation rate of 1.9%. Based on UK government (CM5677, 2002) and European Central Bank (http://www.ecb.int/pub/mb/html/index.en.html).

APPENDIX 1.2

Table A1.2   Details of assumptions used in the simulations in all countries

Assumption	Details	Comments
General		In general, we have based our assumptions on those used by policy-makers in Europe. In some cases, for reasons explained below we have adopted slightly more optimistic assumptions, but we have not adopted any assumptions that are more pessimistic.
Economic data		
Average wages	Annual Gross Earnings in Industry and Services: Eurostat data for 2003. http://epp. eurostat.ec.europa.eu	Gross earnings are remuneration (wages and salaries) in cash paid directly to the employee, before any income tax and social security contributions paid by the employee. Data is presented for full-time employees in industry and services. We used average rather than median earnings because median earnings were not available for all countries.
Inflation	1.9% – based on EU assumptions (www. ecb.int/mopo/html/ index.en.html).	1.9% is the European Central Bank's inflation target.
Gross earnings	Annual rise 2% above inflation.	Gross disposable income rose in the Eurozone by an average of 3.9% in the five years up to 2003 (European Central Bank 2004).
Exchange rate	As of 1.1.2003. For CH: 1 CHF= 0.68951 €; UK: 1 GBP=1.53 €.	
Pension system assumptions		
State pension system	Rules and stipulations of public pension regime as valid in 2003. See country chapters for details.	
State pension age	In Poland the state pension age for	

Table A1.2 (continued)

Assumption	Details	Comments
	women is 60. To allow comparison, the pensions of Polish women on retirement have been projected forward to 65 on the basis of the price index.	
Early retirement	In circumstances where a biography retires early (ie bios 2a, 2c, 4b, 8a and 8b) any pension they receive on retirement has been projected forward to 65 on the basis of the price index.	
Occupational pension scheme stipulations	Rules and stipulations of selected occupation schemes as valid in 2003. See country chapters for details.	
Tax	Our simulations exclude tax and social insurance contributions or benefits. We use gross earnings to calculate pension entitlement and our pension outcomes are gross figures.	Tax and benefits are excluded as a means of simplifying an already complex comparative methodology. Recent research undertaken by the OECD suggests that the effect of tax on pension outcomes is similar across the six countries included in this study. It concluded that 'the differential between gross and net replacement rates for low earners is 17% on average', with little significant variation between countries OECD (2005a, p. 17).
Thresholds Social assistance	The basic social assistance benefit for older people,	Social assistance was not generally used for comparative analysis because of significant variations in social assistance

Table A1.2   (continued)

Assumption	Details	Comments
	excluding allowances for specific items of expenditure, such as housing unless these are an inherent part of the basic benefit (eg Germany). Given that some individual biographies are married at retirement, the social assistance threshold for them is half of couple's social assistance rate in 2050. The threshold for single individuals is the single person's rate.	rates between countries in relation to average income but it is nevertheless important to assess whether each country's pension system succeeds in providing benefits above the nationally determined minimum standard.
Social exclusion	Social inclusion threshold: 40% of average wages; comfortable social inclusion threshold: 50% of average wages.	Median income data from one dataset was not available for all countries, thus we could not use the standard EU threshold for social exclusion – 60 per cent of median income, but used average wage data instead. For social inclusion we chose a 40% average wage threshold rather than the more standard 50% threshold because of concerns that the latter was significantly higher than 60% median figures in some of our countries.
Savings		
Period of saving	All years of employed working life.	This is an optimistic assumption. The earliest age at which Britain's recent Pensions Commission assumed saving started was 25. In savings calculations undertaken by the British Department of Work and Pensions the youngest age included was 20 (DWP 2002: 35).
Scale of saving	Same proportion of earnings during every year of saving.	This is a common assumption made in undertaking savings calculations (see Pensions Commission 2004: 150–156).

Table A1.2   (continued)

Assumption	Details	Comments
Rate of return	For all defined contribution occupational pensions and savings calculations we have assumed a real gross rate of return of 6 per cent.	This is an optimistic assumption which was chosen to assess the potential of personal saving in the best possible circumstances. In simulating pension outcomes up to 2050, the UK government was more cautious: its assumption for annual rates of return was that they would average 2% above average wage growth (DWP 2002), ie 4 per cent in real terms and 5.9 per cent in nominal terms. Our assumption is more in line with data on stock market rates of return in the best-performing countries over the last 100 years (see Dimson et al. 2002).
Annuity rate	5% annuity rate on retirement.	Annuity rate is in line with situation in 2004 (sharingpensions.co.uk, 2004). We have used the same annuity rate for male and female biographies because in some of our countries (Germany and Switzerland) rates are not by law differentiated by gender.

PART II

Case-studies: the veterans

2. The British pension system and social inclusion

Paul Bridgen and Traute Meyer[1]

It has almost become a truism that the main problem with the British pension system is its failure to prevent social exclusion in retirement for many of its citizens. Its comparatively disappointing performance in this regard (Chapter 1; Pensions Commission 2004, p. 69) has often been blamed on the low level of state provision and the prominent role played by private pensions, for example by Lynes (1997) and Walker (1999). Britain it seems is a clear-cut example to support the view that private pensions and social inclusion do not mix.

Our research certainly provides evidence to support this view. Some of our biographies perform extremely badly when compared with those in other countries. However our results also suggest that a life in poverty and/or social exclusion is not the inevitable outcome for individuals in Britain with lower wages or disrupted working lives. Indeed some individuals perform quite reasonably in comparison with the other countries included in this book, with the system capable of providing some of the highest pensions in Europe for some members of the low- to middle-income group studied in this project (Pensions Commission 2004, pp. 68–9).

It is this variability of outcome that we highlight in this chapter. We reconsider the relationship between the social risks generally accepted as determinants of low income in old age – low wages, detachment from the labour market, marriage and divorce – and pension outcome, by paying particular attention to the diverse and patchy coverage of occupational provision in Britain. This advantages some individuals, and excludes others. However we will show that the circumstances that lead an individual to be working for an employer who provides a good-quality occupational pension are structured not only by level of income, qualification or seniority and gender but also by chance – they are an accident of timing, opportunity and/or location (Meyer and Bridgen forthcoming 2008). This variability seems likely to remain, notwithstanding the fact that access to high-quality pension schemes is beginning generally to decline as a result of the current retrenchment in the British occupational sector.

The chapter also shows how changes in the pension system made in the late 1970s, such as Home Responsibilities Protection, together with increased labour market participation, are acting to improve gradually the situation of women in relation to men (see also Pensions Commission 2004). Greater protection for women during periods of caring and part-time work, which seem likely to be extended in coming years (DWP 2006), together with the fact that female employees are concentrated in the public sector where pension provision is more generous, are the main reasons for this improvement. Thus while significant inequalities of income in retirement between men and women seem likely to remain, the system is nevertheless improving in its ability to provide women with a reasonably sized independent income.

To explain more fully these general conclusions, this chapter will firstly provide a brief summary of the main features of the British system. We will then evaluate its inclusiveness for our risk biographies, considering each element. Finally the chapter will assess the extent to which the current policy debate is addressing the deficits our research reveals.

THE BRITISH PENSION SYSTEM

The Public Pillar

The Basic State Pension

The Basic State Pension (BSP) is the foundation stone of the state system (Table 2.1). It is a contributory benefit, with the full pension paid to people who have reached 65, the general pension age by 2050,[2] after paying earnings-related National Insurance contributions on income between a lower and an upper earnings level for at least 44 years. Those who work for a shorter period accrue a lower pension, but an individual must have worked between nine and 11 years to receive the minimum Basic State Pension of 25 per cent of the full rate (IDS 2003, p. 15). This obviously disadvantages those with disrupted working lives, and is currently under review (DWP 2006, p. 104). However even under the existing system on which our simulations are based, many of those who are not in paid work receive some degree of protection from the various credit arrangements.

The value of the Basic State Pension has been declining in relation to wages since 1985, and more people are becoming reliant on means testing after retirement (Pensions Commission 2005, p. 46). In 2006, the Basic State Pension constituted 74 per cent of the social assistance minimum for single pensioners (Pensions Service 2003). Our calculations suggest that on the basis of current policies it will constitute 41 per cent by 2050.

Table 2.1 The three pillars of the British pension system

	1st pillar Public old age pension		2nd pillar Company occupational pensions	3rd pillar Individual pensions	
	Basic State Pension	State Second Pension		Stakeholder	Other
Principle	Universal	Universal for those without suitable occupational provision	Occupational	Personal	Personal
Coverage	Compulsory	Compulsory unless suitable occupational provision	Voluntary	Voluntary, employers must facilitate access	Voluntary
Financing mechanism	Pay-as-you-go	Pay-as-you-go	Funding	Funding	Funding
Contributions	Employment-related	Employment-related	Employment-related	Personal	Personal
Benefits	Flat-rate	Income-related, becoming flat rate	Defined benefit and contributions-related	Contributions-related	Contributions-related
Objective	Poverty prevention	Poverty prevention	Income maintenance	Increased saving among low paid	Complementary individual needs

Comparatively the Basic State Pension is also low: it amounted to 14.5 per cent of average wages in 2004, whereas the equivalent pension in the Netherlands is 19 per cent of average wages (Chapter 3).

The State Second Pension
The State Second Pension is the second mandatory tier of the public pension system. It is a compulsory, and currently still earnings-related pension for those with an income between a lower and upper earnings limit, provided they are not self-employed or covered by a contracted-out occupational or personal pension (Agulnik 1999; see also below). In most cases people who are contracted out into an occupational pension receive no State Second Pension, but there are important exceptions to this general rule (see below). For those on low earnings the State Second Pension is fairly redistributive. Anyone earning above the lower earnings limit (€6126 in 2003) but below a lower earnings threshold (€17 137 in 2003) is treated as though they were earning at the higher level for the purposes of calculating their entitlement. From 2012 it is intended that the State Second Pension pensions will gradually become flat rate up to 2030, meaning that everyone will be treated as if they had an income at a lower earnings threshold regardless of their actual earnings (DWP 2006, p. 119; Government Actuary 1999, p. 21). On the basis of the present system an individual who works full-time earning average lifetime wages would on our calculations secure a pension of 62 per cent of the social inclusion threshold on retirement in 2050. This equates to a replacement rate of only 25 per cent. As a result the United Kingdom has one of lowest projections for spending on the public pension system up to 2050 in the European Union (see Chapter 1; Pensions Commission 2004, p. 61).

Protection of social risks in the first pillar
A number of rules operate to enhance the inclusiveness of the state system for citizens with interrupted employment records, low wages and care responsibilities. Under the Basic State Pension, those economically inactive because they are caring for a child or a sick or disabled person receive pension entitlements through credits or Home Responsibilities Protection. The latter reduces the number of qualifying years needed for a full Basic State Pension for those caring for children under the age of 16 years, or for ill or disabled adults, although a minimum of 22 years in employment is still required for those who will retire in 2050 (Pensions Service 2003). However if somebody combines work and caring within the same year they cannot add Home Responsibilities Protection to their National Insurance contributions (Age Concern 2003; Pensions Service 2003). Recognition of care responsibilities seems likely to be extended in the coming years,

addressing some of these current shortcomings (DWP 2006). Credits are also available for times of unemployment, sickness or disability. In addition divorcees, widows and widowers receive protection (Pensions Service 2003, p. 90).

Credit facilities under the State Second Pension are less inclusive. Individuals caring for a child are only covered if the child is under the age of six, in which case they accrue entitlements based on earnings at the lower earnings limit, and no credit provision is made for unemployment. The self-employed are excluded from the State Second Pension altogether. In contrast disabled people are fully covered and a surviving spouse can inherit half of their State Second Pension (Pensions Service 2003). Finally while divorced and separated people cannot claim the State Second Pension based on their former spouse's contributions, they can, under recent 'pension-sharing' legislation, seek a division of the pension as part of a divorce agreement, although this has only so far occurred very infrequently (IDS 2003, pp. 231–2).

Pension Credit

Pension Credit is the means-tested social assistance minimum available to pensioners, whose income on retirement does not reach a state-designated minimum standard. It is highly redistributive and provides most help to the poorest 20 per cent of pensioners, the majority of whom are women (DWP 2006; TUC 2004). However not all citizens entitled take up this benefit (Evandrou and Falkingham 2005).

Pension Credit is planned to increase in line with earnings while the Basic State Pension will only increase in line with prices or 2.5 per cent, whichever is the higher. Therefore pension commentators have projected that in the future the means-tested Pension Credit would evolve from a safety net for a minority to a significant source of income for the majority of pensioners (Pensions Commission 2005; PPI 2003, p. 17; Rake et al. 2000). However a recent government commitment to increase the Basic State Pension in line with earnings makes such an evolution less likely (DWP 2006).

An increased role for means testing is problematic with respect to private saving, since means testing reduces the incentive for those on modest incomes to save for retirement (Clark 2001). Policymakers responded to this problem by adding a savings element, Savings Credit, which is relevant for those who have an income above the Basic State Pension level but below the Pension Credit level (Clark 2001; DWP 2002). While this element was designed to reward savings it is not yet clear whether it is sufficient to alter savings behaviour substantially (Clark 2002; DWP 2006).

The Second Pillar

In Chapter 1 we showed that Britain has an extensive funded pension system. Yet occupational pension provision is not compulsory which means that coverage is far from comprehensive. Those employers that offer occupational schemes are left with considerable discretion about their operation. They are entitled to establish their own rules with regard to minimum and maximum age conditions and/or minimum length of service. They can also decide whether or not to pay contributions, and whether membership of schemes is automatic upon employment (CBI 2004, p. 16; GMB 2002; TUC 2003). Because of this voluntarism the total size of British funded pension schemes is significantly smaller than the fund sizes in the Netherlands or Switzerland, but still much larger than those of the other countries in this study (Chapters 3 and 4).[3]

However the system is not entirely voluntary. Employers who offer pensions schemes to their employees which require contracting out of the State Second Pension must ensure that employees are covered by one or the other. Moreover where occupational provision is used to contract out of the State Second Pension it must operate at or above minimum standards set by government, which ensure that the size of benefit is equal to or higher than the State Second Pension (IDS 2003, p. 63). In fact most employers operate schemes well above the minimum standard, although recent years have seen a significant retrenchment in this regard (Bridgen and Meyer 2005; Pensions Commission 2004). Generally those individuals who are contracted out receive no state additional pension. However the introduction of the State Second Pension was accompanied by changes in the contracting-out rules which mean that workers with an occupational pension, who earn between the lower and upper earnings limit, still gain some access to additional state provision (IDS 2003).

Until the mid-1970s pensions were outside the remit of equal pay and sex discrimination legislation and therefore employers did not need to admit part-time workers to occupational schemes (Groves 1983, p. 40; Groves 1987, pp. 209, 211). However because of specifications in the 1975 Social Security Act and successive rulings of the European Court of Justice, occupational schemes now also have to maintain the pension rights of women on maternity leave (www.opas.org.uk) and recent pension-sharing regulations for divorce promote a fair split of pension rights (Honeyball and Shaw 1991; IDS 2003, pp. 29–33; Lynes 1997; Mazey 1998, pp. 139–44; Neilson 1998, pp. 71, 73, 75). However workers with incomes below the lower earnings limit can still be excluded from occupational pension schemes (PMI 2004).

The voluntary nature of occupational provision means there are marked differences in coverage with many workers not covered (DWP 2002, p. 75; Pensions Commission 2004, p. 121). Those without access to any scheme are largely concentrated in the private sector, where the likelihood of coverage declines with employer size. In 2003 71 per cent of workers in small, 56 per cent of workers in medium-sized and 40 per cent of workers in large businesses were not covered by any private sector employer-sponsored scheme (DWP 2004, p. 83; Pensions Commission 2004, p. 64). Variation is also evident by industry. In 2003 the majority of the workforce was not covered in hotel and catering (88 per cent), construction (62 per cent), wholesale and retail (59 per cent) and business activities (58 per cent). In contrast only a minority remained without cover in manufacturing (41 per cent), transport and communication (40 per cent), financial intermediation (20 per cent) and mining (20 per cent). The public sector is far more inclusive; in 2003 about 83 per cent of all men and about 81 per cent of women were members of occupational schemes (Pensions Commission 2004, p. 98).[4]

These sector-specific patterns lead to an overall high level of exclusion for female part-time workers; in 2001 about 68 per cent were not covered, however coverage has increased steadily since 1987, when it was only about 10 per cent, and overall, full-time working women are more likely to be occupational scheme members than full-time men: 60 per cent of females were covered in 2002, in comparison with only 53 per cent of males (Pensions Commission 2004, p. 98). It is also important to bear in mind that there is status and income-related variation in each sector too, which puts our risk biographies at a disadvantage. Employees in the highest earning quintile are over three times more likely to have a salary-related scheme than someone in the lowest earning quintile and manual workers are much less likely to belong to a scheme than non-manual workers (Ginn 2003, pp. 26–7; Ginn and Arber 1999; Pensions Commission 2004, p. 97).

Of all workers who are covered by occupational provision in 2004, 71 per cent of them were covered by a few large defined benefit schemes (IDS 2002, pp. 3–4; NAPF 2003, p. 2), whereas only about 10 per cent had access to money purchase schemes. In the public sector there are only defined benefit schemes (GAD 2003, p. 9), while in the private sector money purchase and hybrid schemes are more common even though final salary schemes are still the norm (Table 2.1; DWP 2004, p. 58; Pensions Commission 2004, p. 118). However for people starting their employment, defined contribution schemes are becoming widespread: for example 41 per cent of companies operating a defined benefit scheme have changed to a defined contribution scheme for new members between 2001 and 2003 (CBI 2004, p. 13).

The Third Pillar

In an attempt to address the problems of coverage in the second pillar, and increase private saving particularly among the low paid, Stakeholder Pensions were introduced under the 1999 Welfare Reform and Pensions Act. These are money purchase personal schemes on which charges are limited to 1.5 per cent and to which members can vary their contributions at regular intervals. They were designed to reassure potential investors about the reliability of personal pensions after a series of scandals in the 1990s (Waine 1995). Stakeholder Pensions are administered by private insurance companies, but have a connection to the workplace because all but the smallest employers must compulsorily facilitate access for their employees. However employers are not obliged to contribute and the large majority have not (Pensions Commission 2004, p. 93). Largely as a result of this, take-up rates among the target group have been low;[5] by 2004 'the vast majority of schemes were empty shells with no contributing members' (Pensions Commission 2004, p. 92; see also ABI 2003b). Thus the well-developed nature of the British personal pensions market is largely explained by take-up among individuals on higher incomes.

THE SOCIAL INCLUSIVENESS OF THE BRITISH PENSION SYSTEM FOR RISK BIOGRAPHIES

In this section we consider the microsimulations of the pension entitlements of our constructed risk biographies. Before doing this it is important to be clear about the entitlement assumptions used in undertaking these calculations. Firstly the entitlements of our individuals include all compulsory state provision. Secondly we had to decide what type of second pillar provision to use in a regime where occupational provision is patchy. One approach would have been to exclude all biographies working in sectors and occupations where the majority of workers do not have access to these schemes. This would have meant that only the mother and qualified part-time worker (bio 2), the unqualified worker in the car industry (bio 4), the incomplete resident (bio 9) and the two better-paid biographies (bio 7, 8) would have had access to occupational provision (see Appendix 2.1). However given that this study's overall purpose is to assess the potential of the private sector to contribute to social inclusion, we decided to adopt a more optimistic approach. Thus while no occupational pension has been included for the carer (bio 3) and the small business entrepreneur (bio 6), because it is highly unlikely that they would have such access, the simulations of the construction worker (bio 5) and the retail worker (bio 1) also

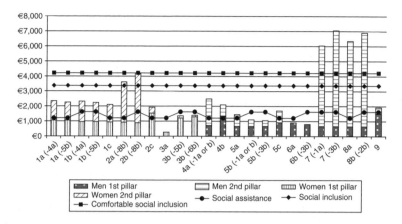

Notes: Social assistance = Social assistance for individuals if person is single on retirement; for married individuals: 50% of couples' social assistance; Social inclusion: 40% average wage; Comfortable social inclusion = 50% average wage.

Second pillars include divorce payments for divorcees; bio 1: dc-stakeholder; bio 2a, b: db; bio 2c: db/dc; bio 3: no 2nd pillar; bio 4: db/dc; bio 5: dc-stakeholder; bio 6: no 2nd pillar; bio 7 and 8: 2 db schemes each; bio 9: dc; see Appendix 1.2, Chapter 1 for details.

Figure 2.1   Projected real monthly pension levels from first and second pillar for British men and women in 2050

include some access to defined contribution occupational pensions. This is on the basis that access for them is more possible: in 2003 around 40 per cent of employees working in these sectors were covered (see above). However we also provide a general illustration of the difference in pension outcomes that would occur on the basis of a different set of assumptions.

Against this background we selected, for all individuals with occupational provision, those schemes that existed for comparable real workers in their sector in 2003. Where our hypothetical individuals changed employers, this is also reflected (see Appendix 2.1 for details).

Protection of Individuals

A first impression when examining the incomes of our individuals (Figure 2.1) is that they confirm the reputation of the British pension regime for its lack of inclusiveness. Only those individuals with earnings above the average, the divorced provider (bio 7: 113 per cent of average wages) and the middle manager (bio 8: 131 per cent of average wages), have a comfortable retirement income, with the mother and qualified welfare workers who stay with a public sector employer throughout their career (bio 2a, b), are the only other individuals to receive a pension above the social inclusion line. No other hypothetical individuals are within 30 per cent of this threshold, with some close to or below the poverty line. Most vulnerable are the carer and informal worker (bio 3), the divorced intermittent construction worker (bio 5b) and the small business entrepreneur (bio 6). The British system thus struggles even to prevent poverty.

The Role of the First Pillar

What explains this situation? To begin with, the first pillar pensions received by our biographies are very low. Thus while an individual on average wages throughout their life course, who is solely reliant on state provision, would have a pension on retirement that reaches 62 per cent of the social inclusion threshold (see below), none of our biographies receive state support close to this level. This is because they are either contracted out from the state second pension for at least some of their working life, or are not fully entitled to state provision for reasons of pay, part-time work and/or self-employment.

However although the state foundation for our biographies is low, the system is nevertheless broad in scope and redistributive, particularly with regard to women. It is noticeable for example that female first pillar pensions are as high, if not higher than males, with the exception of the married carer (bio 3a). For some this situation is the result of the British contracting-out system which as a general rule provides higher state pensions to those without or with less access to occupational provision (bio 3b and 5b, 3b and 6). However it is also a product of redistribution as can be explained by using the examples of the mother and unqualified worker in retail and the best-paid variant of the unqualified car worker.

The retail worker (bio 1a) earns 39 per cent of average wages during her working life while the car worker (bio 4a) earns 79 per cent (Tables 1.1 and 1.2, Chapter 1). Despite this large earnings gap the retail worker's first pillar pension is 32 per cent higher than that of the male worker. This significantly higher first pillar pension for the female biography is largely the product of a state system that mitigates the effect of both women's low level of pay and the years they spend out of the labour market due to caring. Thus the retail worker benefits from the contracting-out arrangements of the State Second Pension, which because of her low pay means she receives some state additional pension even when she is receiving occupational provision, and is covered for both elements of the state pension during her five years as a full-time carer. In comparison the unqualified male worker is less protected: he receives no State Second Pension during the periods when he is receiving occupational provision nor while he is unemployed. Indeed generally periods of unemployment are not as well protected as periods of caring, particularly for State Second Pension entitlement, which is only available to one of our workers while unemployed – the intermittent worker (bio 5c). This is because his unemployment is due to disability.

These examples show that so long as individuals meet the risk-sensitive qualification criteria, they will be entitled to the state pension. However the example of the other variant of the carer who remains married (bio 3a) shows the stark effects of an individual remaining below entitlement thresholds. The married carer suffers from the fact that from aged 25 she only does unregistered work and, as a result, is not entitled to the Basic State Pension and has reduced entitlement to the State Second Pension. This situation might also be experienced by female workers whose participation in the labour market is greater than our married carer because at present the existing credit arrangements do not fully cover caring periods out of the labour force of less than a full tax year (see above).

The Role of the Second Pillar

Thus overall while the state system does quite well to compensate our illustrative individuals for their social risks, the overall level of state pension to which they are entitled is too low to lift them close to inclusion. This means that occupational pensions often play a crucial role for social inclusion and Figure 2.1 shows that they make a substantial difference for many of our individuals. Most obvious beneficiaries of occupational provision are the divorced provider (bio 7) and the middle manager (bio 8) whose state pensions are eclipsed by their large second pillars – worth around 90 per cent of their overall retirement income. These individuals are least at risk – they are our highest earners, and in addition, we assumed that they have access to defined benefit schemes for at least 40 years each, which guarantee them a fixed pension in relation to lifetime earnings. However second pillar pensions also make a dominant contribution – by constituting more than 70 per cent of the overall pension – for the mother and qualified welfare worker (bio 2a, b: 75 per cent, 79 per cent). Her good performance is explained by between 23 (bio 2a) and 35 (bio 2b) years of full-time equivalent membership in a defined benefit public sector scheme. The privileged position in retirement of these two workers is illustrated by considering the other variant of the qualified part-time worker and mother (bio 2c), who spends the last part of her working life in a small private welfare organization without occupational provision. Despite receiving identical lifetime earnings (42 per cent of average income; Table 1.1, Chapter 1) to one of the lifetime public sector workers (bio 2a), she receives a pension 34 percentage points lower as a proportion of the social inclusion threshold.[6] The car worker (bio 4a) is also well covered for occupational provision. He has access to a defined benefit scheme for eight years followed by 38 years of contributing to a defined contribution scheme. He is the person with the longest overall contribution period in our group, which on the one hand explains why his second pillar pension is much more significant than his first. On the other hand if we consider that with 79 per cent of average wages he earns significantly more than the welfare workers, the difference between his and their second pillar pensions demonstrates well the superiority of defined benefit schemes.

The contribution of occupational pensions to overall income is also substantial in the case of the unqualified retail worker (bio 1; between 53 and 58 per cent of average wages), with all variants gaining a significantly higher overall pension because they paid contributions to a defined contribution scheme for between 38 years (bio 1a, 34 years part-time) and 43 years (bio 1b, c, 11 years part-time).

The most disadvantaged of our biographies in the British regime with regard to occupational provision are those who work in small private sector firms or for themselves. In this regard our intermittent construction worker (bio 5a, b) and small business entrepreneur (bio 6) are particularly badly hit despite quite high lifetime wages. The former works in a small business for the first 13 years of his career, gaining access to a stakeholder pension with employer contributions; after that he is self-employed until retirement. As a result while his occupational pension amounts to between 37 and 53 per cent of his overall pension, this is only because his state provision is so low. As can be seen in Figure 2.1, the total pension received by variants of the intermittent worker does not rise above 43 per cent of the social inclusion threshold. The small business entrepreneur receives no occupational provision and thus his pension only amounts to 27 per cent of the social inclusion threshold.

The discussion above has already illustrated the diversity of occupational pensions, and that entitlements depend not only on income or length of contribution period, but also on the availability of good-quality schemes. However it is important to emphasize that availability varies not just between sectors but also within them. This means that individuals working in the same sector might be entitled to a defined benefit scheme, a defined contribution scheme, or to nothing but state provision. To illustrate this situation let us consider again the example of one variant of the unqualified male worker (bio 4b). On the basis of our assumptions in Figure 2.1, he receives an overall pension income of 62 per cent of the social exclusion threshold, 14 per cent of which is provided by the defined benefit pension he obtains in his first employment with Ford, 19 per cent of which comes from his defined contribution pension with Peugeot, with the rest provided by the state pension, including State Second Pension, for which he qualifies during

Table 2.2 Pension income of the unqualified male worker (bio 4b) in Britain in 2050 by different forms of provision

	State provision only*	DB/DC/S2P**	DB/DC***
% of social inclusion threshold			
State pension	51	39	21
Occupational pension	0	23	44
Total pension	51	62	65

Notes:
*   contracted into state second pension throughout working career
**   contracted into state second pension for last 28 years of working life
***   contracted out of state second pension throughout working life

the last 20 years of his working life while he is working for a smaller car component firm (see Appendix 2.1). However, different assumptions about this individual's employers within the car industry would make a significant difference to his pension outcome. For example, if instead of joining one of the big car companies on leaving full-time education at 18 this worker had joined a small component firm, and stayed with it or with similar firms for the rest of his working life, he would have been entirely reliant on state provision. He would thus pay lower pension contributions throughout his working life but, partially as a result, would receive a pension 11 percentage points lower in relation to the social exclusion threshold (Table 2.2). Alternatively if he had remained with his second employer after the age of 37 and up to retirement, his final pension income would have been 3 percentage points higher in relation to the social exclusion threshold due to his longer access to defined contributions provision.

Gender

How does gender map on to this picture? The first point that needs to be made is that the relative performance of our male and female biographies does not conform to a straightforward pattern: the men do not clearly outperform the women. For example if we exclude the higher earners (bio 7, 8) the two highest pensions for our lower-paid biographies are accumulated by women, both by variants of the mother and qualified part-time worker (bio 2). Of the bottom 11 pensions six are received by men, with the self-employed entrepreneur performing particularly badly. This is despite the fact that the female biographies were constructed on the basis of the disadvantaged labour market position of women; thus allowance was made for the fact that women are more likely to experience periods out of the workforce due to caring and, when they are working, tend to be lower paid and undertake longer periods of part-time work (Tables 1.1 and 1.2, Chapter 1).

These results are somewhat at odds with the general view based on current pension outcomes that the British system is clearly gendered (Ginn 2003; Ginn and Arber 1993; Thane 2006). Even allowing for the fact that our biographies are illustrative, not representative, they resonate with findings suggesting a gradual decline in coming years in levels of inequality between men and women, caused by three factors. Firstly the increased entry of women into the labour force means their access to state and occupational pensions has improved, particularly given higher levels of occupational coverage among part-time women workers (Pensions Commission 2004, p. 98). Secondly the entitlement changes made to the state system since the mid-1970s are providing a significant boost to the pensions of women, as was seen most particularly above in the pension outcome of the unqualified worker and mother (bio 1). Moreover many of the continuing weaknesses in this system (Hollis 2006) look likely to be addressed in coming years, although this was not assumed in our simulations (DWP 2006). Thirdly the greater concentration of women's employment in public sector employment (bio 2a, b) means that many women have access to defined benefit occupational provision, an advantage that is accentuated by the recent decline of defined benefit provision in the private sector which seems likely to disadvantage male workers disproportionately (Pensions Commission 2004, p. 96).[7]

However it must also be emphasized that when good occupational provision is not available, women's vulnerability to low income in retirement on the basis of their disadvantaged labour market position strongly reasserts itself (for example bio 2c). Moreover the gendered distribution of social risks, and the lack of protection against these risks afforded by occupational schemes, means that men continue to achieve higher pensions than women when they have access to the same type of occupational provision.

Savings

What scope is there for those of our biographies who do badly in the British system to improve their situation on the basis of private personal savings? This is certainly the type of approach that has been emphasized in recent British policy debates on projected pension shortfalls (see Brown 2004; DWP 2002; Oliver Wyman & Company 2001). However British panel data on savings behaviour is not promising: it suggests that savings level are particularly low among individuals such as our risk biographies, who are on low pay, in part-time work, and/or have broken working careers (DWP

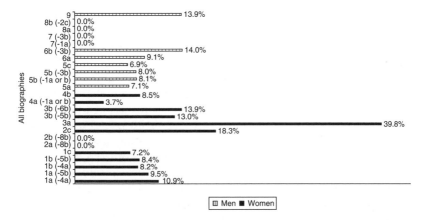

Notes: Each individual linked to another individual receives or pays contributions to divorced partner. Assumptions for private savings: Appendix 1.2, Chapter 1.

Figure 2.2   *Third pillar savings from lifetime income required of British men and women to reach social inclusion line of 40% average wage in 2050*

2002; IFS 2002). Our simulations reinforce this impression: they show that even if more of this group did save, many would face savings rates to avoid poverty and/or social exclusion so large as to be unfeasible (Figure 2.2).

The biography that seems least likely to save at the level required is the worst-performing variant of the married carer (bio 3a) who requires savings of 40 per cent of gross lifetime income to surpass the social inclusion threshold, and an annual savings rate of 12 per cent merely to give her a pension equivalent to social assistance. Even savings at the latter level are highly unlikely given that she receives a lifetime income of 22 per cent of the average wage. It is also extremely unlikely that the other two variants of the married carer (bio 3b, c), with lifetime incomes of 37 per cent of the average wage, will save the 14 per cent of gross income they require to breach the social inclusion line. Moreover there is also the risk for all of these workers that ultimately their savings might prove insufficient to push them over the means-tested minimum. If this did not occur on retirement, it could occur shortly after, making largely pointless their consumption sacrifice during their working life.

The savings rates of the migrant worker (bio 9), the unqualified part-time worker (bio 1) and the qualified male worker (bio 4) are lower. However the particular problem for these workers is that they are already making substantial pension saving through their occupational schemes, which they are likely to perceive as sufficient to provide them with an adequate income in retirement (Pensions Commission 2004). Additional saving in these circumstances seems implausible.

However for some of our biographies private saving seems a more
promising option. This is the situation for the variant of the welfare worker
who leaves the NHS at 40 (bio 2c), the intermittent worker (bio 5) and self-
employed entrepreneur (bio 6). Their low pensions are at least partially
explained by the lower first and second pillar contributions they paid in
comparison with some of our other biographies with greater occupational
provision. Thus in theory they have scope for investing their extra sum of
net pay in a personal saving scheme. For the male workers such saving is
also made more likely by their relatively high lifetime earnings. However
despite these promising factors, there still must be considerable doubt
whether even these biographies would actually undertake the level of
savings required to lift them above the social inclusion threshold on retirement. With regard first to the welfare worker, this is because, while she pays
national insurance contributions for the last 20 years of her working life
that are 4.4 per cent lower than the other variants who remain in the NHS
(bio 2a, b), she requires a savings level of 7 per cent of gross income over
her entire working life to surpass the social inclusion threshold. This level
of sustained savings seems extremely unlikely, particularly given that her
low levels of pay and periods of part-time work put her within two of the
low-saver categories identified by the panel data referred to above. The
reason why the intermittent worker and self-employed entrepreneur are
unlikely to undertake the required level of savings, between 7 and 9 per cent
of gross income, is related to attitudes among self-employed people who
tend not to save because they regard their business as their pension. Thus
only approximately 43 per cent of self-employed men and 35 per cent of
women were contributing anything to a private pension scheme in 2002/03
(Pensions Commission 2004, p. 91).

Protection of Couples and Effect of Divorce

To what extent are the outcomes outlined above consistent with a male
breadwinner model of employment and social support? What is the impact
of divorce?

The fairly balanced distribution of pension income between our male
and female biographies means that the picture with regard to the contribution of individuals to couples' pension income is not consistent with a
simple male breadwinner model (Figure 2.3). Thus while in seven out of 11
couples the man's income is dominant this includes couples that contain the
most affluent male biography (bio 8).[8] If we consider only those couples
that exclude this relatively wealthy individual, men's income is dominant in

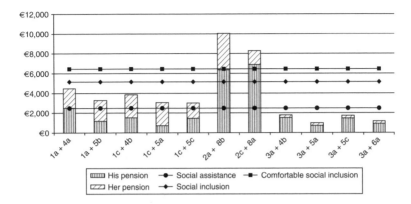

Notes: Social assistance line = Social assistance line for couples; Social inclusion line for couples: 1.5 × 40% average wage; Comfortable social inclusion = 1.5 × 50% average wage.

Figure 2.3   Projected real monthly pension levels of British couples in 2050

only five out of nine couples. Moreover in all four of the cases where the woman was in poverty as an individual, which relates to the experience of the married carer (bio 3a and 4b, 3a and 5a, 3a and 5c, 3a and 6), she remains in poverty in relation to household income as part of a couple. Only her marriage to the unqualified male worker (bio 4b) comes close to lifting her above this threshold. The low level of many male pensions in Britain, in comparison to some of the other countries included in this study, means that women are less likely to be pulled out of social exclusion and/or poverty through marriage. In the four cases where the woman's contribution is greater than her male partner's, this can almost always be explained by differences in the respective access of male and female partners to occupational provision. It is also a result of the reduced entitlement to state provision of self-employed workers.

Overall therefore the results for couples do not suggest that the British pension system performs significantly better on the basis of couples, rather than individuals.[9] However despite the fact that couples do not perform better overall than individuals in relation to our poverty and social exclusion thresholds, choice of marriage partner is not unimportant; it can cause significant variations in the household income experienced in retirement by individuals, as can be seen for example from the sizeable difference in the household income experienced by the unqualified part-time worker and mother (bio 1a) depending on her marriage partners (bio 4a and 5b; Figure 2.3)

Moreover the impact of divorce must also be considered. We have already seen how the protective mechanisms in the state pension system

Table 2.3   The effect of divorce on the pensions of female biographies in Britain, as percentage of social exclusion

Biography	1a/4a	1a/5b	1b/4a	1b/5b	2a/8	2b/8	3b/5b	3b/6
Pension with divorce supplement	68	67	69	66	107	125	40	41
Pension without divorce supplement	63	64	63	63	91	109	36	38
Difference	5	3	6	3	16	16	4	3

Table 2.4   The effect of divorce on the pensions of male biographies in Britain, as percentage of social exclusion

Biography	4a/1a, b	5b/1a, b	6/3b	7/1a	7/3b	8/2a, b
Pension with divorce payment	74	33	25	192	209	188
Pension without divorce payment	80	43	27	259	265	205
Difference	−6	−10	−2	−67	−56	−17

operate to boost the retirement income of some of our female biographies (for example bio 1), thus helping to push their pensions closer to or above those of male biographies (bio 4) who earn considerably more throughout their lifetime. This process is also aided in our simulations by pension-sharing after divorce, which assuming full advantage is taken of the current legislation, involves the transfer of a generally small but significant income supplement from men to women after divorce. Thus as can be seen from Table 2.3 the pension income of women who divorce is raised by between three and 16 percentage points in relation to the social inclusion threshold. Most, and sometimes all, of the divorce supplement received by our women biographies is based on the man's occupational provision, which means that in common with all distributive features of this sector in Britain, there is significant, and largely arbitrary, variation.

In contrast the pension income of men who divorce is significantly lowered, in some cases quite substantially (Table 2.4). In this regard the divorced variant of the intermittent worker (bio 5b) fares particularly badly because he loses half of the employer-supported stakeholder pension he accrues between the ages of 20 and 30, when he divorces aged 32. He suffers a ten-percentage-point loss of pension income in relation to the social inclusion threshold, which while lower than the loss suffered by the higher-paid male biographies (bio 7, 8), is more significant in its overall impact because it is sufficient to push him below the poverty threshold.

The British Pension System and Social Exclusion

In summary our research findings suggest that while the current public–private mix of pension provision in Britain is capable of providing some of our risk biographies with a reasonable pension income it is incapable of delivering a retirement free from social exclusion for most citizens. This disappointing performance is caused by problems in both the state and private sectors, and in the way the two sectors interact.

With regard first to state provision the system works quite hard, particularly for our female biographies, to mitigate the effect of social risks on pension outcomes, yet this by itself does not lift all individuals out of poverty because not all are protected by the first pillar against periods out of paid work (bio 3a). Moreover, even when entitlement is fully secured, pensions are too low. This highlights the limits of entitlement condition reforms by themselves as a means of reducing poverty (see also Rake et al. 2000).

Private occupational pensions can play a major role in protecting citizens. However the variability of coverage between employment sectors and employers of different sizes means that some sectors – self-employment and small business employment as well as informal work which is unrelated to care – are not or are very rarely covered, creating systematic poverty risks for whole groups of workers. For other sectors of the economy variability also means that the process by which some are protected while others are not is to some extent arbitrary (Meyer and Bridgen forthcoming 2008).

Marriage sometimes helps our biographies avoid poverty on retirement but only because those individuals who are married are subject to the couple's social assistance threshold rather than the individual threshold on the basis of economies of scale.

Private saving is the other way in which our individuals might try to surpass the poverty and/or social exclusion threshold on retirement. However our findings indicate that private savings are unaffordable for some, and for others it is far from clear that they represent a good investment. If quite high levels of savings are required on a regular basis merely to surpass the social assistance line – a situation experienced by some of our individuals – there is a considerable risk that ultimately working-time income will have been given up for no material benefit in retirement (see also Clark 2001).

THE REFORM DEBATE IN BRITAIN

Our findings thus suggest that if social inclusion in retirement for all British citizens is a genuine policy goal, significant changes are needed. Indeed quite major reform would be required even to achieve the more limited target of eradicating poverty. To what extent does government recognize these problems?

Until recently the answer would have been that it does not. The Labour government has defended the pension system (DWP 2002) in the face of growing criticism of its performance since 1997 from within the Labour Party (Davies et al. 2003), from the trade unions (TUC 2003) and the Liberal Democrats (Laws et al. 2005). This resistance can be explained in relation to the political underpinnings of the New Labour 'project', and as a consequence of the continued power of the Treasury in social policy-making. With regard to the former, 'New Labour' was conceived in the mid-1990s after four successive Conservative Party election victories, and has involved a move away from the more 'statist' policies associated with 'old' high-tax Labour governments (Ludlum and Smith 2000; Powell 1999). Thus increasing the universal Basic State Pension (BSP) has been regarded as unappealing because it would imply a significant increase in taxation or a transfer of resources away from New Labour's public service priorities, health and education (Powell 1999; Rawnsley 2001). The one exception to this general rule has been that New Labour has shown itself to be gender-sensitive and open to significant change in this regard (DWP 2006), mainly in response to a strong feminist lobby within the party and a concerted campaign by academics and women's pressure groups outside it (Ginn 2003; Hollis 2006).

This resistance to an increase in universal pension provision is strongly supported by the Treasury, the financial department at the heart of British government. It has long been regarded as a major influence over social policymaking (Bridgen 2006; Deakin and Parry 2000; Pemberton et al. 2006) and with regard to the Basic State Pension 'the Treasury line' has always been based on suspicion (Bridgen and Lowe 1998). It is therefore likely that this institution is currently a powerful agent in favour of the status quo. Against this background the New Labour government has opted to emphasize the potential of private provision as a means of lifting most citizens out of poverty on retirement in the longer term. However its policy of removing obstacles to private saving and of emphasizing the importance of occupational provision (DWP 1999, 2002) has run into problems. Reforms to simplify tax rules and pension products, and to improve financial literacy (DWP 2006; HM Treasury and Inland Revenue 2002; Pickering 2002; Sandler 2002), are not expected to lead to a significant change in savings behaviour (Fabian Society 2002, quoted in Evandrou et al. 2003; IPPR 2003; Pensions Commission 2005; Rowlingson 2002; Sandler 2002, para. 91; for a different view, see: ABI 2003a). Indeed many have argued that these initiatives will fail because inadequate income is the biggest obstacle to saving for those on low to middle earnings, particularly given the level of saving that is necessary to avoid means-testing in retirement (for example ABI 2003b; Age Concern 2003; Standard Life 2002). Our results strongly support this view. At the same time New Labour's faith in the reliability of occupational provision has also appeared increasingly misplaced given the substantial and rapid changes in the occupational sphere.

In the face of these developments a wide spectrum of opinion now favours a significant policy change, involving an increase in universal state provision. Importantly supporters of this option include the employers' Confederation of British Industry (CBI 2004), the Association of British Insurers (ABI 2003a), the National Association of Pension Funds (NAPF 2006) and even, to a certain extent, the Conservative Party (Willets and Yeo 2004). This support is largely grounded on the most important perceived flaw in the government's approach: the inconsistency between the growth of means testing, on the one hand, and an encouragement of private saving on the other. Why should people save if they could not be sure that they would gain the full benefits of these savings when they retired? Differences exist about how this problem should be addressed, but all propose a greater increase in the Basic State Pension than envisaged up until recently by the government.

The Pensions Commission and the 2006 White Paper

In response to this pressure for reform, the Pensions Commission was set up in 2002. The remit of this independent body reflected the government's continuing prioritization of private savings; it was asked to 'keep under review the regime for private pensions and long term savings . . . and to make recommendations on whether there is a case for moving beyond the current voluntarist approach' (2004, p. v). The commission recommended no less than a fundamental change of government policy: voluntary saving, the preferred alternative of government, 'was not growing; rather it was in serious and probably irreversible decline'. In particular 'initiatives to stimulate private personal pensions saving have not worked' (2005, pp. 2, 5). Thus without major change pensioners would gradually over time become poorer relative to the rest of society.

To improve the situation a change of the relationship between the individual and the state, and between the public and the private sector, was proposed. The state's responsibility would be to ensure a secure, reliable and transparent foundation for all upon which private saving can take place. It should therefore base entitlement to the Basic State Pension on residency and broaden the scope of the State Second Pension, particularly to include more carers. This could be achieved by linking the Basic State Pension back to earnings from 2010 and by accelerating the planned changes to the State Second Pension. To pay for the increase in public expenditure these reforms would imply an incremental rise in the state pension age to 68 between 2020 and 2050.

However even with a more secure and reliable state foundation, the Commission concluded, many individuals were unlikely or unable by themselves to undertake sufficient private saving to ensure an adequate income in retirement. It therefore proposed the introduction of a National Pensions Savings Scheme into which those not covered by an existing occupational pension of sufficient quality would be automatically enrolled, paying contributions amounting to 4 per cent of their gross earnings. This contribution would be supplemented by a minimum employer contribution of 3 per cent and tax relief amounting to 1 per cent. Anyone would be free to opt out of this scheme.

The Government's response to the Pensions Commission's report contained in the 2006 White Paper accepts many of the most important recommendations made by the Commission, without acceding fully to them. Thus up-rating the Basic State Pension on the basis of earnings has been agreed, but ruled out before 2012 at the earliest. A residency approach to entitlement has been rejected on the grounds of cost, principle and practicality, but a significant easing of entitlement conditions is proposed (DWP 2006, p. 126). Finally, while government has committed itself fully to the introduction of some type of national pensions scheme, which it has labelled Personal Accounts, on an auto-enrolment basis, it is still in negotiations with the private insurance industry about a more market-based proposal than envisaged by the Pensions Commission (see below).

A Fresh Path or a Blind Alley?

Would the implementation of the new public–private mix contained in the White Paper, based on the Pensions Commission report, solve the problems identified in this chapter? Would it move Britain closer to the model adopted in other 'veteran' countries of this study, where a less voluntary approach is taken to non-state provision with better overall results with respect to poverty and/or social exclusion? We suggested above that the existing public–private mix was not generally capable of delivering an income in retirement above the social exclusion line because of problems in both the state and private sectors, and in the way the two sectors interact.

The role of the state

There is no doubt that the proposals contained in the White Paper would involve a change in the nature of state pension provision, but it is also clear that firm limits remain attached to the state's role. Enhanced state pension entitlements are likely to improve the situation for carers and accelerate the progress expected in women's pension entitlement (see above), and therefore have generally been welcomed (PPI 2006). However our simulations show that by themselves they are limited as a means for reducing pensioner poverty and/or social exclusion unless accompanied by a more substantial increase in state provision than is currently being proposed. Moreover the government's rejection of calls by the Pensions Commission and other commentators to move entitlement onto a residency basis means that some vulnerable citizens are still likely to miss out and that an opportunity to simplify the system significantly is lost. The reforms would still leave the British system a long way away from the Dutch universal pensions.

The interaction of state provision and private saving

The White Paper focuses most of all on the disincentives to save that the current system's growing reliance on means-testing creates. However many pension policy commentators suggest that not enough is being proposed to rectify even this problem, notwithstanding the proposal to introduce auto-enrolment into Personal Accounts. The White Paper's failure to make universal state provision a more adequate and reliable guarantee against poverty means that on the government's own reckoning one-third of pensioners could still be entitled to means-tested support in 2050, despite this reform (DWP 2006, p. 122; see also Inman 2006; Pensions Commission 2005, p. 294). Unless the large majority of individuals are fully confident that they will see in retirement the full benefits of any savings they undertake during their working life, savings disincentives are likely to persist (see also Pensions Commission 2005, p. 16), even with the introduction of auto-enrolment. This leaves aside of course the question of whether the level of saving proposed by the White Paper would be sufficient to ensure citizens currently at risk a retirement income above our social inclusion threshold. Our simulations suggest that it would not. They also suggest that if contributions had to be increased it should be the state and/or employers, rather than individuals, who should pay more.

Funded personal saving: savings scheme for the nation or for insurers?

A broad level of support has greeted the government's decision to establish Personal Accounts. There is no doubt they have the potential to reduce some of the arbitrariness that currently exists in the distribution of occupational pension income in Britain (Meyer and Bridgen forthcoming 2008).

However the national, centralized approach for delivering them, recommended by the Pensions Commission, has come under sustained attack, mainly from the private insurance industry which would prefer a more market-based approach (ABI 2006; *Financial Times* 2006). The Association of British Insurers, the National Association of Pension Funds and the Royal London insurance company (Inman 2006) argue that such competition would decrease costs, and that the cost savings claimed for a national scheme are exaggerated (ABI 2006). So far the government seems more sympathetic to the Pensions Commission argument (DWP 2006, p. 56). The other main concern about Personal Accounts is their possible effect on existing occupational provision. There is a concern that existing occupational pension providers might reduce the quality and generosity of their schemes in line with the minimum standard. This is firstly because the introduction of auto-enrolment into existing occupational provision is likely to increase the costs of these schemes (CBI 2006; NAPF 2006), and secondly because the introduction of Personal Accounts might further complicate the already extremely complicated contracting-out arrangements, with some employers having to prove that their existing schemes are of sufficient quality to merit their exclusion from the Personal Accounts system (see also ABI 2006; Pensions Commission 2005).

The government is confident that such an unintended consequence will not occur, on the basis of Department of Work and Pensions research on employer attitudes (DWP 2006). However predicting companies' behaviour in relation to their occupational provision is fraught with difficulties (Bridgen and Meyer 2005). This makes the experience of Switzerland, detailed in Chapter 4 of this book, particularly important from the British perspective. Here there is clear evidence to suggest that the introduction of compulsion, albeit in a different form from that proposed in Britain, led to a levelling-down of existing occupational provision.

CONCLUDING COMMENTS

At this stage in the reform process it is difficult to be sure whether Britain is set to embark on a new path that might significantly improve its performance in relation to poverty and/or social exclusion. However it is possible to say that there *is* now a general acceptance within the British pension policy network that the limits of privatization have been reached. Within government and beyond, few now believe that non-state provision can be extended any further on an entirely voluntary basis. Personal private savings are generally recognized as inappropriate for low- to middle-income earners, because this group cannot afford to pay contributions at a level sufficient to make their savings worthwhile, and because the prospects of profits for private insurers among this group are so low. At the same time it has also become clear that the 'golden age' of British occupational pension provision has passed (Clark 2006).

Yet despite this general acceptance the government has not so far fully committed itself to a state-based solution to Britain's pension problems. In this regard a straightforward proposal to supplement the changes envisaged by the White Paper has been made (PPI 2006): a one-off substantial increase in the Basic State Pension. For those of our risk biographies currently dependent on the Pension Credit or their husbands' pensions, such a step would provide a more adequate minimum by right. It would individualize pensions, widen their scope, preserve their long-term value and it would address the problem of low take-up. Importantly it would also address much more unambiguously than the 2006 White Paper the problem of savings disincentives. Such a proposal is based on the view that the voluntarism of the private sector can only have a more inclusive effect if a more substantial universal minimum for all than is currently available is guaranteed by the state.

The obstacles to the introduction of such a change are significant. There are cost problems, and thus political problems. There are institutional problems both with regard to the British policy legacy and the central role in the pensions policy network of the Treasury. It is not at all clear that these obstacles are surmountable. However if they are not there seems little doubt that the public–private relationship in Britain will remain more of a muddle than a partnership with continuing, and probably worsening, implications for the well-being of the pensioner population.

NOTES

1. The authors thank David Smith for his support during the fieldwork stage of this project.
2. This is set to rise if recent government proposals are passed. There will be a phased move towards a retirement age of 67 for both men and women from 2024. See DWP (2006, p. 18).
3. The Pension Commission is of the view that UK pension assets outstrip the Netherlands (Pension Commission 2004, p. 61).
4. Not all public sector pensions are funded. The NHS scheme for example is a pay-as-you-go system financed from taxation.
5. Employees' take-up of Stakeholder Pensions increases from 13 per cent to 70 per cent when the employer makes a contribution (CBI 2004, p. 16).
6. This is the case even with the exclusion of the supplement the latter receives after divorce.
7. However, Clark (2006) suggests that this imbalance between public sector provision and private sector provision is unsustainable, particularly with regard to the unfunded state schemes such as that provided by the NHS.
8. These figures do not include private saving, but with only two couples (1c and 4b; 3b and 6b) having a gap between the male and female contribution of 20 per cent or less, it is

unlikely that this consideration would greatly change the general picture, particularly given the problems with saving outlined above.
9. There is of course an implicit assumption here about the distribution of household income between partners.

BIBLIOGRAPHY

ABI (2003a), *Stakeholder Pensions: Time for Change*, London: Association of British Insurers.

ABI (2003b), *Simplicity, Security and Choice: ABI Response to the Green Paper*, London: Association of British Insurers, http://www.abi.org.uk/Display/file/300/final-DWP-response.doc.

ABI (2006), *Making a Success of Personal Accounts: The ABI's Response to the Pensions White Paper*, London: Association of British Insurers, http://www.abi.org.uk/BookShop/ResearchReports/Pensions%20%20Personal%20Accounts%20with%20cover.pdf, accessed October 2006.

Age Concern (2003), *Age Concern's Response to the Pensions Green Paper*, London: Age Concern Policy Papers.

Agulnik, P. (1999), 'The proposed State Second Pension', *Fiscal Studies*, **20**(4), 409–21.

Bridgen, P. (2006), 'A straitjacket with wriggle room: The Beveridge Report, the Treasury and the Exchequer's pension liability 1942–1959', *Twentieth Century British History*, **17**(1), 1–25.

Bridgen, P. and Lowe, R. (1998), *Welfare Policy under the Conservatives 1951–1960: A Guide to the Documents in the Public Record Office*, London: Public Record Office.

Bridgen, P. and Meyer, T. (2005), 'When do benevolent capitalists change their mind? Explaining the retrenchment of defined benefit pensions in Britain', *Social Policy and Administration*, **39**(4), 764–85.

Brown, K. (2004), 'Treasury misses a savings chance', *Financial Times*, 29–30 May.

CBI (2004), *Securing our Future: Developing Sustainable Pension Provision in the UK*, London: Confederation of British Industry.

CBI (2006), *CBI Submission to the Department of Work and Pensions: Responding to the Pensions Commission Final Report*, London: Confederation of British Industry.

Clark, G. (2006), 'The UK occupational system in crisis', in H. Pemberton, P. Thane and N. Whiteside (eds), *Britain's Pension Crisis: History and Policy* (pp. 145–66), Oxford: Oxford University Press.

Clark, T. (2001), *Recent Pensions Policy and the Pension Credit*, London: IFS, http://www.ifs.org.uk.

Clark, T. (2002), *Rewarding Saving and Alleviating Poverty? The Final Pension Credit Proposals*, London: IFS, http://www.ifs.org.uk.

Davies, B., Land, H., Lynes, T., MacIntyre, K. and Townsend, P. (2003), 'Better Pensions: The state's responsibility', London, Catalyst Working Paper.

Deakin, N. and Parry, N. (2000), *The Treasury of Social Policy: The Contest for Control of Welfare Strategy*, Basingstoke: Macmillian.

DWP (1999), *Partnership in Pensions*, London: Department of Work and Pensions, HMSO.

DWP (2002), *Simplicity, Security and Choice: Working and Saving for Retirement*, London: HMSO.

DWP (2004), *Income Related Benefits Estimates of Take-up in 2000/2001*, London: Department for Work and Pensions.

DWP (2006), *Security in Retirement: Towards a New Pensions System*, London: DWP, http://www.dwp.gov.uk/pensionsreform/pdfs/white_paper_complete.pdf, accessed October 2006.

Evandrou, M. and Falkingham, J. (2005), 'A secure retirement for all? Older people and New Labour', in J. Hills and K. Stewart (eds), *A More Equal Society? New Labour, Poverty, Inequality and Exclusion* (pp. 167–87), Bristol: Policy Press.

Evandrou, M., Falkingham, J., Johnson, P., Scott, A. and Zaidi, A. (2003), 'Simplicity, security and choice: a response to the Green Paper on pensions by ESRC-SAGE Research Group', ESRC-SAGE discussion paper 13, London, ESRC-SAGE Research Group, http://www.lse.ac.uk/collections/SAGE/pdf/SAGE_DP13.pdf.

Financial Times (2006), 'Financial services guru to help balance personal accounts', 3 August.

GAD (2003), *Occupational Pension Schemes 2000. Eleventh Survey by the Government Actuary*, London: Government Actuary's Department, www.gad.gov.uk/Publications/docs/opss 2000_final_results_final_7april2003.pdf.

Ginn, J. (2003), *Gender, Pensions and the Life Course: How Pensions Need to Adapt to Changing Family Forms*, Bristol: Policy Press.

Ginn, J. and Arber, S. (1993), 'Pension penalties: the gendered division of occupational welfare', *Work, Employment and Society*, **7**(1), 47–70.

Ginn, J. and Arber, S. (1999), 'Changing patterns of pension inequality: the shift from state to private sources', *Ageing and Society*, **19**, 319–42.

GMB (2002), *Response to DWP Consultation Documents: Simplicity, Security and Choice; Simplifying the Taxation of Pensions IR/HM Treasury 03/03*, London: DWP Consultations, http: www.dwp gov.uk/consultations.

Government Actuary (1999), *Report by the Government Actuary on the Financial Effects on the National Insurance Fund of the Child Support, Pensions and Security Bill*, London.

Groves, D. (1983), 'Members and survivors: women and retirement-pension legislation', in J. Lewis (ed.), *Women's Welfare, Women's Rights* (pp. 18–63), London and Canberra: Croom Helm.

Groves, D. (1987), 'Occupational pension provision and women's poverty in old age', in C. Glendinning and J. Millar (eds), *Women and Poverty in Britain* (pp. 199–220), Brighton: Wheatsheaf.

HM Treasury and Inland Revenue (2002), *Simplifying the Taxation of Pensions: Increasing Choice and Flexibility*, London: HMSO.

Hollis, Baroness (2006), 'Gender and the present crisis', in H. Pemberton, P. Thane and N. Whiteside (eds), *Britain's Pension Crisis: History and Policy*, Oxford: Oxford University Press.

Honeyball, S. and Shaw, J. (1991), 'Sex, law and the retiring man', *European Law Review*, **14**, 47–58.

IDS (2002), *Pension Schemes and their Benefits 2002/3*, London: IDS.

IDS (2003), *Pensions in Practice 2003/04, From Primary Legislation to Practical Implementation*, London: IDS.

IFS (2002), 'Retirement, pensions and the adequacy of saving: a guide to the debate', Institute of Fiscal Studies Briefing Note No. 29, October.

Inman, P. (2006), 'National pension plan could bring widespread misselling, says insurers', *Guardian*, 9 October.

IPPR (2003), *Beyond Bank Accounts: Full Financial Inclusion*, London: IPPR.

Laws, D., Alexander, D. and Oakeshott, M. (2005), *Reforming UK Pensions: Liberal Democrat Proposals*, London: Liberal Democrats.

Ludlum, S. and Smith, M.J. (2000), *New Labour in Government*, London: Macmillan.

Lynes, T. (1997), 'The British case', in M. Rein and E. Wadensjö (eds), *Enterprise and the Welfare State* (pp. 309–51), Cheltenham, UK and Lyme, USA: Edward Elgar.

Mazey, S. (1998), 'The European Union and women's rights: from the Europeanization of national agendas to the nationalization of a European agenda?', *Journal Of European Public Policy*, **5**(1), 131–52.

Meyer, T. and Bridgen, P. (forthcoming 2008), 'Class, gender and chance: the social division of welfare and British occupational pensions', *Ageing and Society*.

NAPF (2003), *NAPF Annual Survey of Occupational Pension Schemes 2003*, National Association of Pension Funds, www.napf.co.uk/news/AnnualSurvey.cfm, accessed November 2005.

NAPF (2006), *Security in Retirement: Towards a New Pensions System. NAPF Response*, London: National Association of Pension Funds, http://www.napf.co.uk/publications/Downloads/PolicyPapers/SectionI/2006/whitePaperResponse.pdf, accessed October 2006.

Neilson, J. (1998), 'Equal opportunities for women in the European Union: success or failure', *Journal of European Social Policy*, **8**(1), 64–79.

Oliver Wyman & Company (2001), *The Future Regulation of UK Savings and Investment: Targeting the Savings Gap*, London: Oliver Wyman & Company.

Pemberton, H., Thane, P. and Whiteside, N. (2006), *Britain's Pension Crisis: History and Policy*, Oxford: Oxford University Press.

Pensions Commission (2004), *Pensions: Challenges and Choices. The First Report of the Pensions Commission*, London: Stationery Office.

Pensions Commission (2005), *A New Pensions Settlement for the Twenty-first Century. The Second Report of the Pensions Commission*, London: Stationery Office, http://www.pensionscommission.org.uk/publications/2005/ annrep/annrep-index.asp, accessed November 2005.

Pensions Service (2003), *A Guide to State Pensions*, London: Department of Work and Pensions.

Pickering, A. (2002), *A Simpler Way to Better Pensions: An Independent Report*, London: Department of Work and Pensions.

PMI (2004), *PMI News: The Impact of Anti-Discrimination Laws on Occupational Pensions*, Pensions Management Institute, http://www.pensions-pmi.org.uk/Publications/.

Powell, M. (1999), *New Labour, New Welfare State? The 'Third Way' in British Social Policy*, Bristol: Policy Press.

PPI (2003), *Response to the Department for Work and Pensions Consultation Paper 'Simplicity, Security and Choice: Working and Saving for retirement'*, London: Pensions Policy Institute, http: www.pensionspolicyinstitute.org.uk/news.

PPI (2006), *An Evaluation of the White Paper State Pension Reform Proposals*, London: Pensions Policy Institute, http://www.pensionspolicyinstitute.org.uk/uploadeddocuments/Nuffield/PPI_evaluation_of_WP_state_pension_reforms_20_July_2006.pdf, accessed October 2006.

Rake, K., Falkingham, J. and Evans, M. (2000), 'British pension policy in the twenty-first century: a partnership in pensions or a marriage to the means test?', *Social Policy and Administration*, **34**(3), 296–317.

Rawnsley, A. (2001), *Servants of the People: The Inside Story of New Labour*, London: Penguin.

Rowlingson, K. (2002), 'Private pension planning: the rhetoric of responsibility, the reality of insecurity', *Journal of Social Policy*, **31**(4), 623–42.

Sandler, R. (2002), *Medium and Long-Term Savings in the UK: A Review*, London: HM Treasury.

Standard Life (2002), Unpublished paper prepared for Stakeholder Summit.

Thane, P. (2006), 'The "scandal" of women's pensions in Britain: how did it come about?' in H. Pemberton, P. Thane and N. Whiteside (eds), *Britain's Pension Crisis: History and Policy* (pp. 77–90), Oxford: Oxford University Press.

TUC (2003), *TUC Response to the Pensions Green Paper: Simplicity, Security and Choice*, London: Trades Union Congress.

TUC (2004), *Prospects for Pensions*, London: Trades Union Congress, http://www.tuc.org.uk/pensions.

Waine, B. (1995), 'A disaster foretold? The case of personal pension', *Social Policy and Administration*, **29**(4), 317–34.

Walker, A. (1999), 'The third way for pensions (by way of Thatcherism and avoiding today's pensioners)', *Critical Social Policy*, **19**(4), 511–26.

Willets, D. and Yeo, S. (2004), *A Fair Deal for Everyone on Pensions*, London: Conservative Party.

APPENDIX 2.1

Table A2.1 Periods and type of employer-supported pension coverage assumed for each biography in the British simulations

	Period of employer-supported pension coverage	Type of coverage	Model scheme basis for simulations	Scheme details
1) The mother and unqualified part-time worker in the retail sector				
1a) divorces, remarries and retires early	43 years, 34 years part-time, 5 years of no contributions	DC	Boots stakeholder	Contributions 3% from employer and employee. Charges: 0.65%/annum
1b) divorces, changes to full-time work after child-rearing at 40	47 years, 12 years part-time, 5 years of no contributions	DC	Boots stakeholder	Same
1c) stays married and changes to full-time work at 40	47 years, 11 years part-time, 5 years of no contributions	DC	Boots stakeholder	Same
2) The mother and qualified part-time worker in the welfare sector				
2a) divorces, remarries and retires early	40 years, 23.2 full-time equivalent, 4 years of no contributions	DB	NHS pension	Final Salary: Accrual rate = 1/80th
2b) stays married, changes to full-time work after child-rearing at 42	45 years, 35.4 full-time equivalent, 4 years of no contributions	DB	NHS pension	Same

2c) stays married, changes type of employer and retires early	20 years, 11.2 full-time equivalent, 4 years of no contributions	DB	NHS pension	Same
3) The married carer and informal worker				
3a) stays married and is dependent on partner because of care obligations	None	None	No occupational provision	NA
3b) divorces, is dependent on partner because of care obligations incl. elderly care	None	None	No occupational provision	NA
4) The unqualified worker in the car industry				
4a) divorces, remarries, short spell of unemployment	DB = 8 years, DC = 38 years	DB/DC	Rover/Peugeot pension	Rover: Final Salary (best of final three years); Accrual rate = 1/70th; Peugeot: Matching employer contributions for employee contributions up to 3%; for employee contributions of 4% employer pays 5% and for employee contributions of 5% employer pays 6%. In simulations average DC contributions of 5% employer, 3.4% employees used
4b) stays married, changes employer and retires early after longer spell of unemployment	DB = 8 years, DC = 10 years	DB/DC	Rover/Peugeot pension	Same
5) The intermittent worker in the construction industry				
5a) stays married, employment gaps, change of employer type, further training	13 years	DC	Easybuilder Stakeholder	Contributions: 2003/04 Employer matches employee contributions up to £10 (15.3 Euro)/week

Table A2.1 (continued)

	Period of employer-supported pension coverage	Type of coverage	Model scheme basis for simulations	Scheme details
5b) divorces, remarries, employment gaps, change of employer type, further training	13 years	DC	Easybuilder Stakeholder	Same
5c) stays married, employment gaps, change of employer type, self employment, disabled at the age of 55	13 years	DC	Easybuilder Stakeholder	Same
6) The small business entrepreneur Married, needed to explore risks of type 3	None	None	No occupational provision	NA
7) The divorced provider in the chemical industry Twice divorced, needed to explore impact of divorce on men	45 years	DB/DB	BP and Shell	BP: Final Salary; Accrual rate – 1/60th; Shell: Final Salary; Accrual rate – 1/54th
8) The middle manager in financial services 8a) stays married, retires early	First DB = 7 years, Second DB = 33 years	DB/DB	Lloyds and Nationwide	Lloyds: Final Salary; Accrual rate – 1/60th; Nationwide: Average Salary; Accrual rate – 1/54th
9) The incomplete resident in the electrical industry	None	None	British Oxygen Company (BOC)	Employer contributions are double that of employee between 3 and 5 per cent. We have assumed total contributions of 9 per cent of pensionable pay.

3. The Dutch pension system and social inclusion

Duco Bannink and Bert de Vroom

Citizens at risk in the Netherlands have become used to enjoying comparatively high levels of pension income on retirement. These outcomes are the result of a pension system comprised of an obligatory, collective, public first pillar based on residency; an obligatory, collective, private second pillar based on work history; and an additional voluntary, individual, private third pillar. In contrast to the other five countries featured in this book, the Dutch public pension offers a strong base that lifts virtually all seniors above social assistance level. High levels of social inclusion are then achieved on the basis of a complex system of quasi-compulsory relations between employers and unions, underwritten by the state.

In this chapter we outline how this corporatist pension system functions in the new millennium and how recent changes have affected it, particularly its continued ability to provide socially inclusive outcomes. We argue that the main features of the system are not affected by recent reforms despite greater individualization of risks for employees. In combination the residency-based first pillar and occupational second pillar still allows many citizens to reach incomes in retirement close to or above social inclusion, a result that is better than any other regime discussed in this book.

Yet problems do exist: second pillar coverage gaps remain, affecting irregular workers, the self-employed, care-givers and workers in uncovered sectors. The third pillar cannot fully address these, since the affected citizens often have relatively low working life incomes. The simulations also show significant differences between individuals and they reveal a certain unpredictability in the regime for the individual. Differences are not wholly explained by wage levels and length of employment career, but also by the quality of an individual's pension scheme(s), by the stability of their marriage, by the choice of spouse and by unexpected events such as industrial accidents. As a result, quality of protection also depends on events difficult for individuals to foresee or influence. However more than in the other systems, this increased unpredictability of the life course for risk biographies is cushioned by the highly inclusive first pillar pension, which together with the broad support for a second pillar pension that exists across the pension policy network ensures a strong emphasis upon poverty protection in the Dutch system.

To discuss these issues in the next section we describe the Dutch pension regime; and then assess its inclusiveness for our risk biographies. We conclude by discussing the policy changes required to address some of the gaps the Dutch pension system creates and their political and institutional feasibility.

THE DUTCH PENSION SYSTEM: OBLIGED VOLUNTARISM

The Dutch pension system consists of three pillars (Table 3.1). The first is made up of the compulsory, collective and public General Old Age Pensions Law (Algemene Ouderdomswet, AOW). The second consists of the obliged voluntarist collective, private arrangements. These are tripartite corporatist pensions, in which unions, employers' organizations and the state play a decisive role. The third pillar contains individual savings plans, bought on the private insurance market. The premiums on these are tax deductible under the condition that the person has an acknowledged pension gap, that is if the accrued pension in a year does not allow him or her to reach 70 per cent of their final wage.

Table 3.1 The three pillars of the Dutch pension system

	1st pillar Public old age pension	2nd pillar Sector or company occupational pensions	3rd pillar Individual pensions
Principle	Universal	Occupational	Personal
Coverage	Compulsory for all residents	Compulsory for employees in participating sectors	Voluntary
Financing mechanism	Pay-as-you-go	Funding	Funding
Contributions	Employment-related	Employment-related	
Benefits	Flat-rate, dependent on household status	Contributions-related	
Objective	Poverty prevention	Income maintenance	Complementary individual needs

The First Pillar

The Dutch first pillar pension was constituted by the 1957 General Old Age Pensions Law (AOW) and is available to all Dutch seniors without means testing. It is set at the same level as social assistance. Therefore, by definition (Chapter 1), the AOW reaches poverty level. Yet full entitlement is based on a period of 50 years of residency, from age 15 to 65. For every year 2 per cent of AOW benefit is accrued and every year an individual lives and works outside the country reduces the pension by 2 per cent. Those not reaching the social minimum at 65 may claim means-tested General Social Assistance. The level of the AOW is politically defined as the social minimum. It covers 70 per cent of the net minimum wage for individuals and 50 per cent for each partner in a couple (AOW, art. 9–6; see also Haverland 2001, p. 312; van Riel et al. 2003, pp. 66–7). In 2006 the annual AOW amounted to €11 981 gross for singles and €16 477 for couples (Sociale Verzerkeringsbank 2006). This shows that citizens without supplementary pensions, while not poor, are still some way away from being well off in retirement.

The AOW is indexed to the net minimum wage (AOW art. 9–6) which in turn is linked to the average rise in contractual wages and thus to productivity growth (van Riel et al. 2003, p. 76). However minimum wages systematically lag behind average wages. Our calculations suggest that between 1997 and 2002 the real rise of the gross AOW level was 0.29 per cent lower than average income growth (Dutch Central Bureau of Statistics). As a result, the social inclusiveness of the AOW declines over time, given the link between our social inclusion threshold and average wages.

The Second Pillar

Dutch second pillar pensions are tripartite, corporatist arrangements, based on a joint effort by unions, employers' organizations and the state.[1] In principle, the social partners of each sector are free to choose whether they want to make pension arrangements. However once the first employer in a sector enters an agreement it is assessed for extension by the Minister of Social Affairs, and if approval is granted, all workers and employers in this sector are legally obliged to participate in the system as well (Wet BPF 2000, art. 12).

As a result of this framework coverage is extensive. Only the self-employed generally do not participate in second pillar pension schemes, but of all employers with over 50 employees 99 per cent participate and coverage is complete in the public sector and for all employers with over 200 employees

(SER 2002, p. 14). Altogether around 91 per cent of all workers were covered in 2005, an increase from 82 per cent in 1985 (*National Strategy Report on Adequate and Sustainable Pensions* 2005, p. 7). The remaining roughly 9 per cent are part of the so-called 'white gaps' in the second pillar. They work in areas without branch agreements, such as financial and business services, personal services and retail, cultural and recreational services. Moreover they exist primarily in small, newly established firms (SER 2002, pp. 15–16). In 1996, white gap workers were predominantly female (65 per cent), on short-term contracts (56 per cent) and with many at the start of their employment careers (38 per cent) (SER 2002, p. 89). In our study none of the defined risk biographies work in white gaps so that their effect is not noticeable in the simulations, however our self-employed workers are affected by lack of coverage.

Apart from the relative coerciveness of the system with regard to coverage, the content of pension arrangements is considered the social partners' competency by the Ministry of Social Affairs and the Association of Company Pension Funds. Thus there is scope for negotiations between employers and employees with regard to the details of the pension schemes, which are part of the collective wage arrangements (Anderson 2007). This freedom to negotiate is highly regarded by employers and trade unions alike (van Riel et al. 2003, p. 83) and it has, as will be seen below, on occasion led to major conflicts with government.

As a result of such freedom, conditions for pension rights accrual vary across sector plans, depending on the outcomes of collective bargaining. For example, about 80 per cent of funds apply a minimum entrance age, mostly 25 years (Pensioen- and Verzekeringskamer 2002, p. 28). In some cases employees are excluded from a pension scheme if they have passed a certain age, often 55 years (SER 2002, p. 23); furthermore regulations of pensionable age and early retirement differ, and access to pension schemes can be influenced by the type of work contract.

In addition the level at which the so-called franchise is set differs with significant implications for pension outcome. Typically wage earners with incomes below a level fixed by the pension scheme – the franchise – pay no contributions to this scheme and do not accrue second pillar pension rights. Such individuals are considered sufficiently covered by the public AOW. All employees with wages above the franchise level pay contributions calculated on the basis of the part of their wage above this level. The levels of franchises differ across schemes; as a rule, the higher the level, the more workers are excluded from second pillar accrual. In 2005 the majority of schemes (58.9 per cent) were based on a fixed, indexed amount that lay between the AOW for singles and couples; 22.3 per cent were linked to the higher AOW for couples and 1.3 per cent to the lower AOW for singles (DNB 2006).

If applied without modification the franchise regulation would exclude all low-paid and many part-time workers with incomes below the required level from second pillar schemes. Therefore, to prevent the large-scale exclusion of women in particular, schemes are required to lower the level of the franchise for part-time workers. In fact it is halved for employees on half-time contracts. This legislation is very important for gender equity, considering that in 2005 three-quarters of all women were working part-time (Chapter 1). Potentially, this rule can even advantage a part-time over a full-time worker, if her wage level above the franchise is higher than that of the full-time worker. In our simulations, this is particularly important for the two biographies who experience long periods of part-time work (bio 1, 2).

Average wage pensions are the norm for most employees today, but here also, conditions differ. The dominance of such schemes is fairly recent. In the mid-1990s the Cabinet stated that in order to reduce costs and financial risks it no longer intended to give fiscal support to and to guarantee the compulsory extension of second pillar pension agreements within sectors to final wage pensions. Instead such support was to be limited to average wage schemes (van Riel et al. 2003; 'Werken aan zekerheid' 1996–1997, pp. 82–3, 89). When this plan was strongly resisted by the social partners the government backtracked and gave them the opportunity to develop their own reforms. However the resulting proposals were deemed insufficient, and therefore government set the unions, employers and the insurance industry an ultimatum: within two years they had to find a solution which would lead to a shift towards average salary schemes, otherwise the tax deductibility for final pay schemes would be withdrawn. This pressure led to the 1997 covenant, where the social partners agreed that in order to reduce costs, financial risks and to enhance labour market participation, they would increase the scope of second pillar pensions, contain spending on final salary schemes and limit pay-as-you-go early retirement arrangements, without affecting pension adequacy (Anderson 2007; STAR 1997a [6/97]; STAR 1997b Convenant, [12/97]). In turn the government guaranteed to preserve the existing regulatory framework of 'obliged voluntarism' and tax exemptions (van Riel et al. 2003, pp. 83–4). Subsequently pension arrangements shifted from pure final salary to moderate final salary and average wage schemes. While, in 2000, 60 per cent of the pension funds offered final wage schemes and 32 per cent average wage, in 2004 only 13 per cent of the pension funds still offered final wage pensions and 77 per cent average wage (*National Strategy Report on Adequate and Sustainable Pensions* 2005, p. 11).[2] In addition the voluntary early exit pathway which used to be tax subsidized and resulted in a higher pension at 65 if not taken up is being phased out. At first it was replaced by funded pre-pension arrangements that create incentives against retirement (De Vroom and Guillemard 2002). However after further conflicts with the social partners, in 2004 the government withdrew tax benefits for both types of early exit. As compensation, tax benefits for second pillar old age pensions, which can be taken before the age of 65, were increased. As a result early retirement is still offered today, but it is likely to be more costly for employers and employees than it used to be.

These changes were accompanied by a rise of average accrual rates, which are higher in average wage schemes. Thus while in 1998 94 per cent of participants in a final salary scheme had an accrual rate of 1.75 per cent, the majority (59 per cent) of participants of average wage pension schemes are entitled to an accrual rate above this level (DNB 2006). Nevertheless accrual rates for average wage schemes still vary for our hypothetical individuals, with some being below 1.75 per cent (see below).

Pension indexation is not legally guaranteed and therefore it also varies between schemes. Decisions on indexation are overseen by employers and unions on pension fund boards (Pensioen-en Verzekeringskamer 2002, pp. 31–3). However in 2006 81 per cent of funds applied indexing conditional upon pension fund performance (Anderson 2007; DNB 2006). To improve transparency with regard to indexation, social partners, the Dutch National Bank and the Ministry of Social Affairs agreed in April 2005 to a guideline, which defines under what circumstances pension funds can withdraw from full indexation (Ministry of Social Affairs 2005). This 'indexation matrix' has become an integral part of the control over pension funds by the Dutch National Bank in 2007. Irrespective of its adoption, the fact has remained that indexation differs across schemes, affecting pension levels.

It follows from the above that within the 'obliged voluntarism' framework there is considerable scope for negotiations between the social partners on the specific conditions of schemes. Thus admission regulations, accrual rates and indexation can vary and be changed, in response for example to changed financial circumstances (Clark 2003, pp. 151–2). This variation contributes to the unpredictability of pension outcomes evident in our simulations (De Vroom and Bannink, forthcoming).

The Third Pillar

Dutch pension policy has traditionally been based on the general norm that final pension income at 65 should equate to 70 per cent of final salary after 40 years. Taxation legislation creates incentives for all citizens who fall short of the 70 per cent threshold through the first and second pillar to save into personal schemes.

Thus taxpayers who can prove that they are confronted with a pension deficiency are able to make tax-deductible contributions to a third pillar pension. This deficiency might occur because employees have received salary components without paying pension contributions or because their accrual rate is too low to hit the replacement rate target (Wet Inkomstenbelasting 2001, art. 3.124, 3.127; see also van Riel et al. 2003, pp. 68–9). A maximum of 17 per cent of the income after subtraction of the AOW franchise is eligible for tax deduction.

There are additional tax allowances for the self-employed (Commissie Nationaal Pensioendebat 2002, pp. 82, 84–5; Wet Inkomstenbelasting 2001, art. 3.124, 3.127, 3.129). Since small entrepreneurs often cannot withdraw money from their enterprise, they are allowed to reinvest these savings in their business. Taxation of these savings takes place after termination of the business. At that time the entrepreneur is obliged to invest the tax-exempted savings in an annuity, which is taxed at disbursal. If he or she does not save in this way the tax exemption is treated as profit and taxed straight away.

In a further attempt to encourage private saving, the government recently passed a 'life-course policy' as a solution to various income gaps during working life. This arrangement provides individuals with fiscal incentives to save up to 210 per cent of their yearly wages for career interruptions of up to four years. Although the government originally intended to forbid the take-up of the life-course entitlements in the period directly preceding retirement at 65, this was eventually allowed, under pressure primarily from the unions. As a result, the life-course savings arrangement and the increased tax benefits in the second pillar pension can function as an alternative to the existing pre-pension arrangements. All individuals can take up the life-course arrangement, and employers are allowed to subsidize the individual plans, under the condition that all workers of the company receive such subsidies. It cannot be used to cover gaps in the old age pension collectively.

Risk Sensitivity of the Regime

To conclude despite recent changes the protection offered by the Dutch pension scheme is still high. The coverage of the second pillar pension is relatively good, because of its 'obliged voluntarist' nature and the franchise regulations for part-time workers that particularly assist women. This coverage is built on the strong basic foundation provided by the public old age pension. Gender sensitivity is also evident in second pillar pensions as part of so-called 'pension equalization' arrangements after divorce, under which the pension accrued by both spouses during marriage is divided between the ex-partners with entitlement guaranteed even if ex-partners remarry. Given the lower income of women and the increasing likelihood of divorce and remarriage, this mechanism offers an important protection for women.

However some individuals are still at risk or disadvantaged in the Dutch pension system. Firstly, people with irregular work patterns cannot accrue second pillar pension rights during times when they are not formally employed, for example during career interruptions because of care responsibilities. Secondly, labour mobility can be a problem for workers with final salary pension entitlements because new employers do not normally cover the entire 'back service' required to reach the full final wage pension. Any pension deficit that arises on this basis is not fully eligible for tax deductions (Commissie Nationaal Pensioendebat 2002, p. 86). Thirdly, some workers are affected by 'white gaps', and although they are allowed tax exemptions for private saving, they are worse off than workers in both covered sectors and the self-employed. Finally, the self-employed are not covered by second pillar schemes and the tax deduction arrangement in place for them is not without problems. If termination profits do not cover the full tax exemptions given in the past, the small entrepreneur suffers from a double gap after termination: there is no third pillar pension and there is a remaining tax debt (Commissie Nationaal Pensioendebat 2002, p. 84).

THE SOCIAL INCLUSIVENESS OF THE DUTCH PENSION SYSTEM FOR RISK BIOGRAPHIES

Given that the Dutch system protects individuals effectively in relation to our poverty threshold, our analysis of risk biographies will focus on differences between citizens above this level. As will be seen, despite the existence of a sound safety net, there are still big differences between the pension levels of our biographies. We will discuss below the reasons for these differences and show that they are not merely related to lifetime income but also to scheme quality and other lifetime events. Therefore they are to some extent arbitrary and uncontrollable by the individual.

We will begin with individuals, regardless of whether they are single or a member of a couple. We then turn to couples. However before the simulations are presented we need to explain the choice of second pillar pension scheme for each individual. The pension schemes we have chosen for each hypothetical individual are identical with the pension schemes a real employee with an identical work biography would have in the Netherlands today; that is we selected schemes typical for the industries our workers are in, and applied all their conditions (Appendix 3.2). Due to the strong trend towards average wage or moderate final wage pensions, pure final salary schemes are therefore an exception in our simulations, only relevant for two of our biographies: the middle manager in financial services (bio 8) and the divorced provider (bio 7). However in order to demonstrate the implications of this momentous shift we also simulate final salary pensions for all of our workers.

Applying scheme conditions for 2003 means that most of our hypothetical individuals receive pre-pension benefits because they exist in the respective branches. This implies that unless individuals retire early, their entitlement is transferred to their old age pension, resulting in a higher level.[3] As we explained above, pre-pension benefits are no longer supported by the government. We nevertheless calculate them for these individuals, because they were replaced recently by increased tax benefits for the second pillar old age pension. While the precise effect of these regulations is as yet unclear, and could therefore not be simulated, indications are that the financial room for early retirement under the new regulations is as high as under the old (Jansen 2006). Furthermore the new life-course arrangements could add to this effect, even though accrual for this arrangement is no longer collectivized but subject to individual decisions.

Protection of Individuals

Applying the assumptions explained above, how well protected against exclusion in retirement are our risk biographies? First of all, there is one exception to the encompassing nature of the first pillar. Since AOW is accrued on the basis of residency, the public pension of the incomplete resident (bio 9) is below the social assistance level.[4] Had he or she not had a work history or had he been on a very low income below the franchise level, which is quite common for this group, he would indeed have ended up as a pensioner in poverty. However in our case the incomplete resident's relatively low first pillar pension is compensated for by his second pillar pension, which lifts the total benefits above poverty level. For all other individuals it is second pillar pensions which are decisive in determining whether they are just above the poverty line or much better off.

Figure 3.1 illustrates that all individuals are entitled to pensions above the poverty line, yet 14 of them receive a total pension below the level of comfortable social inclusion and 12 below the social inclusion line. If we focus on the latter group first, their position is relatively precarious because they receive no – or a comparatively small – second pillar pension. For some individuals in this group this is true despite lifetime earnings above 65 per cent of the average. Thus the small business entrepreneur (bio 6), who has 84 per cent of average earnings, is near the bottom of this group because of his fairly long period without second pillar provision while self-employed. Similarly the unqualified worker in the car industry who retires early after a spell of unemployment (bio 4b) also has a pension only just above the

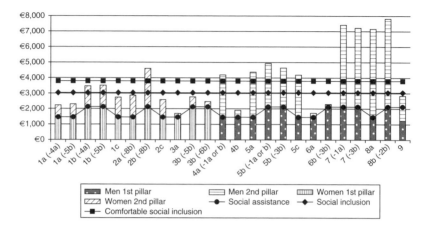

Notes: Social assistance = Social assistance for individuals if person is single on retirement; for married individuals: 50 per cent of couple's social assistance. Social inclusion: 40% average wage; Comfortable social inclusion = 50% average wage.

Second pillar include divorce payments for divorcees. Unless otherwise stated second pillar = average wage pensions. Bio 1: part-time franchise, accrual rate: 2%; bio 1b/c: pre-pension transferred to old age pension; bio 2: part-time franchise; accrual rate: 1.9%; bio 2b: pre-pension transferred to old age pension; bio 3: part-time franchise, accrual rate 2%; bio 4: accrual rate 2.2%; bio 4a: pre-pension transferred to old age pension; bio 5: accrual rate 2.2%; bio 6: accrual rate 2%; bio 7, bio 8: final salary pension, accrual rate 1.75%; bio 9: accrual rate 2%; pre-pension transferred to old age pension; see Appendix 3.2 for details.

Figure 3.1   Projected real monthly pension levels from first and second pillar for Dutch men and women in 2050

poverty line, after earning 65 per cent of the average during his life. In his case this is due to his short membership in an average wage scheme and the fact that he used his pre-pension to finance his early retirement.

The other individuals in this group all have lifetime incomes below half of the average because of part-time work and/or a shorter employment career. Worst off is the married carer and informal worker with very low lifetime earnings (bio 3a: 22 per cent of average wage) who receives an overall pension barely above the poverty line. Her second pillar pension is very low, because her later jobs were informal or she had care obligations while being dependent on her spouse's income so that she made no contributions. The married carer and informal worker who divorces (bio 3b) does better because she works for a large employer in her later years, has a comparatively higher income (37 per cent of average wage) and longer access to pension schemes because she restarts formal work after her divorce. She also receives divorce equalization payments from her ex-husband, which vary depending on her partner (for example bio 5b, 6; Table 3.2).

Table 3.2 Percentage of overall pension gained/lost through divorce in the Netherlands, January 2050

Biography	1a-4a	1a-5b	1b-4a	1b-5b	2a-8b	2b-8b	3b-5b	3b-6b	4a-1a or b	5b-1a or b	5b-3b	6b-3b	7-1a	7-3b	8-2a
Second pillar	10	14	11	17	26	22	134	26	–4	–4	–14	–48	–15	–16	–7
Total pension	3	5	3	4	11	8	15	3	–2	–3	–9	–3	–11	–11	–5

Better off, but still remaining below the social inclusion line, are the unqualified and the qualified part-time worker and mother (bio 1a, c, 2a). One reason they are more comfortable than the married carer discussed above (bio 3) is that they earn more than she does, between 39 and 47 per cent of the average. However their better position is also explained by superior access to second pillar schemes, not least through the impact of the favourable franchise regulations for part-time workers. Without the lower franchise, the mother and unqualified part-time retail worker (bio 1a) for example would accrue no second pillar pension whatsoever during her third, part-time employment, while the mother and qualified part-time worker in the welfare sector (bio 2a) would build a considerably lower second pillar pension during her part-time employment. The higher pension of the retail worker who does not retire early (bio 1c) is also explained by the pre-pension arrangement, which lifts her retirement income by 27 per cent.

There are only two individuals in the second group who have pensions above the social inclusion line but below the comfortable inclusion line. Both are variants of the retail worker and mother (bio 1), and the only difference between them and the retail worker who stays below social inclusion (bio 1c) is that both are lifted above the inclusion threshold because of divorce (bio 1b and 4a; bio 1b and 5b). As a consequence their pensions increase; in addition they are now entitled to the higher state pension for singles.

Our third group comprises ten individuals who make it above the comfortable inclusion line, and while amongst them are those with the highest incomes, this is not always the case. Notably the mother and qualified part-time worker in the welfare sector (bio 2b) has an overall pension level higher than that of individuals with higher lifetime earnings than hers (54 per cent), such as the car and construction industry workers (bio 4a: 79 per cent, 4b: 65 per cent and bio 5a, b: 89 per cent; bio 5c: 62 per cent). This situation is partly explained by the franchise adjustments made during the 12 years she worked part-time; however divorce is a bigger reason. This raises her pension and lowers that of the male. Thus the qualified part-time worker receives a substantial equalization payment after divorce from the middle manager (bio 8), the highest earner in our group; this bolsters her second pillar pension by 22 per cent. She also receives the higher AOW for singles. At the same time, the divorced car and construction workers lose between 2 per cent (bio 4a) and 9 per cent (bio 5b) of their pension because of divorce payments (Table 3.2).

The intermittent worker in the construction industry who suffered an industrial accident is also among the comfortably off, despite his disability (bio 5c). His construction industry pension is designed to protect workers against their specific occupational hazards, and therefore after this accident he continues to accrue pension entitlement up until retirement. As a result, despite earning considerably less than those construction workers who are not disabled (bio 5a, b), and the car worker (bio 4a), the disabled worker's (bio 5c) pension is at a similar level to theirs and he can live a comfortable life as a pensioner. He is also much better off than the car worker who retires early after a spell of unemployment (bio 4b), and who also has a slightly higher lifetime income. These differences demonstrate how the system treats social risks in different ways: unemployment and early retirement lead to a cut in pension entitlements while disability and divorce receives compensation.

All remaining individuals who reach comfortable inclusion (bio 4a, 5a, b, 7a, b and 8a, b) earn between 79 and 131 per cent of the average during long employment careers. Yet again, not only lifetime income, but also the quality of the pension scheme needs to be taken into consideration in explaining their situation. First, they either have the highest accrual rates for average wage schemes in our sample (bio 4, 5: 2.2 per cent) or final salary pension schemes (bio 7, 8). In addition some receive high compensation for their specific social risks, which is not available to others on similar wages. This can be illustrated by a comparison between the construction industry workers (bio 5a, b: 89 per cent of average wages) and the small business entrepreneur (bio 6: 84 per cent of average wages), both of whom are self-employed for long periods of time. Whereas the pension fund in the construction worker's sector allows the self-employed full access (Appendix 3.2), the small business entrepreneur has no second pillar access. Thus despite the fact that there is only a 5 per cent difference in their lifetime earnings the construction workers receive pensions above the comfortable inclusion line, while the small business entrepreneur (bio 6) is amongst our least well-off pensioners.

Most comfortable are the divorced provider (bio 7) and the middle manager (bio 8) whose long working lives, high income and final salary pension schemes make them the best off in retirement by far. Even divorce payments from the divorced provider's second pillar pension of 15 per cent (bio 7, 1a) and 16 per cent (bio 7, 3b) place him nowhere near the social risk threshold (Table 3.2).

To conclude, the analysis above shows that the first pillar guarantees poverty prevention for all of our biographies except the incomplete resident (bio 9). Whether or not our hypothetical individuals are socially included or even comfortably off depends on three main factors: their level of earnings, access to a second pillar scheme, its quality, and their marital history. Access is made easier for part-time workers who benefit from the special franchise regulations (variants of bio 1, 2, 3). By the same token for the small business entrepreneur (bio 6), the married carer and informal worker (bio 3), and the car worker who loses his job leading to early retirement (bio 4b), exclusion from the right to accrue second pillar rights for larger parts of their lives constitutes a risk. Yet amongst those with access to the second pillar the pension level is also affected by the quality of a scheme. Final salary scheme protection is better than average salary scheme, and higher accrual rates lead to higher pensions; in addition, some social risks are better recognized by schemes than others. With regard to marital history, divorce payments explain differences in pension outcome, and protect some of our female biographies (bio 1a, 2a) against risks, while they do not push any of our men below the social inclusion line.

Risks are gendered to some extent. Caring obligations or informal work result in irregular or incomplete work histories and thus an interruption of second pillar pension accrual. However our results show the significant equalizing impact the franchise for part-time workers has and they illustrate the importance of divorce payments for women.

To what extent would these conclusions have been different if final salary schemes were still the norm? Figure 3.2 compares the pension outcomes for each of our biographies in relation to access either to a final salary or average salary scheme. Thus where in Figure 3.1 the hypothetical individual has an average wage pension, this pension is compared to a constructed final wage pension, assuming 1.75 per cent yearly accrual. Where the individual has a final salary pension, this pension is compared to a constructed average wage scheme assuming 2 per cent yearly accrual.

As we can see, for most of our biographies (bio 1–5, 9) who in Figure 3.1 have an average wage pension, a final wage pension would result in a higher pension outcome, although for the lower-paid of this group – the unqualified and the qualified worker and mother (bio 1, 2), the unqualified car worker (bio 4a) and the intermittent worker who is disabled at the age of 55 (bio 5c) – this increase is not substantial. However this is not true for all. Because some individuals do not benefit from the wage rises typical of the latter half of a

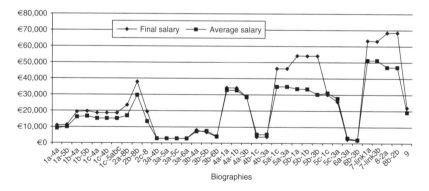

Figure 3.2   Final salary and average salary scheme outcomes for risk biographies in the Netherlands

working life, a final wage pension very slightly lowers their pension outcome. This is true for the married carer and informal worker (bio 3), the unqualified male worker who retires early after a spell of unemployment (bio 4b), and the small business entrepreneur (bio 6a). Of those who have a final wage pension in Figure 3.1 (bio 7, 8) their pension outcome would fall substantially should their second pillar provision shift to an average salary basis. Overall then, a general shift to average wage schemes would make the system more equal because those on higher incomes suffer the most from a shift to average wage pensions.

Savings

Against the background of the shortcomings identified above, we consider in the following section whether personal savings are a viable means for achieving a pension income above our social inclusion threshold. For some of our biographies (bio 2b, 4a, 5a, 5b, 5c, 7, 8) such saving is unnecessary because they surpass this threshold on the basis of their first and second pillar provision. However as has been seen, this is not true for all individuals due to exclusion from good-quality second pillar schemes, the quality of such schemes or short membership times. In Figure 3.3 we can see that the amount of yearly savings these individuals would need to make to reach the social inclusion threshold at 4 per cent real interest and 2 per cent annual charges varies from nil to 34 per cent.

Unsurprisingly those with the lowest income – below 40 per cent of average wages – have to save the most in order to reach the social inclusion line. The carer and informal worker (bio 3a) would need to put aside as much as

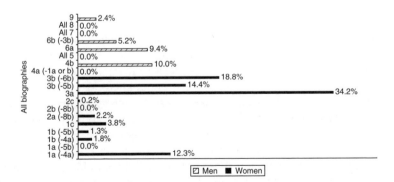

Figure 3.3   Third pillar savings from lifetime income required of Dutch men and women to reach social inclusion line of 40% average wage in 2050

34 per cent of her lifetime income. The situation is less extreme for the divorced carer (bio 3b), who because of her divorce has more years in employment leading to a higher lifetime income and who can rely on her ex-husband's pension equalization payments. Nevertheless she would still need to save a hefty 19 or 14 per cent of her income, depending on her ex-partner's earnings and thus level of contribution. The same, although to a more limited extent, goes for the unqualified part-time worker and mother who divorces and retires early (bio 1a), leading to a lifetime income of 39 per cent of the average; she would need to save around 12 per cent; again the exact amount would depend on which type of husband she had. However if the same individual works longer, boosting her income to 47 per cent, a more manageable amount of less than 2 per cent of her income in savings would lift her above the inclusion line (bio 1b). The significant exception in this group is the unqualified worker in the car industry who retires early (bio 4b). As discussed above, he only pays into a second pillar pension scheme for a limited amount of years, due to change of employers, unemployment and early retirement, with the consequence that despite a lifetime income of 65 per cent average he would need to save an additional 10 per cent to reach the social inclusion line.

All individuals with earnings higher than 40 per cent of the average but with first and second pillar pensions below the social inclusion line need to save between 1 and at most 4 per cent to lift them above this line. The small business entrepreneur (bio 6) is the exception in this group. Despite lifetime earnings of 84 per cent of the average he did not pay any second pillar scheme contributions for most of his life; thus he needs to pay more into a personal scheme.

How feasible are such savings? Research on the use of employee savings arrangements (Tijdens and van Klaveren 2002) suggests it is more likely to occur among our higher earning biographies than the lower earning ones. Thus while 67 per cent of the men and 63 per cent of the women with incomes over €2500 participate in these schemes, only 22 per cent of the men and 31 per cent of the women with monthly incomes below €1500 participate. Thus savings are more conceivable for the small business entrepreneur (bio 6), and to a lesser extent for the unqualified car worker (bio 4b). However because of tax incentives small business entrepreneurs invest their pension contributions in their businesses and thus are unlikely to save that much (see above). Moreover our car worker's wages, while relatively high in relation to some of our biographies, are at the lower end in relation to research referred to above. It is thus unlikely that they would put aside more than nine per cent of their income. In conclusion, we consider it unlikely that personal savings point the way towards better protection for those at greatest risk. For all workers not reaching 70 per cent of the final wage and fulfilling the conditions of the third pillar regulation, tax incentives apply.

However this arrangement is not feasible for our constructed low wage workers, because the majority of them reach 70 per cent of final wages on the basis of the public old age pension alone.

Protection of Couples

Above we argued that individual savings are an unrealistic way to improve protection for those at greatest risk. Yet many individuals do not live alone and thus may not need to rely exclusively on their individual income in old age. In this section we discuss whether inclusiveness increases if we assess the income of couples together and if we assume that they share this income (Figure 3.4). The following paragraphs will show that if we take this perspective some biographies achieve a higher standard of living. Unsurprisingly this is particularly relevant for the female biographies, which generally have lower lifetime earnings and lower pensions than their partners, although this is not always the case.

All couples are protected against poverty, but they have to rely to a greater extent than singles on second pillar protection to reach the social inclusion line. This is because a couple's public pension is less valuable in relation to our inclusion thresholds than that for individuals. It reaches 51 per cent of comfortable social inclusion for couples as opposed to 56 per cent for individuals, assuming the couple's threshold is set at 1.5 times the level of individuals. This means that based on the AOW alone, couples are less well protected than singles.

In our analysis of individuals we have shown that the married carer and informal worker (bio 3), the small business entrepreneur (bio 6), the

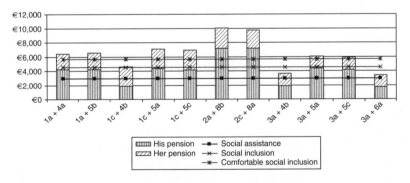

Notes: Social assistance line = Social assistance line for couples; Social inclusion line for couples: 1.5 × 40% average wage; Comfortable social inclusion = 1.5 × 50% average wage.

Figure 3.4   Projected real monthly pension levels of Dutch couples in 2050

unqualified car worker who retires early (bio 4b), the unqualified mother and worker (bio 1a, c) as well as the qualified mother and worker (bio 2a, c) and the incomplete resident (bio 9) were below the social inclusion line and thus most at risk. Is this situation improved if we consider their household status? Much depends on the choice of partner. For the carer (bio 3a), our lowest earner and a prototype of a traditional homemaker, living standard in retirement is strongly influenced by this factor. If she marries someone who also has a very low pension, like the unqualified worker in the car industry (bio 4b) or the small business entrepreneur (bio 6), she will be part of a couple whose pension income barely rises above the social assistance line. She and her spouse suffer a double disadvantage because of a compilation of risks. In contrast our carer's marriage to the construction worker would bring her a more comfortable life in retirement (bio 3a and 5a; bio 3a and 5c), yet how close to the comfortable inclusion level this would be again very much hinges on his employment career. A similar situation is evident for our car worker who retires early (bio 4b) – his shared standard of living in retirement is low if he marries the carer (bio 3a), and considerably higher if the unqualified worker (bio 1c) becomes his partner.

In all these cases risk equalization takes place, with one person benefiting from the other. This is normally the woman because women's earnings and pensions are usually lower. However where the female has a more stable employment career covered by a second pillar scheme (for example bio 1c), and the male's employment career is interrupted, not covered by a second pillar scheme or ends early (for example bio 4b,) the beneficiary can be the male partner.

Thus in summary, a partner's career can be very important for the standard of living of less well-off pensioners but the impact of this factor is to a significant extent dependent on chance. Even if an individual had the unlikely intention to choose a future spouse according to their pension, it is impossible to know upon marriage what type of pension scheme her or his partner is likely to have during their working life.

Discussion of Results

The Dutch system continues to protect well against poverty on the basis of its generous first pillar. Upon this comparatively generous base an extensive second pillar system can flourish. The shift from final to average wage pensions in this tier means an overall loss in income after retirement, but this is least costly for our lower-waged biographies. It is only those who are excluded from second pillar schemes altogether, or who suffer risks like unemployment or work outside the formal labour market which is unrecognized by the second pillar, that fail to surpass the social inclusion threshold.

Personal savings do not seem likely to compensate for these shortfalls. The savings rate for those at greatest risk seems to be too high because these groups often do not have the means to spare. However any money that they would save counts towards a better retirement income due to the universal nature of state provision.

However our analysis also highlights that for many individuals, even those for whom the system works relatively well, their pension level remains unpredictable (De Vroom and Bannink forthcoming). This has to do with the heterogeneity of the second pillar and is also due to changes in people's lives. The quality of pension schemes varies, yet individuals are unlikely to choose them strategically. Thus for example, some individuals are better off than others because of more generous accrual rates or final salary schemes (bio 4, 5, 7, 8). Likewise disability does not mean poverty for the intermittent construction worker (bio 5c) only because he is a member of a pension scheme with good protection. It is unlikely that when individuals start their careers and when they make career moves the type of pension scheme is the driving force behind their decisions; this is even more the case for those individuals whose changes of employer were prompted by redundancies (bio 4), disability (bio 5c) or care-related interruptions (bio 1, 2). Overall, this heterogeneity implies a degree of random inequality resulting in unpredictability for employees, although the consequences of this situation are less stark than in the UK (Chapter 2) due to a more generous Dutch first pillar and greater compulsion in the second. The level of unpredictability is also mitigated by the shift from final to average wage pensions, at the cost of an overall decline of pension levels.

With regard to changing life patterns, individualization and a corresponding destandardization of life courses seem to make the level of retirement income harder to predict for many. Thus while choice of partner has important implications for pension levels, none of our individuals will know when first married the value of their partner's pension 40 years later, and whether they will be able to share their pensions in one household when they retire. The unpredictability of such factors grows if the interaction between the work decisions and marriage choices is taken into account. Risk biographies are particularly affected by this unpredictability because certain choices for them could spell a retirement close to the poverty line.

THE REFORM DEBATE IN THE NETHERLANDS

Despite the generally good performance of the Dutch pension system, our simulations illustrate that further reform would be necessary for the system to guarantee a socially inclusive pension to the types of citizens illustrated by our risk biographies. As we have seen above, incomplete residency and insufficient or no access to second pillar schemes, due to unemployment, self-employment or informal work, are risk factors. In addition the system provides unpredictable results for individuals leading modern lives. Moreover it has also been seen that the public pension level lags behind average wage rises. How have these issues been addressed by policymakers?

The system is fiercely debated. Against the background of negative economic developments, demographic ageing and liberal-conservative government incumbency, the Dutch pension system has not escaped from programmatic and systemic (Pierson 1994) welfare state reforms. The basic framework of the system appears safe, but the social partners, the government and other relevant actors in the network are aiming at a recalibration (Pierson 1994) of responsibilities. At least three general tendencies can be observed: (1) individualization and privatization of the system; (2) an increased emphasis on lifelong labour market participation signalled by the current discouragement of pre-pension arrangements; and (3) implicit privatization of the public pension by incomplete indexation and pressure to increase the pensionable age. Our expectation is that all three tendencies will increase the risks of social exclusion of those groups that are already vulnerable under the existing system.

Below we discuss the reform processes and outcomes concerning all three pillars. Our understanding of the preferences of policy network actors is based upon policy documents and interviews conducted in 2003 and then repeated between April and July 2005 on which occasion we asked interviewees to comment on our research results (see Appendix 3.1 for details).

The Public Old Age Pension AOW

The role of the basic state pension for the social inclusiveness of the Dutch system cannot be overestimated. But given that its value is falling in relation to social inclusion thresholds (see above), most relevant for our citizens at risk is the question of how probable it is that the state pension will decline further and that the Dutch system will come closer to the British situation, for example. At present the danger of a strong relative decline in public pension levels seems slight because, firstly, the state ensures that the pension rises faster in net terms. This commitment has reassured the Coördinatieorgaan Samenwerkende Ouderenorganisaties (CSO; the umbrella organisation of the elderly), for example (interview CSO, 19 May 2005). Secondly any systematic attempt to reduce the pension level would provoke severe social protest. In addition to the CSO (interviews CSO, 8 May 2003 and 19 May 2005), employers, the association of company pension funds and trade unions would resist such a proposal out of fear that they would have to increase their own efforts in the second pillar as a consequence (interviews VB, 7 May 2003 and 28 April 2005; AWVN, 20 May 2005; SER, 30 May 2005). As they see it, this would undermine the basic principle of the Dutch system that state and social partners have a shared responsibility for pensions, but that their costs are limited by adequate state provision (STAR 1997b [6/97]). Against this background the Ministry of Social Affairs has restated its commitment to the status quo (interview, 2 June 2005).

While the status quo seems guaranteed, it is improbable that the public old age pension will return to full indexation. Employers and right-wing political parties do not want social assistance to rise on this basis due to work disincentives, but at the same time, detaching the public old age pension from social assistance to facilitate bigger pension increases is also unfeasible, because labour and leftist political parties consider the linkage to be a means to protect the level of social assistance.

The second problem of the otherwise very inclusive AOW we identified in our simulations is incomplete residency. A growing number of individuals – migrants, global workers – do not meet the requirement of 50 years of residency for a full AOW. In 2005 the Social and Economic Council highlighted the urgency of this issue (SER 2005), but no proposals are currently being worked on by the Ministry of Social Affairs. Reducing the residency requirement to 40 years without raising the cost of the public old age pension would imply lowering the level of the public pension, which is politically unlikely, as we have just argued. However an approach based on the third pillar involving greater tax exemptions, for example, does not appear feasible for migrant workers given that their low levels of income make investments in additional savings difficult.

The Second Pillar

As our simulations show, in the Netherlands private pensions and social inclusion sometimes go together because of the state's fiscal support and legislative encouragement and regulation of second pillar provision. This highly differentiated pattern of corporate actors – trade unions, employer associations, big companies, task specific pension organizations and so on – integrated in policymaking networks both on the sector and the national level, offers a relatively flexible and low-cost system that is able to accommodate pensions to new pressures and specific circumstances. However as has been seen, a concern with this system is the unpredictability of second pillar pension outcomes for our risk biographies. This unpredictability is reinforced by life-course events such as employment gaps, care obligations, periods of informal work or divorce. How are these issues addressed in current debates?

Regarding differences in pension scheme quality, firstly, it is unlikely that the trend towards average salary schemes is going to be reversed, given the strong agreement between government and social partners on containing spending and increasing the flexibility of the second pillar. Recent reforms all strongly point in the direction of pension schemes that are more flexible and conform more to labour market outcomes. It is likely that average salary schemes will become the norm everywhere, increasing the risks for our individuals slightly, but to a lower proportion than those of higher earners as was shown above. Secondly, despite some trend towards stronger homogenization of schemes there is no sign that differences in accrual rates and franchise levels by sector or differences in indexation will disappear. They are likely to continue because social partners have a vested interest in keeping this autonomy in order to be able to adjust pensions to labour market outcomes. The trade-off of such autonomy and flexibility is (limited) inequality. The resulting pension differences for individuals and the unpredictability of pension outcomes are therefore likely to remain.

With regard to gaps in coverage, there are firstly the self-employed. However despite their poverty risks resulting in exclusion from the second pillar, this insufficient protection is not a public policy issue. The example of the construction worker (bio 5) above who was integrated into an existing scheme as part of a small construction business is one potential solution to this problem. However such an approach conflicts with current policy that allows the small business self-employed to invest such pensions contributions into their business and buy an annuity later. This may explain the lack of attention to the issue.

The situation is different with regard to the 'white gaps' in sectors where employees have no occupational pension rights. The Ministry of Social Affairs and social partners have made continual efforts to decrease the number of white gaps (SER 2005). Even though none of our existing risk biographies is assumed to work in white gap sectors, workers that share their characteristics are employed there, in particular unskilled, part-time and irregular workers. Some citizens at risk will therefore benefit from such efforts.

The Third Pillar

A more individualized solution to the issues described above would be increased support for the third pillar. This seems likely to acquire greater significance in particular for higher earners as second pillar entitlements are lower and less predictable for the employee. As we explained above, a life-course savings arrangement exists to compensate for the abolition of early retirement rules. Currently however a possible complementary role for the third pillars is not being discussed with regard to the old age pension.

In conclusion, considering current reform trends, it is obvious that changing economic and demographic conditions have led to a certain deterioration of first and second pillar pensions in the Netherlands, but this has not hit those at risk particularly hard. With regard to the main reform initiatives, we can conclude that nothing is being discussed that would change the picture painted by our simulations in a major way. Our risk biographies seem likely to remain fairly well protected by the first pillar, while diversity in the second is going to continue, because of the voluntarism of social partners. As a consequence, our research suggests that the Dutch regime continues to live up to its social democratic reputation.

NOTES

1. The second pillar pension system is regulated by the Pensioen- en spaarfondsenwet (Pension and Savings Funds Act) and the Mandatory Participation in a Branch Pension Fund Act. The National Civil Pension Fund Act regulates the second pillar pensions of employees in the public sector. Further public support for second pillar pensions is given through tax deductions.
2. In 2006 10.1 per cent of active participants built a final wage pension and 76 per cent of participants built an average wage pension (DNB 2006).
3. The pre-pension arrangement lifts the pensions of the following individuals as follows: Retail workers who retire at 65: bio 1b, 4a: 20 per cent; bio 1b, 5b: 20 per cent; bio 1c: 27 per cent. Qualified part time worker in the welfare sector: bio 2b, 8b: 23 per cent; the carer who stays married, bio 3a: 15 per cent; the unqualified car worker: bio 4a: 27 per cent; the small business entrepreneur: bio 6a: 6 per cent, bio 6b, 3b: 4 per cent; the divorced provider: bio 7, 1a and 7–3b: both 22 per cent; the incomplete resident: bio 9: 22 per cent. The intermittent worker (bio 5) does not have a pre-pension, and the middle manager (bio 8) has a substantial one but he uses it for retiring early.
4. Residency is 29 years (2021–2049), so her AOW is 29.2 per cent equating to 58 per cent of a full AOW.

BIBLIOGRAPHY

Anderson, K.M. (2007), 'The Netherlands: political competition in proportional system', in E.M. Immergut, K.M. Anderson and I. Schulze (eds), *Handbook of West European Pension Politics* (pp. 713–57), Oxford: Oxford University Press.
AOW, Act of 31 May 1956, Stb. 1956, last changed 23 December 2006, Stb. 2006.
Clark, G.L. (2003), *European Pensions and Global Finance*, Oxford: Oxford University Press.
Commissie Nationaal Pensioendebat (2002), *Zorgen over morgen*.
De Vroom, B. and Bannink, D. (2006), 'De onberekenbare toekomst. De verschuivende overgang van werk naar pensioen in Europese verzorgingsstaten', *Tijdschrift voor Arbeidsvraagstukken*, **22**(2), 93–108.
De Vroom, B. and Bannink, D. (forthcoming), 'Changing life courses and new social risks: the case of old age pensions', *Journal of Comparative Policy Analysis*.

De Vroom, B. and Guillemard, A. (2002), 'Institutional changes at the end of the worklife: from externalisation to integration of ageing workers', in A. Goul and P.H. Jensen (eds), *Changing Labour Markets, Welfare Policies, and Citizenship*, Bristol: Policy Press.

DNB (2006), *Uitgebreid bestand met tabellen pensioenmonitor*, Dutch National Bank, http://www.statistics.dnb.nl/statistics/verz_pens/PM_uitgebreid_nl.zip, accessed 27 October 2006.

Dutch Central Bureau of Statistics, www.cbs.nl.

Haverland, M. (2001), 'Another Dutch miracle? Explaining Dutch and German Pension Trajectories', *Journal of European Social Policy*, **11**(4), 308–23.

Jansen, S. (2006), 'De besluitvorming pond VUT, pre-pensioen en levensloop', Masters thesis, Enschede: University of Twente.

Ministry of Social Affairs (2005), *Gezamenlijk vastgestelde uitkomsten van het overleg op 12 april 2005 tussen het Ministerie van Sociale Zaken en Werkgelegenheid, De Nederlandsche Bank en de werkgroep Pensioenen van de Stichting van de Arbeid*, The Hague, (AV/PB/2005/27030; 12 April 2005): Ministry of Social Affairs and Employment.

National Strategy Report on Adequate and Sustainable Pensions (2005), The Hague: the Netherlands, http://ec.europa.eu/employment_social/social_protection/docs/2005/nl_en.pdf, accessed 27 October 2006.

Pensioen- and Verzekeringskamer (2002), *Pensioenmonitor. Stand van Zaken 1 januari 2002*, PVK: Apeldoorn.

Pensioen- en spaarfondsenwet (2007), *Act of 15 May 1952, Stb. 1952; retracted 1 January 2007, Stb. 2006, 200, Pensioenwet, Act of 7 December 2006, Stb. 2006, 705; last changed 1 January 2007, Stb. 2006*, (Pensions and Savings Funds Act).

Pierson, P. (1994), *Dismantling the Welfare State?*, Cambridge: Cambridge University Press.

SER (2002), *Rapport witte vlekken op pensioengebied*, The Hague: Social and Economic Council.

SER (2005), *Van alle leeftijden: Een toekomstgericht ouderenbeleid op het terrein van werk, inkomen, pensioenen en zorg*, The Hague: Social and Economic Council.

Sociale Verzerkeringsbank (2006), www.svb.nl, accessed 15.01.2007.

STAR (1997a), *Convenant inzake de arbeidspensioenen. Overeengekomen tussen het Kabinet en de Stichting van de Arbeid op 9 december 1997*, The Hague: Foundation of Labour.

STAR (1997b), *Nota, Aanbevelingen gericht op vernieuwing van pensioenregelingen*, The Hague: Foundation of Labour.

Tijdens, K. and van Klaveren, M. (2002), *Hoe belangrijk is de spaarloonregeling?* Amsterdam: AIAS, University of Amsterdam.

van Riel, B., Hemerijck, A. and Visser, J. (2003), 'Is there a Dutch way to pension reform?' in G. Clark and N. Whiteside (eds), *Pension Security in the 21st Century* (pp. 64–91), Oxford: Oxford University Press.

'Werken aan zekerheid' (1996–1997), Parliamentary dossiers, TK 25 010, no. 1.

Wet BPF (2000), *Wet verplichte deelneming in een bedrijfstakpensioenfonds 2000*, Act of 21 December 2000, Stb. 2000, 628; last changed 1 January 2007, Stb. 2006, p. 605, 706.

Wet Inkomstenbelasting 2001 (2002), Act of 11 May 2000 (Stb. 2000, p. 215); last changed 1 January 2007 (various changes) (Income Tax Act).

APPENDIX 3.1:   LIST OF INTERVIEWED ACTORS IN THE POLICY NETWORK

4 April 2003, civil servant, pension specialist, Ministerie van Sociale Zaken en Werkgelegenheid (Ministry of Social Affairs and Employment)

10 April 2003, three civil servants, Pensioen- en Verzekeringskamer (PVK; Chamber of Pensions and Insurance, supervisory organ)

16 April 2003, two officials, pension specialists, Sociaal-Economische Raad (SER; Social and Economic Council)

7 May 2003, official, Vereniging van Bedrijfspensioenfondsen (VB; Association of Company Pension Funds)

8 May 2003, two representatives, Centrale Samenwerkende Ouderenorganisaties (CSO; Association of Cooperating Organizations for the Elderly)

28 April 2005, official, Vereniging van Bedrijfspensioenfondsen (VB; Association of Company Pension Funds)

12 May 2005, civil servant, pension specialist, De Nederlandse Bank (DNB; the Dutch Central Bank, functions as supervisory organ; the respondent was employed at the former supervisory organ for the pension sector PVK, which was integrated into DNB in 2005)

19 May 2005, two representatives, Centrale Samenwerkende Ouderenorganisaties (CSO; Association of Cooperating Organizations for the Elderly)

20 May 2005, official, pension specialist, Algemene Werkgeversvereniging Nederland (AWVN; General Employers' Association the Netherlands)

30 May 2005, two officials, pension specialists, Sociaal-Economische Raad (SER; Social and Economic Council)

2 June 2005, two civil servants, pension specialists, Ministerie van Sociale Zaken en Werkgelegenheid (Ministry of Social Affairs and Employment)

APPENDIX 3.2

Table A3.1   Pension schemes used for simulations

	Years occupational coverage	Type of coverage	Accrual rate; franchise level (2004)
1) The mother and unqualified part-time worker in the retail sector	Pension fund for retail sale food sector, *Bedrijfstakpensioenfonds voor het Levensmiddelenbedrijf*		
1a) divorces, remarries and retires early	35 years	Average wage	2.0%; €15 153
1b) divorces, changes to full-time work after child-rearing at 40	38 years	Average wage	2.0%; €15 153
1c) stays married and changes to full-time work at 40	38 years	Average wage	2.0%; €15 153
2) The mother and qualified part-time worker in the welfare sector	Pension fund for the civil service, *Algemeen Burgerlijk Pensioenfonds*		
2a) divorces, remarries and retires early	36 years	Average wage	1.9%; €13 000
2b) stays married, changes to full-time work after child-rearing at 42	39 years	Average wage	1.9%; €13 000
2c) stays married, changes type of employer and retires early	36 years	Average wage	1.9%; €13 000
3) The married carer and informal worker	Pension fund for retail sale food sector, *Bedrijfstakpensioenfonds voor het Levensmiddelenbedrijf*		
3a) stays married and is dependent on partner because of care obligations	1 year	Average wage	2.0%; €15 153
3b) divorces, is dependent on partner because of care obligations incl. elderly care	1 year	Average wage	2.0%; €15 153
	Pension fund for processing of fruits and vegetables sector, *Bedrijfspensioenfonds voor de groenten- en fruitverwerkende industrie*		
3b) third job, different sector	11 years	Average wage	1.5%; €14 600
4) The unqualified worker in the car industry	Pension fund for metal and electrics, *Bedrijfstakpensioenfonds Metalektro**		

Table A3.1 (continued)

	Years occupational coverage	Type of coverage	Accrual rate; franchise level (2004)
4a) divorces, re-marries, short spell of unemployment	39 years	Average wage	2.2%; €16 489
4b) stays married, changes employer and retires early, after longer spell of unemployment	11 years	Average wage	2.2%; €16 489
5) The intermittent worker in the construction industry	Pension fund for the construction sector, *Bedrijfspensioenfonds bouw,* *'Bouwpensioen 2000'*		
5a) stays married, employment gaps, change of employer type, further training	36 years; the fund is accessible for self-employed	Average wage	2.2%; €15 348
5b) divorces, remarries, employment gaps, change of employer type, further training	36 years; the fund is accessible for self-employed	Average wage	2.2%; €15 348
5c) stays married, employment gaps, change of employer type, self-employment, disabled at the age of 55	36 years; the fund is accessible for self-employed	Average wage	2.2%; €15 348
6) The small business entrepreneur	Pension fund for the retail sale food sector, *Bedrijfstakpensioenfonds voor het Levensmiddelenbedrijf*		
Married, needed to explore risks of type 3	5 years; accrual only during first employment; the fund is not accessible for self-employed	Average wage	2.0%; €15 153
7) The divorced provider in the chemical industry	Dutch State Mines Pension Services		
Twice divorced, needed to explore impact of divorce on men	40 years	Final salary	1.75%; €13 401
8) The middle manager in financial services	Constructed final salary pension; based on traditional pension objective and franchise equal to single AOW		
8a) stays married, retires early	36 years	Final salary	1.75%; €16 421

Table A3.1   (continued)

	Years occupational coverage	Type of coverage	Accrual rate; franchise level (2004)
9) The incomplete resident in the electrical industry	Philips 'Flexpension'		
9a) incomplete resident	29 years; incomplete public old age pension coverage (29 out of 50 years accrual)	Average wage	2.0%; €13 863

Note: * This biography works in car manufacturing. The only car manufacturer in the Netherlands is Nedcar. Nedcar has a company pension arrangement, the text of which was not available. The Nedcar arrangement is based upon the general metal and electrics pension fund arrangement. Therefore, we used this arrangement as an indicative arrangement for the one used at Nedcar.

4. The Swiss pension system and social inclusion

Fabio Bertozzi and Giuliano Bonoli

In international comparisons and reports published by international agencies the Swiss multi-pillar pension model has often been praised for its ability to combine a sustainable financing method, involving pay-as-you-go and funding, with a high degree of inclusiveness.[1] The inclusiveness of the system depends on the universal and redistributive character of the basic first pillar pension, so that people with low lifetime earnings fare rather well as far as this scheme is concerned. Career interruptions, as long as they occur in the context of child rearing or marriage to a working spouse, are not penalized in the first pillar. Inclusiveness is also comparatively strong in the second pillar, thanks to its compulsory character and the presence of guaranteed minimum regulations, known as the Obligatorium.

In this chapter we test this assumption and assess the performance of the Swiss multi-pillar pension system in providing adequate pension benefits that enable citizens to avoid old age poverty and social exclusion, in particular for individuals with low wages and/or disrupted working careers. First of all we provide a short description of the main features of the current Swiss pension system. Secondly we discuss the results of the pension simulations for the risk biographies at age 65, in year 2050. In other words we assess the extent to which some social risks such as unemployment, divorce or low wages have an impact on the old age benefits provided by the mandatory pension system in Switzerland. The contribution of each pension pillar of the Swiss system to social inclusion will also be discussed. In this section we show that as a result of recent retrenchments, particularly in the second pillar, the high reputation of the Swiss regime for inclusiveness is becoming much more open to question. Finally, on the basis of these findings, in the last part we present some reform options for the Swiss system and discuss the feasibility of the proposals. To do this we focus on the main problems of the pension system in terms of social inclusion and we present the point of view of the most important actors involved in pension policymaking: political parties, insurance companies, trade unions and employers.

THE SWISS PENSION SYSTEM

The Swiss pension system is based on a three pillar model: a threefold system of public, occupational and private insurance. The first pillar (AVS/AHV)[2] is compulsory for the entire population and is aimed at guaranteeing a poverty-free retirement. It is moderately earnings related and includes a means-tested pension supplement (PC/EL)[3]. The second pillar (LPP/BVG)[4] has the task of providing retirees with a standard of living close to the one they experienced while in work – an income maintenance objective – and consists of mandatory occupational pensions for employees. The official objective of the compulsory pension system – the first two pillars together – is to provide a replacement rate of at least 60 per cent of final salary. Finally, the third pillar allows people to tailor pension coverage to their individual needs through non-compulsory private pension savings supported by tax concessions (Table 4.1).

The three pillars structure of the Swiss pension system is the result of more than 50 years of institutional developments (Bertozzi et al. 2005; Bonoli 2000). Historically the first compulsory element, the first pillar (AVS/AHV), was introduced in 1948. The principle of a multi-pillar pension system was adopted only in 1972: the functional division between the three levels of pension provision was included in the federal constitution. Nevertheless occupational pensions became compulsory only many years later. In fact although occupational pensions developed substantially throughout the twentieth century, on a voluntary basis, their coverage remained patchy. In 1970 only 50 per cent of employees were covered by an occupational pension. For women the proportion was a much lower 25 per cent. However since 1985 second pillar occupational pension coverage has been compulsory for all employees earning at least twice the amount of the first pillar minimum basic pension, corresponding to approximately 40 per cent of the Swiss average wage. The third pillar of the Swiss pension system, private provision, consists of tax concessions for payments made to personal pension schemes. Tax concessions are more substantial for people who are not covered by an occupational pension, such as the self-employed. Personal pensions play a relatively small role in the Swiss pension system, although the size of this industry is expanding fast.

State Provision: The First Pillar

The first pillar (AVS/AHV) provides universal coverage and is a fairly redistributive scheme, due to a compressed benefit structure: the highest pension is worth only twice as much as the lowest one. In 2006 the lowest and the highest pension were set at about €740 and €1480 per month respectively,

Table 4.1   The three pillars of the Swiss pension system

	1st pillar		2nd pillar	3rd pillar
	Old-age insurance (AVS AHV)	Complementary benefits (PC EL)	Occupational pension schemes (LPP BVG)	Individual provision
Principle	Universal	Need	Occupational	Personal
Coverage	Compulsory for all residents	Compulsory for all residents	Compulsory for employees*	Voluntary
Financing mechanism	Pay-as-you-go	General taxation	Funding	Funding
Contributions	Employment-related	–	Employment-related	
Benefits	Almost flat-rate	Means-tested	Contributions-related	
Objective	Poverty prevention	Basic needs	Income maintenance	Complementary individual needs

Note: * Coverage is compulsory for all employees earning more than €13 470 (19 350 CHF) a year (2006).

109

corresponding to approximately 20 per cent and 40 per cent of the Swiss average wage.[5] Within these limits, the amount of the benefit is related to the contributions paid while in work, with about a third of retirees receiving the maximum amount. The strong vertical redistribution is due to the fact that contributions are proportional to earnings without a ceiling. Even though its benefits are moderately earnings related, the Swiss basic pension is a scheme of Beveridgean inspiration, geared towards poverty prevention rather than income maintenance. In international comparisons this pillar is actually often considered as a flat rate pension scheme (Hinrichs 2000; Weaver 2003).

As far as financing is concerned, the AVS/AHV works on a pay-as-you-go basis. It is mainly financed through employment-related contributions, but also receives a state subsidy financed by general taxation equal to 19 per cent of total expenditure. Coverage is universal: those who are not working after age 21, for instance students, are required to pay an annual flat rate contribution of about €290 or, if providing informal care, are entitled to contribution credits.[6] Benefits are adjusted every two years according to a so-called 'mixed index' resulting from the arithmetic average between inflation and wage increases. Unemployed people pay contributions calculated on their unemployment benefit, which is treated as a salary, the unemployment insurance fund contributing 4.2 per cent of the unemployment benefit on their behalf. Contribution credits are provided for those with children younger than 16, and a contribution-sharing system between married people called 'splitting' makes sure that non-working spouses are credited with half of the contributions paid by their partner. In case of divorce each partner of the former couple keeps their shared contributions for the period of their marriage.

AVS/AHV is clearly the most socially inclusive component of the Swiss pension system. However first pillar benefits in Switzerland do not guarantee pension benefits over the old age social assistance level, unlike in the Netherlands for instance. The Swiss basic pension is thus not fully poverty preventing like in other Beveridgean countries (Hinrichs 2000, p. 356). This means that people who are either not entitled to second pillar benefits, who have very limited second pillar benefits or cannot rely on their spouse's pension, might get pensions below the old age social assistance threshold. In this case they can claim supplementary benefits (PC/EL). These are means tested and available on application. They are financed out of tax revenue by the federal state, the cantons and partly by the municipalities.

Supplementary benefits were introduced in 1966 as a transitional measure, to span the period until pensions would be high enough to guarantee a satisfactory minimum income. However over the years it became clear that this measure would become a structural benefit, since first pillar minimal benefits have never been raised over the social assistance threshold. Data on recipients of complementary benefits confirms that the mandatory pension system in Switzerland is unable to prevent old age poverty for the entire population. In 2005 up to 12 per cent of first pillar beneficiaries, 149 600 persons, also received supplementary benefits (OFAS 2006). These recipients are particularly concentrated in some categories of the retired population. In fact the female share of first pillar supplementary benefits recipients (14.4 per cent) is noticeably higher than the male share (8.4 per cent). Even more important differences are evident in relation to marital status: on average unmarried persons (21.8 per cent) turn much more often to supplementary benefits than married persons (5.4 per cent). Among those not married at the age of retirement, divorcees confront the biggest problems in getting a pension over the social assistance level: indeed 30.8 per cent of them get supplementary pension benefits. Among both unmarried and divorced persons, women are represented disproportionately. There are also relevant regional disparities: depending on the selected Swiss canton, the share of first pillar benefits recipients that get means-tested complementary benefits can vary from 5.8 per cent (Canton of Wallis) to 20.8 per cent (Canton of Ticino).

The Privately Administered Compulsory Occupational System: The Second Pillar

The second pillar of the Swiss pension system, occupational pensions, were first granted tax concessions in 1916 and became compulsory in 1985 for all employees earning at least twice the amount of the minimum AVS/AHV pension. The first LPP/BVG revision, adopted in 2003 and implemented in 2005, has lowered this threshold to 1.5 times the minimum AVS/AHV benefit. Since January 2005 it is about €13 093.[7] This, in contrast to the Dutch second pillar, is not reduced for part-time workers.

In the 1990s coverage was virtually universal among male employees but reached only around 80 per cent among employed women (DFI 1995, p. 10), mainly because part-time employment and wages below the threshold are more common in female employment. A full occupational pension is granted to employees with a contribution record of 39 years for women and 40 for men, although this might be equalized over the next few years. When affiliation to an occupational pension became compulsory in the mid-1980s, many employees were already covered by voluntary arrangements of this kind. The situation was such that legislation needed to take into account the existence of a relatively well-developed system of occupational pension provision. As a result it was decided to introduce a compulsory minimum level of provision, the Obligatorium, which is calculated on the basis of notional contributions, leaving relatively wide room for manoeuvre to existing pension funds regarding how to deliver and finance this minimum level of provision. The employer bears ultimate responsibility for ensuring that their employees are subscribed to a second pillar scheme capable of achieving this minimum standard. However many pension funds – especially in the public sector or those sponsored by large employers – still offer better conditions than the Obligatorium (Bonoli and Gay-des-Combes 2003; Vontobel 2000).

The objective of the new law was to aim at a combined first and second pillar's Obligatorium replacement rate of 60 per cent of gross earnings up to a ceiling wage equal to three times the maximum AVS/AHV benefit. For low-paid workers this goal could be achieved by the moderately earnings-related benefits provided by AVS/AHV. As a result insured earnings were those comprised between one and three times the maximum AVS/AHV benefits, that is between approximately 40 and 120 per cent of average earnings.

The minimum second pillar pension threshold is calculated on the basis of notional contributions. Depending on the employee's age, individual accounts must be credited with a percentage of insured earnings, ranging from 7 to 18 per cent; rates are higher for older people. Pension funds are free to finance the set amount as they wish, with the proviso that contributions must at least be equally split between workers and employers; the latter can contribute more than half of the contribution bill, if they so wish. For instance a pension fund could decide to apply an age-neutral contribution rate of 12.5 per cent, or alternatively to charge employees on the basis of their age, thus reflecting the pre-set notional contributions. In fact, because of the way notional contributions are calculated and financed, the system is not purely funded but includes some intergenerational redistribution. The rationale for this was to guarantee adequate coverage to workers who were already in employment before the 1985 law came into force, and thus were not going to have a full contribution record. In theory this pay-as-you-go element should disappear once, and if, every worker spends their whole working life in the system.

Besides notional contributions, the occupational pension law also prescribes a government-set minimum nominal interest rate, which must be credited to second pillar pension funds. At the time of the introduction of the new law, this rate was set at 4 per cent and remained at this level until 2003 when, as a result of the crisis in the stock market, it was reduced to 3.25 per cent. In 2004 the rate was further reduced to 2.25 per cent, and for 2005 and 2006 it was set at 2.5 per cent, which is the rate used in the simulations. The impact of these decisions on the level of the benefits depends on their duration. If limited in time it will be negligible; otherwise the 60 per cent target replacement rate will be out of reach for many current workers.

When a worker reaches retirement age, or decides to take early retirement, which is possible from the age of 62, but with an actuarially determined benefit reduction, the capital resulting from the notional contributions credited and the applicable minimum interest (compound) is converted into a pension, on the basis of a conversion rate set by the government. The conversion rate was originally set at 7.2 per cent in the law of 1985 but was recently lowered to 6.8 per cent with a transition period of ten years (until 2014). The Swiss government is currently (in 2007) planning to further lower this rate to 6.4 per cent with a shorter transition period (until 2011).[8] The rate is used to convert the capital into an annual pension. There is no annuity market for (compulsory) occupational pensions, as the price of annuities is de facto determined by the government in the shape of the conversion rate, which does not take into account sex-based differences in life expectancy. The result of this complex calculation represents the minimum occupational pension entitlement.

As was suggested above, in reality a large but decreasing number of pension scheme members enjoy more favourable conditions than those guaranteed by the occupational pension law. This is particularly the case with respect to defined benefit plans, common especially in the public sector. However it should be noted that in common with developments in Britain their number has declined rapidly over the last few years. In 1994 33 per cent of insured persons were covered by defined benefit plans. In 1996 this was only 29 per cent and in 2000 the figure was down to 23 per cent. The sharpest decline has taken place in public sector pension funds (OFS 1999, 2004).

In the Swiss second pillar there is no automatic contribution-sharing system for spouses. Nevertheless, according to the new Swiss legislation on divorce implemented in 2000, second pillar pension savings have to be equally split between partners in case of divorce. Despite this legal requirement, a recent research project has shown that the splitting of second pillar savings in case of divorce is still far from being equally and generally implemented in Switzerland at this time.[9] Contrary to what happens for the splitting of first pillar contributions, where this occurs automatically, the sharing of second pillar savings has to be negotiated by the partners in the framework of the divorce arrangement. In this case calculations can be rather complicated and precise information on the exact amount of professional savings collected by both partners is sometimes difficult to obtain. This is why the implementation of the new legislation is still incomplete. Moreover pension savings are sometimes traded against other property belonging to the former spouse such as houses.

The Third Pillar

The third pillar of the pension system, voluntary private provision, consists of tax concessions for payments made to personal pension schemes.[10] In 2006 employees who are already covered by a second pillar occupational pension can deduct from their taxable income contributions paid into a third pillar pension up to about €4270 per year.[11] Tax concessions are more substantial for people who are not covered by an occupational pension such as the self-employed who can deduct up to 20 per cent of their income from their income tax return. Personal pensions play a relatively small but fast-growing role in the Swiss pension system. The number of personal pensions went from 560 000 in 1990 to just over 2 million accounts in 2003, but the assets held by third pillar pension providers, banks and insurance companies, amounted to 'only' about €20 billion in 1999, or 13 times less than those held by second pillar funds (OFAS 2004).

The third pillar, individual pension schemes encouraged through tax concessions, is one of the constitutive elements of the Swiss three pillar pension system. According to an important report by the federal government on the future of the Swiss pension system, the third pillar 'offers to each individual the choice about the means he wants to dispose of at age of retirement' (DFI 1995). The function of the third pillar is to allow individuals to adjust their pension coverage on the basis of their individual preferences, which may differ, and as a result cannot be satisfied by the one-size-fits-all solutions represented by the first and the second pillar. As such, third pillar pensions are widely considered as a somewhat marginal element in the system. Unlike pillars one and two, third pillar pensions are seldom in the news, have not been subjected to any in-depth investigation and do not seem to play any significant role in the politics of pensions.

Yet there are reasons to believe that third pillar pensions are being wrongly ignored. Firstly as already mentioned, over the last few years we have seen a massive increase in the number of third pillar accounts. Secondly recent economic and demographic developments suggest that in an increasing number of cases the pensions provided by pillars one and two may not be sufficient to cover even basic needs. An increase in atypical career profiles, lower returns on second pillar pension fund assets and higher life expectancy for retirees suggest that the target combined replacement rate of 60 per cent of earnings may be unachievable for many current workers, a scenario which is confirmed by our simulations.

THE INCLUSIVENESS AND THE PROTECTION AGAINST POVERTY PROVIDED BY THE SWISS PENSION SYSTEM

The Protection Provided to the Risk Biographies

In this section we focus on the results of the pension simulations for the risk biographies to assess the outcomes of the Swiss pension system. The pension simulations include mandatory first pillar benefits and compulsory second pillar professional provisions. Only minimum mandatory second pillar savings have been considered – the Obligatorium. As already mentioned, several second pillar professional pension schemes, particularly in the public sector and those sponsored by large companies, still provide more generous pension benefits than legal minimum requirements. However supplementary provisions have been reduced in recent years because of the bad economic performance of pension funds and population ageing. With scope in law to modify supplementary pension regulations, those pension funds offering more than the Obligatorium have gradually begun to reduce their provision to that level. Given this situation, pension funds have started in recent years to use savings above the compulsory level to fill the gap that has resulted in the compulsory part of the second pillar. The future of supplementary savings looks very uncertain. As previously mentioned, the Swiss government recently suggested that the conversion rate which is nowadays guaranteed by the Obligatorium (6.8 per cent) will have to be lowered again in the near future to adapt the system to the changing demographic structure of the insured persons. In these conditions of uncertainty we have chosen in the simulations to use the current conversion rate, but not take into account supplementary, non-compulsory, provision. This means that we focus exclusively on what is currently guaranteed by the national legal framework.

It must also be underlined that some of the biographies included in our sample do not have access to second pillar coverage. For instance self-employed persons are not compulsorily insured. They are likely to opt for third pillar private savings, since tax concessions are more substantial for people who are not covered by a second pillar occupational pension. This is by far the most usual attitude among the self-employed in Switzerland (see below).

Individual risk biographies
The results of the simulations are presented in Figures 4.1 and 4.2. The first figure shows results for individuals, including both married and unmarried persons at age of retirement. The second figure deals with the situation of households.

In each figure the level of the pension benefits (in euros) that the risk biographies will get according to current pension regulations at age of retirement is indicated and compared to three different thresholds: the national old age social assistance level is the poverty line, below this level retired persons can apply for means-tested complementary benefits; 40 per cent and 50 per cent of the Swiss average wage are thresholds for social inclusion and comfortable social inclusion respectively.[12]

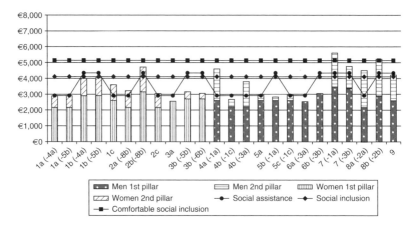

Notes: Social assistance: social assistance for individuals if person is single on retirement. Corresponds to the first pillar subsistence level, under this level means-tested supplementary old-age benefits can be obtained. For married individuals: 50% of couple's social assistance. Social inclusion: 40% average wage. Comfortable social inclusion: 50% average wage. See Appendix 2, Chapter 1 for details. Second pillars include divorce payments for divorcees. Second pillar yearly interest rate 2.5%.

Figure 4.1   *Projected real monthly pension levels from first and second pillar for Swiss men and women in 2050*

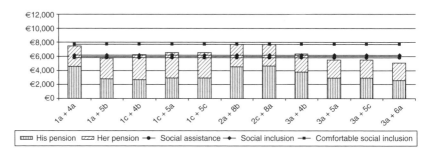

Notes: Social assistance line: social assistance line for married couples. Corresponds to the first pillar subsistence level, under this level means-tested supplementary old-age benefits can be obtained. Social inclusion line: 1.5×40% average wage. Comfortable social inclusion: 1.5×50% average wage. Second pillar yearly interest rate 2.5%. Other details: see Appendix 2, Chapter 1.

Figure 4.2   *Projected real monthly pension levels of Swiss couples in 2050*

Figure 4.1 summarizes the results of the pension simulations for individuals at age of retirement.

Overall our results show that the large majority of our biographies are at risk of receiving incomes below the social inclusion threshold on retirement, with a significant number reliant on means-tested benefits to lift them out of poverty. However in terms of a comparison with the other countries in this study the poverty result is somewhat misleading: the comparatively large number of Swiss biographies who fall under the poverty threshold is at least partially a product of the comparatively high level of old age social assistance in Switzerland. In 2003 the old age social assistance benefit for individuals was actually above our social inclusion threshold of 40 per cent of average wages. Thus while the Swiss pension system appears to be becoming decreasingly good at delivering pensions above the national social minimum, the Swiss threshold is high by international standards.

When individuals fall below old age social assistance, lack of access to second pillar provision is normally the most important reason. This is often linked to, or exacerbated by, low lifetime income, caused by either low wages or prolonged periods of labour market absence. Whether an individual is married or single on retirement also plays a role. There are nine individuals who are in this situation: the single variants of the unqualified mother and part-time worker (bio 1b), the married carer and informal worker (bio 3), the unqualified male worker in the car industry who retires early after a long spell of unemployment (bio 4b), a variant of the intermittent worker (bio 5b) and the male small business entrepreneur (bio 6).

For most of these individuals the first pillar pension is comparatively generous, reaching at least 50 per cent of the social exclusion threshold. This result for the first pillar is broadly comparable with the situation in the Netherlands (Chapter 3), the best-performing country in this book. It is a product of the redistributive nature of the first pillar and the splitting mechanism introduced in the Swiss first pillar in 1995, according to which contributions paid by each of the two spouses are added, divided by two and the resulting sum attributed to each member of the couple. This reduces first pillar benefit differences among spouses (see below). Combined with the contribution credits paid to persons with children under age 16, these measures protect household members during periods of inactivity or informal work, and prevent very low first pillar benefits.

Second pillar provision is more problematic for this group of biographies. For the carer the main reason for her limited access to second pillar provision is the periods she spends in informal work, a problem especially acute for the first variant (bio 3a) whose 35 years of informal employment mean she does not contribute anything to a second pillar fund. However even with a longer spell in the labour market (for example bio 3b) this individual is in any case disadvantaged by the low wages she receives from part-time work. The car worker who retires early after unemployment (bio 4b) has higher wages and works full-time for a long period of his adult life, but he again suffers from the fact that 20 years of this employment are undertaken without second pillar contributions. This is rather an unlikely scenario in the Swiss system, given the compulsory nature of second pillar provision for most full-time employed workers. However it can sometimes occur for workers who are employed on short-term contracts of less than three months, and who are thus not covered by the compulsory occupational pension stipulation. The intermittent worker (bio 5b) and the small business entrepreneur (bio 6a) are even better paid than the car worker but because they are self-employed for long periods of their working life they are not compulsorily covered by the second professional pillar. However in their cases they are much more likely to invest in a private third pillar fund allowing important tax concessions (see below).

The unqualified mother and part-time worker (bio 1b) has fewer problems qualifying for a second pillar pension: her dilemma is that her low lifetime wages mean that even with such access she cannot build up sufficient second pillar provision to lift her above social assistance. This is also the main problem for the eight individuals (bio 1a and 4a; 1a and 5b; 1c; 2a and 8b; 2c; 4b and 3a; 5a; 5c and 1c) whose pensions surpass the poverty threshold but remain significantly below the social inclusion line (Figure 4.1).

The biographies that definitely escape the risk of old age poverty and social exclusion among both married and unmarried persons are the mother and qualified part-time worker (bio 2b), the unqualified male car worker (bio 4a), the divorced provider (bio 7) and the middle manager (bio 8). All these biographies have lifetime earnings above 55 per cent of average (Figure 1.1, Chapter 1), but even more importantly they all have good access to second pillar provision because they spend most of their working life in full-time employment.

It is possible that our simulations underestimate the performance of those of our biographies who work with public sector employers and large employers, particularly that of the worker in the welfare sector (bio 2). Traditionally such employers have provided more comprehensive second pillar schemes than the legally binding Obligatorium provided in small private firms. Nevertheless, as has been seen, the current 'race to the bottom' convergence in the second pillar in the direction of the Obligatorium might be expected to decrease these differences in the long term, that is at the time when our risk biographies will retire.

There are three other factors affecting the performance of our biographies that are worthy of comment. The most important of these is retirement age, which has an important impact on the amount of first pillar benefits. In fact, according to the current first pillar regulations, early retirement at age 63 instead of 65 indeed leads to a lifelong reduction of the first pillar benefit by 13.6 per cent. This is illustrated by the reduced first pillar benefit of all the biographies retiring at age 63 instead of 65: the unqualified female part-time worker in retail (bio 1a), the qualified female part-time worker in the welfare sector (bio 2a, c), the unqualified car worker (bio 4b) and the middle manager (bio 8).

The second factor is marriage. The relative performance of all our single individuals is affected by the fact that they are liable to the single person's social assistance line, which is noticeably higher than 50 per cent of the one for married households. Thus despite the fact that our single variant of the unqualified part-time worker and mother (bio 1b), for example, has a higher overall pension than many married individuals who are not in poverty on the basis of the married person's social assistance line (such as bio 1a); she is nevertheless in poverty herself. This situation occurs despite the fact that in general, individual first pillar benefits for married persons are relatively low in Switzerland. This is because the sum of the first pillar pension of both partners of the couple cannot exceed 150 per cent of the maximum first pillar benefit (see also Figure 4.3).

The final significant factor affecting the performance of our biographies is divorce. In this regard, despite some already mentioned implementation problems, we have strictly applied the new Swiss divorce rulings concerning the sharing of second pillar savings. This means that we might overestimate the size of second pension pillars for divorced women in our simulations, who benefit most from this ruling given that their second pillar pension entitlements are generally lower than their former spouses. Nevertheless it can be expected that the new rulings will be implemented more strictly and systematically in the next years. A comparison of the two divorced variants of carer and informal worker (bio 3b and 6b, 3b and 5b) clearly illustrate this point: while the level of first pillar benefit does not change, second pillar benefits are different depending on the husband's biography. The divorce from the small business entrepreneur (bio 6) does not provide her with any supplementary second pillar savings, since he has no access to a professional second pillar scheme. In contrast, when she divorces from the intermittent construction worker (bio 5b), who has some second pillar savings, her savings increase because of the sharing of the savings collected during the marriage years.

In summary the factors having the most relevant impact on final pension level for the individuals included in our simulations are twofold. Firstly entitlement and extent of second pillar benefits significantly affect the chance of getting a pension above the social assistance line, as was seen with regard to all biographies. In this respect self-employment or informal employment and low wages, often as a result of part-time employment, are the main obstacles to accede to second pillar schemes. On this second point, the extension of the coverage of the Swiss second pillar that was implemented in January 2005 should have a positive impact as it meant a 25 per cent reduction in the minimum wage for compulsory affiliation. The use of these new second pillar rulings in the simulations has led to an increasing coverage of professional schemes among the selected biographies. Secondly retiring earlier than 65 is particularly risky for low-wage biographies because of its effect on the first pillar. In conclusion the Swiss system relies on its almost universal first pillar to prevent old age poverty. In fact this pillar provides moderately earnings-related benefits that can be complemented with supplementary means-tested old age benefits for those below the social assistance level. From this point of view, basic needs are largely covered. The income maintenance objective of the second pillar is less fulfilled, in particular for those categories that are not compulsorily covered by the scheme: employees with low wages and the self-employed. Since it is strongly correlated with low wages, part-time employment can be a risk factor in building up adequate pension rights. It must be added that part-time employment in Switzerland is extremely widespread among women: whereas only 12 per cent of male workers had part-time jobs in 2005, 59 per cent of female workers were in this situation (Table 1.2, Chapter 1).

Households' risk biographies
The simulation results for individuals married at age of retirement (Figure 4.1) can also be compared in terms of households (Figure 4.2), in order to assess how individualized the Swiss pension system is. In this regard we have already seen that an automatic sharing mechanism exists in the first pillar which boosts the pension entitlement of the lower-paid partner in a couple. This helps to explain the quite similar contributions to total household income made by males and females in a couple (Figure 4.2). Nevertheless some individuals, as has been seen, are vulnerable to poverty and/or social exclusion on the basis of their own pension. To what extent are these individuals protected better as part of a couple? This type of redistribution – normally from the man to the woman – is built on personal dependency; it is therefore less reliable than individualized social rights. Nevertheless it can be assumed that spouses share their pension benefits to a certain extent. Moreover living together enables them to share housing costs and other types of expenditure. This is why in the Swiss system the sum of the first pillar benefit of both spouses cannot exceed 150 per cent of the maximum first pillar benefit. Following the same logic, the old age social assistance level for households corresponds to 134 per cent of the level for single persons that are not married.

When compared in terms of households, the lower-paid partner in a couple can improve their situation. This is particularly the case for the carer and informal worker (bio 3a) married to the unqualified car worker (bio 4b), and for this same individual when he is married to the mother and unqualified part-time worker (bio 1c). However this transfer is not always from male to female, as the example of the mother and unqualified part-time worker (bio 1c) married to the unqualified car worker (bio 4b) or the intermittent male worker (bio 5a, c) shows. If the woman is in stable employment and the man is not, men can improve their situation through their spouses' pensions. In contrast when biographies perform well individually inter-personal redistribution is less important: because both partners do well as individuals they also do well as a household. By the same token, when both partners have individual pensions below the social assistance line, their household pension benefit remains under the households' social assistance level. This is illustrated by the marriage between the carer and informal worker (bio 3a) and the small business entrepreneur (bio 6b).

To sum up, the performance of the Swiss pension system does not radically change when analysing the risk of old age poverty for couples instead of the same risk for married individuals. The already mentioned factors of low wages, part-time work and self-employment represent once again the main risk factors for old age social inclusion. Marriage is still a protection for the weaker partner in those households where one partner earns significantly more than the other, provided they share earnings.

Contribution to Social Inclusion by the Different Pillars of the Swiss Pension System

The strength of the public regulatory framework decreases, going from the first to the third pillar. The first pillar is strictly regulated by the state and the central fund is managed by the federal administration. However the social partners do take part in the management of the scheme by running some branch funds. For second pillar occupational schemes, state regulation mainly concerns the guarantee of the minimum requirements (Obligatorium) and other technical details such as portability. The law also prescribes the obligation to involve employees' representatives in the joint steering bodies of the funds. Nevertheless scheme managers have a large degree of freedom in deciding how to attain the objectives of the minimum requirements and in providing supplementary provisions. The legal regulations for third pillar private pension savings are even less binding, and are rather similar to the directives concerning any private insurance contract.[13] The main state limitation concerns the maximum amount of savings that can be deducted from taxable earnings.

In the Swiss three pillar pension system each pillar caters for a distinct level of provision. The functional division between three levels of pension provision is upheld by the federal constitution, and it is widely regarded as an important constraint with regard to policy change in the area of pensions.

As shown by the simulations, most pensioners obtain their income from a combination of these different pillars. In aggregate terms, the first pillar (AVS/AHV) contributes 60 per cent of retired people's income and second pillar occupational pensions 22 per cent (own calculations, see Bonoli and Gay-des-Combes 2003). However the latter figure is set to rise with occupational pension scheme maturation.

In the following sections we discuss the role played by each pension pillar and its contribution to social inclusion, with a special focus on the role of the third pillar, which has been poorly analysed until now.

Role of state provision

As already mentioned, the first pillar component of the Swiss pension system contributes by far the most to social inclusion of retired persons. First of all the entire resident population is compulsorily covered by this scheme, which is not the case for the two other pillars. Secondly as seen in our simulations, it is fairly redistributive, both vertically and by gender, and thus guarantees an important degree of solidarity. Thirdly it is set at a comparatively high level. It fails to perform better in relation to the Swiss social minimum mainly because this threshold is itself comparatively generous.

Role of privately administered, compulsory occupational systems

As has been seen in our simulations, second pillar occupational pensions play an important role in lifting a number of our individuals above the poverty and/or social inclusion threshold. The main problem with this pillar is coverage, notwithstanding the fact that the level of compulsion is comparatively high and pressure for retrenchment. With regard to the former, in 2006 only employees with annual earnings above €13 093[14] were compulsorily covered by the scheme and the self-employed were excluded. As well as affecting employees with very low wages, the earnings stipulation excludes the non-working population and some part-time workers. Indeed employees cumulating several part-time jobs are not compulsorily insured, even if their total earnings are higher than the threshold unless one of the jobs provides a salary above the previously mentioned threshold. Within these groups female workers are particularly prevalent. Since the first pillar provides pension benefits below old age social assistance level, persons excluded from the second pillar and who cannot rely on a spouse's pension can only escape old age poverty by applying for means-tested complementary benefits (PC/EL) or by relying on third pillar voluntary savings or any other form of private savings.

In addition to this situation of incomplete coverage, another issue challenges the role and objectives of the professional pension pillar. The pension funds' decreasing performances in recent years and the ageing of the population put into question the capacities of second pillar benefits to guarantee income maintenance during retirement. On the one hand, professional schemes providing more generous conditions than the Obligatorium are, as have been seen, progressively reducing their non-compulsory part, often in order to fill the gaps that have emerged in the compulsory component. On the other hand, the benefits guaranteed by the Obligatorium are decreasing as well. In fact the two government-set technical variables which have an essential impact on final benefits, the minimum nominal interest rate and the conversion rate, have been reduced in recent years. Even if the reduction of the minimum interest rate is only a short-term decision dependent on the performance of pension funds, it looks unlikely that this rate will be increased again to the level set in the 1980s and 1990s, which was 4 per cent. The reduction of the conversion rate is linked to population ageing and is thus a long-term change. Moreover most of the actors involved in pension policymaking stress that the conversion rate will have to be further reduced very soon to comply with demographic realities and, as already mentioned, the Swiss government has recently published a proposal to this effect. To sum up, second pillar benefits have already decreased and are very likely to decrease even further in coming years.

The incomplete coverage and decreasing benefits of the Swiss professional pillar challenge its original function. The outcome might be that second pillar benefits fail to guarantee preservation of living standards any more, that is to provide for full social inclusion, but become a limited supplement to the basic pension benefit, enabling individuals merely to avoid the risk of old age poverty. This scenario might be particularly realistic for middle-wage employees. In this case third pillar voluntary savings might become necessary for everybody to guarantee income maintenance.

Savings

It seems essential to improve our knowledge of third pillar voluntary pension provision. Two issues need to be explored. First of all who needs third pillar benefits in order to prevent old age poverty? That is, whose first and second pillar benefits are likely to be insufficient to guarantee a poverty-free retirement and how much should they save privately to fill this gap? Second who has nowadays voluntarily subscribed to a third pillar scheme in Switzerland? To answer the first question we go back to our simulations and show how much our biographies should save in order to fill their final pension gaps. The underlying question is whether third pillar private savings can be considered a solution for persons who are likely to be confronted by the risk of old age poverty.

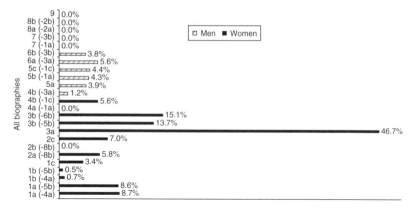

Notes: Each individual linked to another individual receives or pays contributions to divorced partner. Assumptions for private savings: Appendix 1.2, Chapter 1.

Figure 4.3   *Third pillar savings from lifetime income required of Swiss men and women to reach social inclusion line of 40% average wage in 2050*

Figure 4.3 shows the amount of private savings needed by each risk biography on the basis of their first and second pillar benefits in order to attain the 40 per cent of the average wage line at age of retirement. The amount of savings required is measured as the average percentage of their annual wages that should be devoted to this type of instrument. The real rate of return that has been applied is 4 per cent, which looks very generous in the Swiss context compared to the conditions that are usually applied in third pillar schemes (Appendix 1.2, Chapter 1).

The amount of earnings our biographies need to devote to private pension savings during their working years to reach the social inclusion line of 40 per cent average wage after retirement is often very high and seems unrealistic, most especially for the biographies with low wages. This is particularly the case for the carer and informal worker (bio 3) and partly for the unqualified part-time worker and mother who retires early (bio 1a). Willingness to save among this group is also likely to be affected by the fact that individuals not married at retirement age can attain the social inclusion line as well, through the means-tested supplementary pension benefits (PC/EL).

To answer the second question concerning the voluntary subscription to a third pillar scheme in Switzerland, we focus on the Swiss household panel survey.[15] This contains a question asking respondents whether they have a third pillar pension scheme or not.[16] This question is asked in the household questionnaire, so it is impossible to know who within a household is the legal owner of the third pillar plan. However we can estimate the number of people living in a household that have at least one private pension. For our analysis we have decided to focus on a sub-sample of respondents aged 25 to 60. The lower limit reflects the beginning of compulsory second pillar coverage for employees (if applicable) whereas 60 is the earliest age for the withdrawal of a third pillar pension. In the 2002 wave of the survey, 68.4 per cent of respondents aged between 25 and 60 lived in households that have a third pillar.[17] However what socio-economic factors affect adoption of third pillar private pension schemes? At least five different hypotheses can be formulated: third pillar pensions are used only to adapt pension coverage to individual preferences; they are a luxury good; they are essentially used in order to reduce the tax bill; they are used to compensate for substandard pension coverage; or the inclination to buy a third pillar is related to how pressing the need to save for retirement is because of the age of the respondent.

The Swiss household panel data allow us to test these hypotheses.[18] In fact the prevalence of third pillar pensions in the population varies dramatically according to socio-economic group. The probability of having a third pillar pension depends most strongly on household income (positively) and on being self-employed. Least likely to have a third pillar are single parents. Other significant variables include age (positively) and the respondent's degree of satisfaction with his or her financial situation. Variables measuring the lack of pension coverage, for example being a part-time worker, were not found to be associated with having a third pillar.

The most important outcomes for our study cases are that while the self-employed usually tend to compensate for the lack of a second professional pension pillar by private third pillar pension savings, other categories without or with a very limited second pillar – such as part-time workers or employees with very low wages – do it less frequently. From this point of view, voluntary private pension savings seem inadequate to prevent old age poverty for most social groups.

THE REFORM DEBATE IN SWITZERLAND

The issue of pension coverage for atypical workers, particularly part-time workers, highlighted by our simulations, has been prominent on the agenda for several years, in the context of the first important reform of the legislation on occupational pensions (first revision of the LPP/BVG). On that occasion the minimum annual earnings needed for compulsory affiliation to a pension fund was lowered by 25 per cent with the result of including many more low-income employees in the system, mostly part-time workers,

and of extending the portion of earnings covered.[19] As a direct consequence of the adoption of this reform in late 2003 the debate on how to
improve the inclusion of atypical workers in the pension system has somewhat faded away. The modest lowering of the access threshold was the
result of a compromise, as the trade unions and the Socialist Party were in
favour of scrapping the threshold altogether. However presumably because
of political realism, they have not pressed this issue lately.

On the basis of our simulation work, where we applied the new second
pillar regulations, it is nonetheless possible to identify coverage problems
for selected groups of workers, in particular low-income employees and the
self-employed. Similar simulation work carried out in a previous project
had also shown that divorced women with a weak connection to the labour
market are also exposed to the risk of pensions below poverty level (Bonoli
and Gay-des-Combes 2003). These potential problems are likely to be com-
pounded by the more recent developments in the regulatory framework for
second pillar pensions. As we discussed above, in the early 2000s a number
of crucial parameters determining the final amount of second pillar pensions, such as the minimum interest rate and conversion rate, were altered.
This was partly a result of the stock markets crisis of 2001–2002 and partly
in anticipation of longer life expectancy. The precise consequences of these
decisions are still uncertain, but it is clear that they will have a downward
impact on pension levels. In addition the current debate on the setting of
these parameters seems to be dominated by the position supported by
the insurance industry, that both the minimum interest rate and the conversion rate should be set on the basis of returns on risk-free investments.
According to the insurance industry these two important parameters
should not assume returns higher than the interest rate guaranteed by Swiss
federal government bonds, a risk-free investment par excellence. Other
actors – the trade unions, the left – have challenged this view, arguing that
more optimistic assumptions can be made, taking into account higher rates
of return that can be achieved, in the long term, in real estate and stock
market investments (interview USS/SGB, 14 March 2005). But this view
seems to be less influential in the present context.

The adoption of this position by the insurance industry has two different
sorts of consequences, depending on the regulatory level of second pillar pensions. With regard to law-based parameters, it translates into political pressures to reduce the commitments that must be taken up by providers. With
regard to parameters that are not regulated by law, such as the conversion
rates applied to coverage above the legal minimum, insurance companies
enjoy almost complete freedom. As a result many providers have dramatically reduced the conversion rate for non-compulsory coverage to a level that
is far below what is being debated in the context of the law. Since 2004 a

number of providers apply a conversion rate of 5.45 per cent for women and 5.84 for men on coverage above the legal minimum (Lelièvre 2004).

These developments suggest that, all other things being equal, future pension benefits are likely to be lower than today's. Their impact will be felt regardless of income level, but it may push those who on the basis of current regulations just manage to be above the poverty line, below it. In addition the fact that we increasingly see a decoupling in the rules applied to compulsory provision and to coverage above the legal minimum suggests that the importance of the latter component in the system is going to diminish over time. As the costs of retirement increase because of longer life expectancy, it is reasonable to expect employers, pension funds and private insurance companies to save where it is easier to do so, such as in the field of non-compulsory coverage, which, unlike the legal minimum, is not strictly regulated by law.

On the basis of these observations, we conclude that the recent LPP/BVG reform has probably not solved the problem of pension coverage for atypical workers once and for all. However this reform is rather recent, and this makes political mobilization and debate on this issue more difficult. In addition the impact of the changes to the minimum interest and conversion rates remains somewhat uncertain, and certainly obscure to the majority of voters. As a result the lack of debate is not particularly surprising.

However absence of debate does not necessarily mean that political actors are not thinking about these issues or that they do not have a position on them. In this final section we present and discuss the positions of the main actors in relation to the issue of how to improve pension coverage for risk-exposed atypical workers. Several options are discussed, belonging to each of the three pillars of the Swiss pension system.

Debate and Options for the First Pillar

As seen above, the first pillar of the Swiss pension system fares rather well insofar as its ability to include atypical employment is concerned. This is so notwithstanding proposals on how to improve further the quality of coverage and the redistributive function of the scheme that have been made in recent years. These concern both the general level of pension and the more specific issue of early retirement. The key actor behind each of these proposals is the trade unions (USS/SGB 2005).

In response to their failure to obtain the abolition of the access threshold to second pillar pensions in the 2003 reform (first LPP/BVG revision) the unions refocused their strategy on the first pillar. In spring 2005 they published a proposal for strengthening the role of the first pillar in the pension system (USS/SGB 2005). According to this, the minimum monthly pension should be set at €2000 for single persons and €3000 for couples (respectively 55 per cent and 82 per cent of average earnings). This should be achieved by reducing mandatory contributions to the second pillar and increasing contributions to the first pillar. Thus the proposal entails a shift of resources from the second to the first pillar. This project has little chance to be adopted by the federal government and parliament, which are both dominated by centre-right political parties that are usually opposed to an expansion of the first pillar. In spite of its potentially controversial character, it has generated little debate, which is understandable given the extremely unfavourable political outlook.

The second element in the trade unions strategy, an improvement of early retirement benefits for low-income workers, has generated considerably more debate. Our simulations have shown that early retirement is strongly and permanently penalizing in the Swiss first pillar, in particular for those persons having low or not very high earnings. Retiring before the legal age strongly increases the risk of old age poverty for the persons mainly relying on first pillar benefits. To improve early retirement benefits for low-income workers was the objective of a reform started in 2000 (11th AVS/AHV revision). However the measures planned to that effect were overturned by the right-wing majority in parliament (Bonoli 2005, 2007). As a result, the trade unions challenged the reform with a referendum in 2004 and won.[20] The government was forced back to the drawing board and came up in late 2005 with a new proposal which provides a means-tested benefit for non-working persons aged between 60 and 65 which is slightly more generous than social assistance. This more modest proposal is unlikely to be considered satisfactory by the trade unions, which have collected the 100 000 signature needed to call a referendum on the lowering of the standard age of retirement to 62. A vote will take place in 2007 or 2008.

These demands for the improvement and the strengthening of first pillar pensions are contrasted by expenditure projections showing growing imbalances in the finances of the basic pension scheme. It is expected that in order to ensure the solvency of the scheme in 2040, the VAT rate will have to be raised by five percentage points. In response to this some influential actors, including the minister of social affairs, have been calling for an increase in the age of retirement to 67.

Debate and Options for the Second Pillar

Further lowering or abolition of the access threshold to compulsory second pillar pensions

Such a measure would undeniably further extend the coverage of second pillar pensions. It is difficult to estimate how many workers would benefit from this measure, as some of those whose earnings are currently below the access threshold may already be covered by a pension fund thanks to more generous regulations than the legal minimum. The main likely objections to it would be in terms of costs, particularly administrative costs, which are proportionally higher for low-wage workers. Atypical workers, to the extent that they may also be more likely to experience career interruptions and job changes, are particularly costly for pension funds, as each change requires administrative actions to be taken. In addition it should be mentioned that this measure would have no impact on the self-employed, who have been shown in the simulations to be a particularly risk-exposed group.

From the point of view of political feasibility, one can assume that the compromise reached on the access threshold in the context of the first LPP revision (see above) is the lowest level on which a sufficient level of consensus can be found at the present time. In the deliberations that preceded the final adoption of the law, the threshold was at one stage halved to about €8730 per year, but it was later raised again.[21] In fact finding an agreement proved hard and the pension reform bill went back and forth several times between the two houses of parliament. As a result we do not think that this measure would stand any serious chance of being adopted in the foreseeable future. Moreover trade unions and left-wing parties, which were in favour of further lowering the access threshold at the time of the reform, have apparently changed their political strategy since then. In order to address the problem of pensions for low-wage workers and atypical workers they now focus more on the first pillar than on the second pillar (cf. the previous section).

More freedom of choice in second pillar pensions
Part of the problem with second pillar pensions is the tight link between the insured person and the employer. Atypical workers, either because they do not have an employer (the self-employed), because they change employers frequently or because their connection is too weak (short working hours) may be penalized by this situation.[22] A less stringent system, allowing for instance those who change jobs frequently to have their own, individual, pension plan which receives their own and their employer's contribution, may be of help in allowing greater continuing access to second pillar pension coverage without increasing administrative costs.

From the point of view of political feasibility, this solution may prove more interesting. In fact for completely different reasons, there is an ongoing debate on whether more freedom of choice is needed in second pillar pensions. The proposal originates from the observation that the performance of pension funds varies enormously, and from the belief that more freedom of choice will bring about more competition and as a result a better overall performance.

In the late 1990s an informal consultation exercise was carried out by a consulting firm on behalf of the Federal Office of Social Insurance on this issue. Employers turned out to be strongly opposed. The reasons mentioned included the fact that company pension funds are an important tool for human resources management, especially at times of restructuring when early retirement can be used to reduce the workforce peacefully, and some other less obvious reasons, such as the risk of a generalized reduction in the level of coverage. Pension fund managers were also overwhelmingly against the freedom-of-choice option, arguing that the scope for improvement in performance was limited, while on the other hand several practical problems could be expected. Other groups with a stake in pension policy were not interviewed (Prasa 1999).

The partial but consistent evidence uncovered in this consultation exercise suggests that the introduction of free choice of pension fund is an unlikely development over the next few years. It should be noted however that the consultation has not stopped the debate, as the idea comes up regularly in policy debates. However at the beginning of 2006 the Swiss government expressed once again its opposition to more freedom of choice concerning professional pension schemes.[23]

Affiliation to a 'default fund'

For the reasons mentioned above, it is conceivable that all those who cannot be efficiently insured with their employers may obtain second pillar pension coverage from a central public default fund. In Switzerland this option would be facilitated by the fact that such a fund already exists (Fondation Institution Supplétive LPP 2004).

The Swiss default fund is run by the social partners and has, among other things, the task of guaranteeing coverage to employees of employers who do not fulfil their obligation with regard to compulsory affiliation. In addition the default fund can provide coverage to self-employed workers on a voluntary basis and to employees working for more than one employer, whose total earnings exceed the access threshold to second pillar pension coverage but are not covered by the various individual employers. In the latter case affiliation takes place on a voluntary basis too. However this option is very seldom used: in 2002 only some 400 workers were insured under this heading (Fondation Institution Supplétive LPP 2004). It should be noted that the administrative costs per insured person are currently comparatively high in the default fund, which may be seen as an argument against extending its coverage further. However this is largely due to the fact that the fund 'inherits' the most difficult situations, such as those where employers are reluctant to pay their share of contributions, which generates high expenses.

An extension of the coverage of the default fund could take several forms. The simplest option would be to advertise more openly that it is possible to file a request for voluntary affiliation. The very existence of the default fund is currently probably unknown to a majority of Swiss residents, let alone the possibility of voluntary affiliation. More ambitious reforms could include the extension of compulsory affiliation to those earning below the threshold, combined with the possibility of choosing the default fund. This would be a favourable option only assuming that an extension of the default fund will lower its administrative charges per insured person, otherwise they would be better off with a standard private insurance company. Alternatively one could also imagine the establishment of a second default fund only for atypical workers, which would not be forced to share the burden represented by the administrative costs caused by the difficult situations described above.

Support for such measures is however unlikely to be forthcoming. With the exception of a stronger effort in making known the already existing options of voluntary affiliation, a fairly consensual measure, it is difficult to see sufficient support emerging for the extension of the tasks of the fund, employers and the right being generally opposed to expansionist social policy measures.

Debate and Options for the Third Pillar

The third pillar is surprisingly completely absent in the public and political debate on pensions in Switzerland. Nevertheless, when they are asked, pension network actors have very widespread and different opinions about this pillar. On the one hand, trade unions and left-wing parties have a very bad opinion of the third pillar, which they consider essentially as a means to build fiscal facilities for high-wage workers. They suggest that this instrument should not be considered as a real pillar of the pension system. On the other hand, right-wing parties and insurance companies support the third pillar and even think that reliance on this pillar should be further stimulated.

Better regulation of third pillar pensions

An analysis of access to third pillar pensions based on survey data shows that while these are considerably more common among high-income households, presumably because of the tax advantages they entail, there are also many low-income people who have a third pillar. The proportion of individuals living in households which do have a third pillar pension reaches 51 per cent among those in the first quartile of the income distribution and 50 per cent among single parents (against 80 per cent in the top income quartile). These are individuals for whom having a third pillar does certainly not lead to significant savings on the tax bill. More likely third pillar pensions are for them an instrument of saving for retirement or other contingencies (the survey question on which our analysis is based was phrased so as to include life insurance in general).

The current regulatory framework for third pillar pensions is however based on insurance law and takes into account only financial requirements such as those concerning minimum funding levels. There is no provision aimed at insuring that a third pillar pension can fulfil a social function, such as protecting insured people who at some stage in their life may not be able to make payments, limiting charges or ensuring transparency and consistency in the information provided in the marketing of these saving vehicles. The social dimension of a third pillar pension could easily be improved by adopting some sort of quality label, such as the British 'Stakeholder Pension' (Chapter 2) that would signal that a product is particularly suitable as a saving vehicle for people on low, intermittent income. However such proposals are completely absent from the current debate.

Tax financed subsidies for atypical workers

It may not be sufficient for atypical workers to be included in a second pillar pension to obtain adequate pension coverage. The strict correspondence between payments and benefits in these systems means that long spells of non-employment or underemployment will result in low pensions. One group identified as particularly at risk – divorced women with a weak labour market connection for instance – may not profit that much from formal inclusion into a second pillar arrangement unless additional payments are made to their accounts. These could, for instance, take the shape of subsidies paid for periods of inactivity due to child rearing, as is the case in the German Riester pensions (Chapter 5). Like most of the policy measures reviewed in this section, however, this idea has not as yet been brought to the public debate.

CONCLUSION

In 2000 the World Bank published a report on the Swiss pension system, subtitled 'The triumph of common sense?' (Queisser and Vittas 2000). This flattering qualification may have been well deserved at the time. The Swiss system managed to combine a not-so-worrying financial outlook with the guarantee of a decent coverage to the most disadvantaged in society. Our analysis has focused on the second element, and while it basically confirms the views put forward by the World Bank, it also raises issues with regard to the sort of future developments that can already be identified on the basis of current labour market trends, of recent decisions taken concerning the regulation of second pillar pensions and the reduction in supplementary, non-compulsory second pillar provision. If the effects of these two developments are considered jointly, then the prospect of seeing problems on the benefit side may not be so remote. Of course, the Swiss pension system includes a rather generous means-tested pension that should make a return of a serious poverty problem for older people unlikely. More likely is the increase in inequity and the reduction in savings incentives that are inherent in a largely means-tested pension system. Equity problems are already apparent now, when comparing the final disposable income of pensioners who have a small second pillar pension that lifts them just above the access threshold, to the means-tested pension and those relying on it. Very often, because the means-tested pension opens access to a number of other benefits, the latter are considerably better off than the former. If in the future more pensioners have earnings in the region of the means-tested pension, this problem will become more frequent.

More generally the developments reviewed above are also likely to shatter the rather high levels of trust in the pension system and in second pillar pensions in particular. If the benefits turn out to be much lower than expected because of the changes adopted in the early 2000s, trust will be undermined. This may result in more working-age people turning to private individual pensions. As the history of pensions shows, when income in retirement is not guaranteed by the state, workers are prepared to sacrifice current consumption for a pension. But their ability to do so depends strongly on their financial situation while in work. Low-income workers are unlikely to be able to afford the costs of large third pillar pension provision. In the end they may be the main losers of the reforms adopted in the 2000s.

NOTES

1. For example Queisser and Vittas (2000) for the World Bank.
2. Old age and survivors' insurance (Assurance Vieillesse et Survivants – Alters und Hinterlassenenversicherung).
3. Supplementary benefits (Préstations complémentaires/Ergänzungsleistungen).
4. Occupational pension (Prévoyance professionnelle/Berufliche Vorsorge).
5. These pension amounts are respectively 1075 and 2150 CHF (Swiss francs). See Chapter 1, Appendix 1.2 for exchange rate used.
6. 425 CHF in 2006.
7. 18 990 CHF.
8. This government proposal should be submitted to the parliament at the end of 2007 and, if accepted, implemented on 1 January 2008.
9. Only 8 per cent of the analysed divorce cases have led to an equal splitting between former partners. In all other situations, the sharing out has favoured men in 89 per cent of the

analysed cases. Swiss National Research Program 45 'Future Problems of the Welfare State', research project 'Evaluation de la compensation de la prévoyance – Evaluation Vorsorgeausgleich' (4045-64783), 28 January 2004, http://www.snf.ch/downloads/prr_arh_04jan26_f.pdf, http://www.snf.ch/downloads/prr_arh_04jan26_d.pdf.

10. The regulatory framework for third pillar schemes is weak and relies on article 82 of the LPP/BVG and on the OPP 3/BVV 3 (Ordonnance sur les déductions admises fiscalement pour les cotisations versées à des formes reconnues de prévoyance – Verordnung über die steuerliche Abzugsberechtigung für Beiträge an anerkannte Vorsorgeformen) adopted in 1985.
11. 6192 CHF.
12. The old age social assistance level in Switzerland has to be differentiated from ordinary social assistance. These two thresholds are not set at exactly the same level.
13. The regulatory framework for the third pillar mainly relies on OPP 3/BVV 3 (Ordonnance sur les déductions admises fiscalement pour les cotisations versées à des formes reconnues de prévoyance – Verordnung über die steuerliche Abzugsberechtigung für Beiträge an anerkannte Vorsorgeformen) adopted in 1985.
14. 18 990 CHF in 2006.
15. http://www.swisspanel.ch
16. The precise phrasing of the question was: 'Have you got a third pillar (for instance a private pension scheme, a life insurance)?'
17. In the 2002 wave of the Swiss household panel, 3564 individuals aged 25 to 60 have responded to the question on the third pillar.
18. Empirically we have first performed some bivariate analysis in order to measure the prevalence of third pillar pensions in different socio-economic groups. Second, we performed a multivariate analysis using the strongest predictors.
19. The threshold has been lowered from €17 458 to €13 093 (from 25 320 to 18 990 CHF). This change was implemented in 2005.
20. The Swiss constitution provides different kinds of referenda. Firstly constitutional change always requires acceptance in a referendum. In this case an amendment must be accepted by a majority of voters both nationally and in a majority of cantons (double majority). The second kind, which is called 'popular initiative', is a proposal for constitutional change, has to be backed by 100 000 valid signatures and also requires a double majority in order to be successful. Thirdly on any piece of legislation a referendum can be called if backed by 50 000 valid signatures. Here a simple majority of voters nationally is sufficient for a referendum to be successful.
21. 12 660 CHF.
22. Employees with working contracts shorter than three months are not compulsorily covered by the second pillar, regardless of the wage level.
23. Press release by the Federal Department of Home Affairs, 17 March 2006.

BIBLIOGRAPHY

Bertozzi, F., Bonoli, G. and Gay-des-Combes, B. (2005), *La réforme de l'État social en Suisse. Vieillissement, emploi, conflit travail-famille*, Lausanne: Presses polytechniques et universitaires romandes (PPUR).
Bonoli, G. (2000), *The Politics of Pension Reform: Institutions and Policy Change in Western Europe*, Cambridge: Cambridge University Press.
Bonoli, G. (2005), 'Switzerland: adapting pensions within tight institutional constraints', in G. Bonoli and T. Shinkawa (eds), *Ageing and Pension Reform Around the World* (pp. 137–56), Cheltenham, UK and Northampton, MA, USA: Edward Elgar.

Bonoli, G. (2007), 'Switzerland: development and crisis of a multipillar pension system', in E.M. Immergut, K.M. Anderson and I. Schulze (eds), *Handbook of West European Pension Politics*, Oxford: Oxford University Press.

Bonoli, G. and Gay-des-Combes, B. (2003), *L'évolution des prestations vieillesse dans le long terme: une simulation prospective de la couverture retraite à l'horizon 2040, Aspects de la sécurité sociale, Rapport de recherche no.3/03, 26 mai 2003*, Berne: OFAS.

DFI (1995), *Rapport du Département Fédéral de l'Intérieur concernant la structure actuelle et le développement futur de la conception helvétique des trois piliers dela prévoyance vieillesse, survivants et invalidité*, Berne: OFAS.

Fondation Institution Supplétive LPP (2004), *Fondation Institution supplétive LPP*, 'Exercice 2003', Berne.

Hinrichs, K. (2000), 'Elephants on the move: patterns of public pension reform in OECD countries', *European Review*, **8**(3), 353–78.

Lelièvre, F. (2004), 'L'assureur Swiss Life présente sa réponse au modèle Winterthur', *Le Temps*, 11 June.

OFAS (2004), *Statistique des assurances sociales*, Berne: OFAS

OFAS (2006), *Statistique des prestations complémentaires à l'AVS et à l'AI 2005*, Berne: OFAS.

OFS (1999), *La prévoyance professionnelle en Suisse*, Neuchâtel: OFS.

OFS (2004), *La prévoyance professionnelle en Suisse*, Neuchâtel: OFS.

Prasa (1999), *Rapport partiel relatif au mandat de recherche sectoriel de l'Office fédéral des assurances sociales sur le libre choix de la caisse de pension*, Neuchâtel: Prasa.

Queisser, M. and Vittas, D. (2000), *The Swiss Multi-Pillar Pension System: Triumph of Common Sense?*, Development Research Group, Washington, DC: the World Bank.

USS/SGB (2005), *Endlich existenzsichernde Renten: Erste Säule stärken – 3000 Franken für alle, Dossier 34*, Berne: USS.

Vontobel, W. (2000), 'Die Säulen-Scheinheiligen – Pech hat, wer in einem Kleinbetrieb arbeitet: Die Versicherung behält die Zinsen Zurück', *CASH*, 1 December, 44.

Weaver, K. (2003), 'The politics of public pension reform', Center for Retirement Research Working Paper, 2003–06.

PART III

Case-studies: the newcomers

5. The German pension system and social inclusion

Barbara Riedmüller and Michaela Willert

Protection against poverty is not an explicit objective of the German public pension scheme. Rather the equivalence principle is the core of the Bismarckian-type system that ensures a strong link between contributions and outcomes. During the economic growth period after the Second World War benefits increased in a way sufficient to maintain the income of full-time workers and their dependants above the poverty line in old age (Kaufmann 2003). The system was perceived to be working quite well because of its high inclusiveness and the below-average ratio of pensioners who received social assistance compared to the total population.

In the face of the problems posed by an ageing population for the sustainability of the social budget and public debt, the government reformed the system between 2001 and 2004. These reforms decreased the benefit level of the statutory pension, increased the legal retirement age and abolished several provisions for early retirement. Before the reform a target living standard was defined and the social contributions of the employees and employers were calculated according to spending.[1] These priorities have now been reversed. The objective is to maintain constant contributions, particularly for employers, with the level of pension benefits determined by the revenues collected (see also Schmähl 2002, p. 3; Trampusch 2005).[2] As a result projections of the public pension administration suggest that the share of former gross income of an average worker that is replaced by the statutory pension scheme after 45 years of employment will decrease from 47 per cent to 39 per cent in 2030 (VDR 2003a). Occupational and private pension plans are being promoted as the main means by which this gap can be reduced, with the government facilitating easier access to voluntary savings in either occupational pension schemes or in subsidized and licensed private schemes. However there is little evidence yet that these alternative forms of provision are able to provide anything approaching 100 per cent coverage.

Given this policy context it might be expected that the financial position of more vulnerable citizens, like our risk biographies with incomplete and/or low-wage careers, would be uniformly worse than that of the average

Table 5.1   The three pillars of the German pension system

	1st pillar GRV*	2nd pillar	3rd pillar	
			State subsidized plans	Non-subsidized plans
Principle	Employment related	Occupational	Personal	Personal
Coverage	Compulsory for employees	Voluntary**	Voluntary	Voluntary
Financing mechanism	Pay-as-you-go	Pay-as-you-go/Funding	Funding	Funding
Contributions	Employment-related	Employment-related		
Benefits	Defined Benefit	Contributions-related/ Defined Benefit schemes		
Objective	Main fraction of income maintenance	Income maintenance	Income maintenance	Complementary individual needs

Notes:
* Gesetzliche Rentenversicherung. Only employees are mandatorily covered. Special schemes exist for civil servants, farmers, and self employed like lawyers or health care professionals.
** In some sectors of economy mandatory by collective agreements.

worker. However the situation is more complex. It is true that many of our biographies are at substantial risk of social exclusion in retirement under the new regime. However important variations occur with regard to the relationship between social risk and pension outcome due either to the protective devices that exist for some groups, such as women, in the first pillar or to the incomplete access to second pillar pensions.

In the following sections we will first present the structure of the German pension system and explain its main features, particularly those that influence pension outcomes and opportunities for private saving. Next we will assess the potential of this reformed system to promote social inclusion among future pensioners on the basis of our simulation results. Here we show that, while the German first pillar still provides a basic income that compares well with the other countries included in this study, particularly with regard to our women biographies, the total pensions of our individuals compare less well because of the underdeveloped and variable nature of the second pillar. Voluntarism in the second pillar has not so far worked to fill the gaps left by the state, and the third pillar shows limited potential to assist in this regard. In the following sections we will discuss the impact of certain features of the system on social inclusion and the proposals of political actors to increase social inclusion.

THE GERMAN PENSION SYSTEM

The Public Pillar

The constituting principle of the German mandatory defined benefit pension scheme is the strong link between contributions and outcomes. The earnings-related pension takes into account the individual's whole employment career and therefore reproduces existing working life income differences, for instance between men and women. The scheme is financed by contributions paid in equal parts by employers and employees. In 2006 the total contribution rate was 19.5 per cent.

Voluntary payment by the self-employed is also possible, but not widespread.[3] Low-wage workers with earnings below a certain limit are permitted to opt out of social insurance and there is an upper income limit of twice the average wage, with earnings above this threshold not covered by the scheme, reducing the replacement rate of public pensions for high earners.[4] Occupational pensions have traditionally been used by this group to decrease the gap between final salary and public pensions.

Almost uniquely among European pension systems there is no guaranteed minimum pension (Kaufmann 2003, p. 284). However pensioners with low pensions are entitled to a special variant of means-tested social assistance. In order to become eligible for a pension a person has to fulfil a qualifying period. For old age pensions this is normally 60 months. However periods of unemployment and care responsibilities help to qualify for this pension. As a result 96 per cent of all pensioners drew first pillar scheme benefits in 2001 (Bundesregierung 2006, Table B.3), making the quantitative inclusiveness of the public pension system high. The system also has several other features that aim to protect carers from pension losses.[5] For example, the federal budget contributes to the pension scheme of a mother by default, or of the father on application, for three years per child as if he or she was earning an average income. These credits add to contributions paid due to employment. Furthermore since 2001 periods of caring up to the tenth birthday of a child gain pension entitlements if the mother combines caring duties and part-time work or if she cares for two children under ten at the same time (Sozialgesetzbuch VI, §§ 56, 57, 70, para. 2, 3a).

Other parts of the social insurance system also help to bridge employment gaps. Long-term care insurance pays pension contributions for non-professional carers, benefiting women in particular. The short-term unemployed receive pension entitlements based on earnings slightly below final salary, reducing their public pension losses. However long-term unemployment will become an increasing risk for the social inclusion of pensioners because since 2003 their contributions to the pension system have been decreased to a flat rate contribution no longer linked to their pre-unemployment income.

The Second Pillar

In the 1990s the second pillar did not play an important role for the majority of the workforce because the first pillar provided sufficient retirement income. In Western Germany in 1999, 56 per cent of male and 90 per cent of female retirees did not receive occupational pensions after working in the private sector (Bundesregierung 2001, p. 157). Those employees who did were mainly highly qualified male employees with high earnings in large companies. In the private sector companies initiated schemes voluntarily as a means of attracting and retaining high-skilled workers (Bundesregierung 2001, p. 85; Kaufmann 2003, p. 284; VDR and BMA 1999, Graph 2-3a). Employers were also motivated to provide occupational pensions because they were permitted to fund their schemes by book reserves, which are tax exempt and could be reinvested into the company (Ebbinghaus 2000, p. 25). In 2003 these schemes made up 60 per cent of occupational pension assets (Schwind 2005). Less-qualified and lower-paid workers thus only tended to have access to occupational provision in the public sector, where provision has been mandatory since 1929 (VBL 2004), and in the construction industry, where unusually unions took the initiative to press for occupational pension provision from 1957 (Trampusch 2004).

Despite employers' freedom about how to launch and organize occupational pension schemes, the state tightly regulated these schemes by law (Betriebsrentengesetz 2006). Before the pension reform in 2001 only defined benefit schemes were permitted. Employers were obliged to inform employees about their scheme, administer them and assume liability for the taxing of outcomes. Moreover pension benefits had to be indexed regularly. To protect employees against company bankruptcy the assets invested in occupational pension schemes had to be reassured or supervised by a public authority. To receive the benefits the statutory framework relating to vesting specified an age threshold of 35 and a ten-year qualifying period of employment before employees' occupational pension assets became vested, an arrangement that was strongly criticized for disadvantaging women (Deutscher Bundestag 2000, p. 68).

The 2001 reform has heralded some important changes in the occupational sphere. A main element of the 2001 pension reform was to introduce the right of employees to require their employer to transfer a share of the payroll into an occupational pension scheme. This deferred compensation is designated for investment in pension schemes for which the employer is responsible; investments are free of tax and social insurance contributions. It was hoped that this would make them attractive to employers and employees and accelerate occupational pension development.[6] However because these contributions mean a loss for social insurance funds, the government plans to phase out this incentive in 2009.

Another change is that employers are allowed to implement defined contribution schemes under the condition that they guarantee pensions with a zero rate of return at least in order to protect assets against risks.

The vesting arrangements of employer-financed occupational pensions have also changed. Vesting now occurs after five years' participation in the scheme with the threshold age reduced to 30 (Sozialbeirat 2001, para. 37). This is an important development for less-skilled and shorter-term workers, many of whom are women. For the latter in particular, the 2001 pension reform improved the possibility to accrue assets within the company. In contrast to the employer-financed schemes, deferred compensation benefits become vested with the first paid contribution (Betriebsrentengesetz 2006). This enables fixed-term workers to participate in occupational pension schemes even if they do not fulfil the qualifying period for pensions that are offered by the employer.

These pension arrangements also raise the profile of the unions because which part of an employee's payroll is permitted to be deferred compensation hinges on collective agreements negotiated by the union. Unions have reacted positively to the opportunities offered by this legislation. By 2006 all sectors of the economy were covered by collective agreements that permit deferred compensation. As yet however occupational schemes to which employers pay high levels of contributions exist only in the mandatory public and construction sectors and the food and textile sectors. However even when employers pay contributions this is often based on reductions in other existing fringe benefits (BDA-Tarifabteilung 2006). Only in the construction and food sectors were additional employer contributions negotiated, in exchange for a slower wage increase (interview with construction workers union, Trampusch 2004, p. 246). This issue is important because generally employee take-up rates are higher when employer contributions occur (Bundesregierung 2006, p. 201).

In the metal industry, chemistry and hostelry unions and employers' associations have founded collective sectoral investment institutions (Versorgungswerke), which administer the voluntary retirement investments of employees and reduce costs (Karch 2005, p. 168). However up to 2005 the scope of these sectoral institutions was limited: for example of the more than three million metal workers only 150 000 used the 'Metallrente' for retirement savings (Metallrente 2006).

Overall therefore, despite the fact that coverage of occupational pension schemes increased by 10 per cent between December 2001 and June 2004, the scope remains partial. By 2004 60 per cent of employees were covered of whom one-third worked in the public sector. Only 46 per cent of private sector employees had second pillar entitlements (tns Infratest 2005, p. 14f). In small and medium-sized enterprises in 2004 coverage ranged between 21 per cent in very small enterprises and 39 per cent in enterprises with 50–99 employees. In contrast coverage in companies with more than 1000 employees amounted to 86 per cent (tns Infratest 2005, p. 48). However many of the new schemes differ from pre-2001 arrangements in terms of the contributors, with a significant fall in the number of employer-only financed schemes and a significant rise in the number of joint employer–employee-funded schemes (tns Infratest 2005, p. 72). There is a strong trend away from the traditional 'book reserve' approach (Ebbinghaus 2000) towards 'out-of-company' administered pension plans (tns Infratest 2005, p. 126).

The Third Pillar

Personal pension provision is not new in Germany; indeed life insurances have a long tradition. But in the course of the 2001 pension reform the establishment of the 'Riester pension' increased the importance of this sector. For those employees without occupational provision the government recommends that 4 per cent of gross income be invested in these new plans. This is not compulsory, but individuals who buy such contracts receive either tax subsidies or direct allowances on contributions up to the recommended level. To be eligible for subsidy Riester contracts have to fulfil several qualifications in relation for example to rates of return, charges and consumer information (Altersvorsorgeverträge-Zertifizierungsgesetz 2004). The direct allowances paid to contributors can be substantial, particularly for low earners. Moreover assets that are accrued by means of Riester contracts are not set off against social assistance. Even so take-up has been disappointing. At the end of 2005 many more people were covered by occupational pensions than invested in Riester pensions: only 5.6 million private pension plans were sold representing 15 per cent of the eligible population (Verbraucherzentrale Bundesverband 2006) and some of these were higher-paid workers.

Everyone covered by the public pension scheme is eligible to claim state support for a Riester pension. This includes unemployed people, who apply for unemployment benefits, but excludes the self-employed.[7] An attempt has also been made to ensure the inclusion of full-time carers, with the spouses of housewives permitted to place a Riester contract and receive subsidies, even when they only contribute the allowance from the state and do not make additional savings. At first glance this seems to promote the strong breadwinner model. However it can also be interpreted as an attempt to implement an individualistic type of social protection within traditional arrangements. Moreover the promotion of child credits in the third pillar was driven by discussions about the poverty risk of single mothers. Finally a long-lasting discussion about disadvantages for women on the private insurance market caused by their higher risk of longevity resulted in unisex annuity rates, three years after the introduction of Riester plans (Alterseinkünftegesetz 2004).

Given the exclusion from Riester pensions of the self-employed, a new type of subsidized private pension plans was established in 2004, the so-called 'Rürup' plans. They are less flexible compared to life insurances, and were therefore criticized by some in the financial and employers' sector (Beck and Uttich 2004; GDV 2004; ULA 2004). However their advantage is that contributions are tax free up to a certain limit, and that the accrued assets are protected in case of bankruptcy of the self-employed.[8]

THE SOCIAL INCLUSIVENESS OF THE GERMAN PENSION SYSTEM FOR RISK BIOGRAPHIES

To assess the consequences of the new German pension system for our risk biographies (Table 1.1, Chapter 1), we have had to make decisions about the likely coverage of occupational provision for each individual (Table 5.2). In this regard three of our biographies are compulsorily covered by occupational pensions. These are the mother and qualified part-time worker in the welfare sector (bio 2), the intermittent worker who is employed in the construction industry (bio 5) and, for part of her working life, the married carer (bio 3b) who works in the food industry. The scheme in the construction industry includes a mandatory and a voluntary part.

We also include second pillar entitlements for the unqualified car worker (bio 4), the divorced chemical worker (bio 7) and the middle manager in the financial sector (bio 8) in our simulations because they are likely to gain access to occupational pensions on an auto-enrolment basis; their large companies offer such schemes. In 2004 95 per cent of companies in finance provided occupational pensions (BVV Versicherungsverein des Bankgewerbes a.G. 2006). For our chemical worker we use the defined benefit scheme available in his industry. It is financed by a contribution rate of 4 per cent, shared equally between employer and employee.

In contrast our mother and unqualified part-time worker in retail (bio 1) and our construction worker (bio 5), with regard to his additional fund, have to indicate that they wish to participate in these schemes. Yet we know that where employers' contributions are higher than employees' it is very likely that a person starting employment will enter the scheme (Bundesregierung 2006, p. 201). This is the case in retail, where employers pay flat-rate pension contributions of €300 annually for all full-time workers, reduced in proportion to working time. In construction employers guarantee a minimum rate of return of 3 per cent and in 2005 they contributed €30.68 if the employee paid at least €9.20 or up to 4 per cent of his or her income voluntarily (TV TZR 2005).[9] For these reasons we included the occupational scheme for our retail worker and the additional provision for our construction worker in the simulations. However we did not allow for voluntary employee-only deferred compensation schemes.

Protection of Individuals

Despite preserving status differentiation, before 2001 the German pension system was sufficiently generous to ensure that a good proportion of citizens rose above the social assistance line in retirement. This outcome was also the result of the steps taken to protect vulnerable groups, such as carers. Our simulations suggest (Figure 5.1) that for many of our biographies the reformed 'public' pension continues to provide a reasonable income in retirement, albeit that this is lower than under the old system. The equivalence principle remains effective but where individuals have regular access to the public scheme, they accrue a state pension comparable with the more

Table 5.2   Second pillar schemes used for simulations in Germany

Biography	Kind of agreement	Access of employees to pension scheme
1) **The mother and unqualified part-time worker in the retail sector**	Collective agreement[1]	Employees have to claim the benefit, no employee contribution required
2) **The mother and qualified part-time worker in the welfare sector**	Collective agreement[2]	Mandatory
3b) **The married carer and informal worker (low-paid work at large food manufacturer)**	Collective agreement[3]	Mandatory
4) **The unqualified worker in the car industry**	Employer led on company level[4]	Automatic enrolment
5) **The intermittent worker in the construction industry**	Collective agreement[5]	Pensions allowance: mandatory Additional pension: Employees have to claim the benefit, own contribution required
6) **The small business entrepreneur**	No second pillar	–
7) **The divorced provider in the chemical industry**	Employer led on company level[4]	Automatic enrolment
8) **The middle manager in financial services**	Employer led, most in branch scheme[6]	Automatic enrolment
9) **The incomplete resident in the electrical industry**	No information available	–

Sources:
1 Tarifvertrag über tarifliche Altersvorsorge im Hamburger Einzelhandel 20. Juli 2001 (expanded to Germany), para. 2.
2 Tarifvertrag über die betriebliche Altersversorgung des öffentlichen Dienstes 12. März 2003.
3 Rahmentarifvertrag zur Altersvorsorge im deutschen Bäckerhandwerk 18. Dezember 2002.
4 Information provided by companies for this project.
5 Tarifvertrag über eine Zusatzrente im Baugewerbe (TV TZR) vom 15. Mai 2001 in der Fassung vom 27. Februar 2002 und 31. März 2005; Tarifvertrag über Rentenbeihilfen im Baugewerbe (TVR) vom 31. Oktober 2002.
6 BVV Versicherungsverein des Bankgewerbes a.G. (Bundesregierung 2006, p. 201).

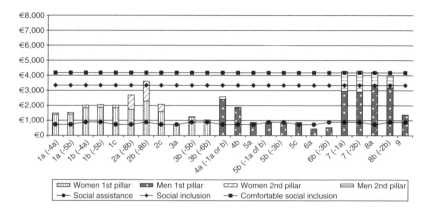

Notes: Social assistance = social assistance for individual retirees if person is single on retirement, including basic needs and housing costs; for married individuals 50% of couple's social assistance; social inclusion: 40% average wage; comfortable social inclusion = 50% average wage, see Appendix 1.2, Chapter 1 for details.

Figure 5.1   Projected real pension levels from first and second pillar for German men and women, 2050

generous countries included in this study. This is true even when their life-time income is low and they spend much of their working life in part-time employment, as is the case with the unqualified mother (bio 1a) and the qualified part-time worker (bio 2a, c).

However while the public pension scheme lifts most of our individuals above the poverty line, the incomes of very few are above the social inclusion line. Thus the provision and generosity of occupational pensions becomes a major factor influencing social protection. As yet this still-developing pillar does not seem generally capable of filling the gap left by the reformed public pension scheme, with the consequence that a significant number of our biographies fail to breach the social inclusion threshold even when their second pillar income is counted; indeed most are still substantially below it. They would have to save voluntarily to reach the social inclusion line, but there is good reason to believe that they will not be able to set enough aside.

If we examine Figure 5.1 in more detail it becomes apparent that most at risk are all employees whose coverage by the statutory pension scheme is either incomplete or non-existent. In this group, which we will consider first, are those whose informal work, self-employment or labour market detachment results in short contribution records and lower pensions: the married carer and informal worker (bio 3), the intermittent construction worker (bio 5), the small business entrepreneur (bio 6) and the incomplete resident (bio 9). Nearly all of these short-term employed biographies would have to claim social assistance if they rely solely on the state's pension system, taking into consideration that taxes and contributions to health and long-term care insurance are deducted from pensions. An exception is the migrant worker (bio 9).

The result for the housewife with the weakest labour market attachment (bio 3a) is of special interest because it shows the level of redistribution to women in the German public system. Thus while this individual receives a pension below social assistance on retirement, due to the credit system this income is significantly greater than would have been expected on the basis of her lifetime income. However while these protective measures are sufficient to provide her with a higher independent pension income than might otherwise have been expected, she is reliant on marriage or private savings (see below) to rescue her from poverty. The incomplete resident is similarly at risk in this respect. Both individuals have to be considered as vulnerable to social exclusion. Our self-employed individuals (bio 5, 6) are also vulnerable, but as will be seen this reflects problems with the take-up of private saving among this group.

Occupational provision is not much help to our group of short-term employed individuals. Only the intermittent worker (bio 5) and the carer who starts formal employment with a large food manufacturer after divorce at 45 (bio 3b) have some occupational pension entitlements, although both are very small. The intermittent worker starts his career in the building sector with a mandatory second pillar scheme, which only provides him with 2 per cent of his overall pension because of the limited time in which he makes payments. Moreover he is not eligible for the mandatory part of the construction industry scheme, because he remains below its 18-year entitlement threshold. He leaves this scheme at the age of 34 with pension entitlements based on paid contributions and accrued interest; but he loses all the interest that his assets would otherwise accrue in the 30 years up to his retirement. The divorced carer's occupational pension amounts to less than 1 per cent of her overall entitlement, again because of her short con-tribution period. Moreover in 2005 her employer contributed only €40 annually to her occupational pension.

If we turn to individuals who have longer periods of membership in the public system we can see that their pension outcome is significantly above those of the short-term employed. All individuals included in this group receive public pensions more than 90 per cent higher than the social assis-tance line. However only the qualified part-time worker in the public sector (bio 2b), the divorced provider (bio 7) and the middle manager (bio 8) exceed the social inclusion threshold, with only the divorced provider cross-ing the comfortable social inclusion line.

The first pillar results for this group are comparatively good, even when compared with the social inclusion threshold: the German public system performs only slightly worse in this respect than the Swiss and significantly better than the British and Polish. Moreover the pension of the female biographies is quite well protected in the public pillar against the effect of lower lifetime earnings due to caring, on the basis of the credit system described above.[10] Long-term unemployment is less well protected, as is illustrated by the result for the low-qualified worker in the car industry, who was made redundant at the age of 57 (bio 4b). This is an important reason why his pension is 21 per cent lower as a proportion of the social inclusion threshold than the other low-qualified worker (bio 4a), although this is also a product of his lower wage.

Consideration of the total pensions of the long-term employed biographies highlights the significant variations in second pillar coverage between economic sectors, with the public sector and the chemical industry having the most generous schemes, both providing defined benefits. In particular the pension income of the part-time mother working in the welfare sector (bio 2) and the medium-qualified chemical worker (bio 7) increases significantly. Despite her relatively low lifetime earnings, the former is advantaged because of the generosity of the public sector scheme: employers contribute 8.5 per cent of the wage, while employees contribute 1.4 per cent, with the scheme also including child-rearing credits, unique for collective agreements.

Thus the medium-qualified woman in the public welfare sector who starts working full-time after child rearing (bio 2b) is the best covered among the women. Full-time work and occupational entitlements amounting to one-third of her overall pension lift her above the social inclusion threshold. The importance of this additional pension scheme is shown by comparing the results of the other two variants of the medium-qualified woman (bio 2a, c). Both have equal biographies in terms of remuneration, but the latter leaves the public sector and its additional pension scheme at the age of 40. This change of employment reduces her pension by more than 40 per cent.

The lack of a significant second pillar also disadvantages the mother and unqualified part-time worker (bio 1). Her part-time work combined with low income ensure she receives a low first pillar pension despite her nearly lifelong employment career and pension insurance coverage. But this situation is exacerbated because she works in a sector with an ungenerous occupational scheme.

The relative position of the low-qualified worker in the car industry (bio 4) is also lowered due to a small second pillar pension. His Volkswagen scheme involves an employer contribution of only 1 per cent of gross income to a pension fund (*Autogramm* 2003). He works in a sector where the unions have resisted the development of company schemes because they favour a more generous public pension scheme.[11] As a result while the public pension of the variant with a lifetime income of 79 per cent of the average and a working life of 46 years (bio 4a) lifts him significantly above the public pension of the qualified worker in the welfare sector with life-time earnings of 47 per cent and 42 working years (bio 2b, c), this position is lost once the second pillar is included. His occupational defined contri-bution scheme pension only contributes 5 per cent to his total pension. This leaves him reliant on Riester pensions for a retirement income above the social inclusion threshold (see below).

Savings

How likely is it that private personal saving could fill the gaps left by pen-sions provided in the first and second pillar? As was seen above, the gov-ernment has supported the development of third pillar pensions with the introduction of Riester and Rürup schemes. The structure of the direct allowance, which includes child bonuses, was intended to attract low earners or large families particularly to the Riester plans. They are also gender sensitive. Our calculations concerning the part-time worker in the retail sector (bio 1) demonstrate the effects of state allowances: in 2005, she would receive direct subsidies of 12 per cent of her investment in Riester plans. In 2015, when she re-enters the labour market after full-time caring for two children, the direct subsidies and the child bonus will amount to 60 per cent of her investment. The regulation of the private plans as well as the direct allowances make private saving particularly attractive for those people who often change their employer, have intermittent careers due to unemployment or who are full-time carers.

However notwithstanding these positive features, overall our results suggest that the private personal saving option is unlikely to provide a route out of social exclusion for most of our biographies. This is for two reasons. Firstly Riester pensions were introduced on the basis of individuals saving 4 per cent of their gross income. This is the amount that the government subsidizes. However as can be seen from Figure 5.2 most of our individuals, including our retail worker, would have to save significantly more than this to reach the social exclusion threshold. This seems unlikely particularly given their low level of pay. Secondly these savings figures are based on individuals saving throughout their working life. However many of our individuals are already paying contributions to occupational schemes for some of their working life. They are unlikely during these times to under-take additional private pension saving. Thus their private saving period

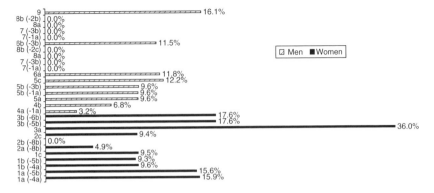

Notes: Each individual linked to another individual receives or pays contributions to divorced partner. Assumptions for private savings: Appendix 1.2, Chapter 1.

Figure 5.2   *Third pillar savings from lifetime income required of German men and women to reach social inclusion line of 40% average wage in 2050*

is likely to be shorter, pushing higher the level at which they would need to save.

The position of the low-qualified worker in the car industry (bio 4a) is somewhat different. He can be seen as a benchmark: all people who earn lower lifetime wages than he does are vulnerable to social exclusion, unless they participate in a generous second pillar scheme and/or save privately a greater portion of their payroll than the state actually subsidizes. As was seen above, his public and occupational pension provides him with 77 per cent of the social inclusion threshold, which leaves him with a required savings rate of only slightly above 3 per cent (Figure 5.2), below the government's recommended Riester savings rate of 4 per cent. The likelihood of this individual lifting himself out of social exclusion with private saving is thus greater than for the other biographies, although the low take-up of Riester schemes must throw doubt on whether this would in fact occur.

In contrast to our lower-paid biographies, our self-employed individuals (bio 5, 6) should theoretically have no problems in avoiding poverty in old age and in maintaining a decent standard of living. Both are capable of saving the required parts of their gross income to reach the poverty line as indicated in Figure 5.2. The calculated necessary private saving contributions of between 10 and 12 per cent are only slightly higher, respectively, than the payroll contributions of employees, which are 9.75 per cent in 2006. They would also receive some assistance through the Rürup schemes to which they may contribute an amount of €20 000 annually, which is exempt from tax. However if the self-employed are not able or willing to save the required amount throughout their lifetime, perhaps because of the start-up costs of their business or in times of low profit, they too will have to claim social assistance. In this regard Fachinger (2002) has found that 15 per cent of the self-employed have no explicit old age provision, and even if they have, the invested assets are generally rather low (Fachinger 2002, Table 12).

Protection of Couples and Effect of Divorce

Due to the absence of couple-related entitlements, German household pension income is just the sum of the incomes of all household members. The spouse's income is not taken into account, unless he or she draws survivor's benefit or social assistance. On this basis most individuals improve their income situation in relation to the poverty threshold when they live as part of a couple, mainly because economies of scale of living in a couple are reflected in the couple's social assistance rate. Nevertheless despite this improved position, only one type of couple, the mother and qualified welfare worker and the middle manager (bio 2a and 8b), generates a pension above the comfortable social inclusion line. This is because of the husband's above-average income and the wife's generous public sector pension. Those couples who accumulate several risks, like employment gaps due to caring (bio 3a) combined with self-employment of the partner (bio 5, 6), will be vulnerable and may have to draw social assistance. This is also likely for the combination of constant part-time work and self-employment within one household (bio 1a and 5b).

Women are able to contribute substantially to the household income because as was seen above in most cases they gain access to a reasonably sized first pillar pension. In five out of 11 couples the wife's pension from the first and second pillar schemes provides the bulk of income. Two further couples have an income gap of less than 20 per cent. However women's contribution to the total income of the household depends on the husband's occupation (Figure 5.3). For instance, the retail worker (bio 1a) contributes one-third to the household income when married to the low-qualified car worker (bio 4a), while in combination with the intermittent worker (bio 5b) her pension is the main income source. This illustrates again the effects of variable coverage in the second pillar. At the same time in four of the couples women are in a state of high relative dependency. This nevertheless generally positive picture with regard to the economic independence of women would change somewhat if it were assumed that self-employed husbands saved sufficiently to pull them out of social exclusion, but as has been seen there is good reason to believe that this would not happen.

If the inclusion of an individual as a part of a couple increases, are divorcees more vulnerable to social exclusion? The results of the first and

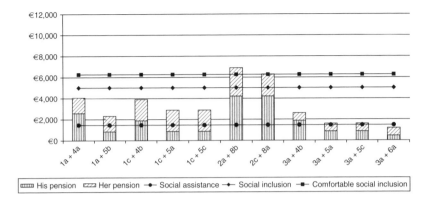

Notes: Social assistance line = Social assistance line for couples; Social inclusion line for couples: 1.5 × 40% average wage; Comfortable social inclusion = 1.5 × 50% average wage.

Figure 5.3   Projected real monthly pension levels of German couples in 2050

second pillar pension simulation do not show that divorcees are generally worse off than couples in relation to poverty and social inclusion lines. For the part-time worker in public service (bio 2) and the full-time carer (bio 3b) this results to some extent from the reasonable assumption that their work patterns after divorce change, such that they respectively start to work full-time or re-enter the formal labour market.

The direct impact on women's pensions in the first and second pillar of legislation regulating divorce is rather low. To calculate this we optimistically adopted the divorce law in force, which decrees that first and second pillar pension entitlements of ex-spouses accrued during marriage are shared equally. In most of the cases the share of derived pension entitlements in female pension income is only between 2 and 10 per cent. The losses of the male individuals through divorce are equally low. The reason for this is that women are able to accrue substantial entitlements through child-rearing credits within the first pillar during marriage and therefore partners have similar pensions in most of our cases. It is also because both partners split only modest occupational pension assets. Large-scale redistribution of pension entitlements between the ex-spouses on divorce would take place only where levels of inequality between partners were greater.

The German Pension System and Social Inclusion

In summary the current German pension system preserves first pillar pensions as the most important source of retirement income. The public pillar

lifts most of our individuals above the poverty line but leaves most significantly below the social inclusion line. Given the close association between
pay and pension outcome it works best for full-time workers with lifetime
incomes on or around 50 per cent of average wages, provided they are not
self-employed. Thus, according to our calculations, in 2050 a pensioner
who can look back on a lifetime income of 45 per cent of the average
income of a full-time worker and employment from age 18 to 65 will receive
a public pension well above the social assistance threshold. Those in part-
time work and/or on low wages are more vulnerable. However the public
pension is highly sensitive with regard to gender where caring duties and
employment are reckoned to have an equal value. Thus all of our female
biographies benefit substantially from the credit facilities for child-caring.
For example, these credits add up to one quarter of the first pillar pension
of the part-time retail worker and carer (bio 1). The system is less sensitive
towards long-term unemployment.

The current operation of additional pension schemes is only able to mitigate these effects in a limited way. Although the role of occupational
schemes is changing, the existence of adequate schemes remains patchy and
the pension levels promised remain lower in comparison with the 'veteran'
countries included in this study. Particularly for women the 2001 pension
reform improved the possibility to accrue assets within the company. But
assets invested by women are still rather low. As a result some commentators now argue that more will need to be done if occupational provision is
to fulfil the role the framers of the 2001 reform envisaged for it. The same
could also be said for Riester pensions.

THE REFORM DEBATE IN GERMANY

Among the main pension policy actors in Germany a strong consensus
exists about the most important current challenges, based on the principles
that informed the 2001 reform. The main objectives of this reform were to
limit the increase of non-wage labour costs to enhance Germany's international competitiveness (Deutscher Bundestag 2000, p. 1; Lindlar and
Scheremet 1998, p. 14ff), and to minimize the effect of demographic change
on spending (for a critical review see Schmähl 2005). Accordingly most
redistributive elements within the public pension scheme were reduced,
while individual responsibility was strengthened. Individual responsibility
as a core principle of social protection is accepted by Conservatives and
Social Democrats alike (Seeleib-Kaiser et al. 2005, p. 21f).

Moreover concerns about fiscal sustainability have recently been reinforced by government calculations which show that while the system will

attain the defined minimum benefit levels, it is likely in the long run to exceed the target for maximum pension contributions (Bundesregierung 2006). Most discussions of public pension reform focus on proposals to attain lower contribution rates (Koalitionsvertrag von CDU, CSU und SPD 2005, p. 28) and long-term financial sustainability. The most recent reform in this vein is the decision to increase the retirement age to 67 years except for those who worked 45 years or longer (for a critical assessment see Sozialbeirat 2006, p. 12).

In contrast social inclusion is only very slowly surfacing on the policy agenda. The salience of this issue is further reduced by the fact that poverty among retirees is very low. Consequently raising the generosity of the public pillar is not high on the political agenda in the short term. Instead the operation of the second and third pillar of the pension system has been the focus of considerable attention in relation to proposals for reducing the risk of social exclusion.

Reform Proposals to Increase Social Inclusiveness of the Public Scheme

Nevertheless proposals do exist for improving the projected performance of the public pension in relation to social exclusion. These are mainly concerned with increasing pensions for low earners and citizens with intermittent careers. Thus the Christlich Demokratische Union (Christian Democratic Party: CDU) and the Greens propose to introduce a means-tested minimum public pension (Bündnis 90 / Die Grünen 2002, p. 89; CDU 2003, p. 42). This would replace the current need for poor retirees to claim social assistance, which is considered stigmatizing. There are also proposals to improve and make more flexible pension entitlements for those on low incomes (interview with representative of the Pension Insurance for Employees BFA; DGB 2005; Langelüddeke et al. 1999; Michaelis and Thiede 1999).

However these proposals conflict with the equivalence principle of retirement provision in Germany. This principle is still seen as its major strength by many policy actors, including the representatives of the Ministry of Social Affairs, the Ministry of Financial Affairs, the Social Democrats and the Employers' Association who were interviewed for this book. They argue that it facilitates individual responsibility, minimizes the tax character of social insurance contributions and, therefore, works as incentive to increase employment (Börsch-Supan 2003; Deutscher Bundesrat 2002, p. 6). This makes the introduction of these proposals unlikely.

Proposals by the Greens and the unions for a more citizenship-based public pension are also unlikely to be successful (Bündnis 90 / Die Grünen 2002, p. 80, Bündnis 90 / Die Grünen 2005, p. 40; DGB 2005). Significantly the main argument for this proposal is not based on concerns about social exclusion; rather it is that the public pension scheme's contribution base would increase, thus reducing the burden of demographic change on employees. These proposals are highly contested by the employers' association and by the Liberals (interviews with Representatives of Employers' Association, FDP 2003). Moreover two expert commissions appointed by the former governing coalition of Social Democrats and Greens and by the CDU, respectively, have rejected these proposals on the basis of cost and because of fears of their effect on existing provision (BMGS 2003; Herzog-Kommission 2003; see also Kaufmann 2003; p. 282).

Occupational Pensions

The broad coalition in favour of the status quo in the public pension system makes paradigmatic shifts highly unlikely. This increases the importance of proposals for change in the second and third pillar. The 2001 reform marks the beginning of active involvement by unions and individuals in the pensions field. From 2001 to 2004 one-quarter of all companies established new pension schemes or increased the scope of existing ones (tns Infratest 2005, Table 5.1). However coverage of occupational provision remains partial, and even where provision exists it is often not very generous. In this regard the main problem is in small and medium-sized businesses. As was seen in the simulations, this significantly increases the risk of social exclusion of a number of our risk biographies.

Various proposals exist with the policy network for addressing this issue. For example the German Social Advisory Council, the official advisor of the government, suggested that social insurance exemptions for contributions to occupational pension schemes should be extended past the 2009 cut-off date (Bundesregierung 2006, p. 199; Sozialbeirat 2006, para. 94). This proposal is supported by the employers' association, private insurers and the lobby of occupational pension providers. However other network members believe more needs to be done if coverage is to be significantly extended. The main proposals in this regard can usefully be divided into supply- and demand-based proposals.

Supply-based proposals
The employers' association claims that excessive regulation is part of the reason why coverage within small and medium-sized enterprises has not developed more rapidly. They point to the stipulations which prohibited 'pure' defined contribution schemes as a means of protecting employees (Blomeyer and Otto 2004, para. 87). The employers' association, with the support of the Liberal Party, argue that these regulations inhibit small

and medium-sized enterprises from providing occupational pensions (Bundesregierung 2006, p. 200). However opposition to this proposal is not confined to the parties responsible for the 2001 reform; it is also upheld by the Christian Democrats (CDU/CSU – Bundestagsfraktion (Arbeitnehmergruppe) 2000).[12] For this reason it is unlikely that the current situation will change in the short run.

Demand-based proposals
In contrast to the approach of the employers, the unions' confederation Deutscher Gewerkschaftsbund (DGB) argues that only limited progress will be made under conditions of voluntarism. They favour mandatory occupational pensions, facilitated by collective agreements (DGB 2005). At the very least the DGB argues for employees to be automatically enrolled in occupational pension schemes when they are hired by a company, with the option to leave ('opt out') once they start work. This proposal is also supported by pension experts at the Bertelsmann-Foundation (Bertelsmann Stiftung and Leinert 2003), and is also endorsed by the Liberal Party, the CDU and the Association of the German Financial Sector (FDP Bundestagsfraktion 2005; Stanowski and Tigges 2004; Storm 2005). Supporters argue that automatic enrolment decreases individual psychological barriers to take-up, because employees actively have to leave the occupational scheme rather than actively join it (Leinert 2003; 2004). Moreover auto-enrolment would allow low-income workers to stop saving if their income became too low. It would also mean that individuals who are already saving voluntarily for old age are not forced into double savings.

However the auto-enrolment proposal is opposed by the employers' lobby and by the association of private insurers (BDA 2005; Bundesregierung 2006, p. 199; Ruprecht 2004), who argue that auto-enrolment would undermine individual responsibility and that comprehensive coverage would weaken occupational pensions as a means to attract high-skilled workers.[13] They also fear higher administration costs, particularly if low-wage earners or intermittent workers are included in such schemes (BDA 2005; see also Bundesregierung 2006, p. 199).

Other problems
Other coverage problems with occupational pensions relating to self-employed individuals and women are largely absent from debate within the pension policy network. With regard to the former, so far the only development in this sphere has been the introduction by the former governing coalition of Social Democrats and Greens (1998–2005) of the Rürup pension (Alterseinkünftegesetz 2004). With regard to women, the most important issue is contribution gaps in occupational pension plans

during periods of child-rearing or caring, which employers are not obliged to cover. Thus only the public sector scheme provides such coverage (Tarifvertrag Altersversorgung 2003, para. 37). German unions tend to be conservative in relation to gender roles and have said little about this issue but have instead tended to concentrate on protecting the male core workforce (Koch-Baumgarten 1999; Taylor-Gooby 2005).

Private Pension Plans

As has been said above, the introduction of 'Riester pensions' in 2001 was intended to facilitate the growth of private savings as one means of filling the pension gap left by the state. However the take-up of third pillar products lags behind expectations. Various reasons have been suggested to explain this problem. These suggestions, like those in the occupational sphere, can be usefully divided into supply-based and demand-based explanations.

Improving the operation of the market

A criticism of the new Riester pensions was that they were much more regulated than existing life insurance schemes. This, it was argued, made them unattractive to potential providers and consumers alike. The red–green government responded to these concerns. Since 2005 there have been new regulations which intend to simplify the administration and procedures of the private saving plans, although reaction to these changes has been mixed (Verbraucherzentrale Bundesverband 2006, p. 10f).

Demand-based proposals: knowledge and subsidies

There were also concerns that consumers found Riester pensions complicated and were not sufficiently confident in financial matters to purchase them. This is supported by a survey revealing uncertain economic and legal conditions as the main reasons for not saving (Bundesregierung 2006, p. 194).[14] Many citizens appear to be unaware of how they could benefit from the Riester pensions. Thus in 2003, two years after the pension reform, more than one-quarter of those who were eligible to receive state subsidies were unaware of this fact, and therefore less likely than informed citizens to acquire a scheme (Bertelsmann Stiftung and Leinert 2003). However other surveys now cast some doubt on the claim that complicated regulation is the main reason for non-saving. Instead people indicate that they already invest enough money in private provision, that there are more profitable investment products or that they do not have enough money left (Deutsches Institut für Altersvorsorge 2006).

To widen the scope of the Riester pension a broad coalition of political actors suggests making eligible all taxpayers or the entire working

population on the basis that universal provision almost always ach-
ieves higher take-up than targeted provision (BDA 2004; BMGS 2003;
FDP Bundestagsfraktion 2005; GDV 2004; Herzog-Kommission 'Soziale
Sicherheit' 2003; Sozialbeirat 2006).[15] This proposal would also address the
problems created by current eligibility conditions for people who oscillate
between employment (when they are entitled to a Riester subsidy), and entrepreneurship or informal work (when they are not). However the government
rejects this demand because of budgetary constraints (Bundesregierung
2006, p. 203). One of the aims of the Conservative–Social Democrat coalition government (since 2005) is to improve financial literacy among the population with courses in adult education centres.

More general changes to Riester
Other policy actors want to change private provision more generally. The
Green Party, the Liberal Party and the financial sector suggest creating
individual old age provision accounts on which all investments could be
accumulated (FDP Bundestagsfraktion 2005; Stanowski and Tigges 2004,
p. 184; Scheel 2003). These investments should be tax exempt up to a
certain limit. Private provision as well as occupational pensions could be
acquired with one personal account, which would make retirement provision more flexible, more portable when changing employer and more transparent than the existing system. Because this proposal requires substantial
changes to the system, it is unlikely that it will be realized in the near future.
The grand coalition government prefers stabilizing the existing framework,
at least until 2007 (Bundesregierung 2006, p. 203).

Private Provision of the Self-Employed

As the simulations show, the self-employed are vulnerable to old age poverty
if they are not covered by a pension scheme provided by a professional association or if they do not save voluntarily. There are strong indications that
they are not saving enough (Fachinger 2002, Table 12). There are some types
of self-employed workers, for example midwives, freelance teachers and
skilled craftsmen within the first 18 years of self-employment, that the government has regarded in the past as particularly in need of protection and
they are currently obliged to contribute to the public pension scheme.
Additionally since 2005 the self-employed are able to contribute to the subsidized Rürup pension. However some policy actors would like further reforms.

Inclusion in the public pension scheme
As the debate about the public pension scheme showed, the Greens and the
unions aim to include the self-employed in the mandatory first pillar,

although their arguments for doing so are not concerned with retirement provision for this special group (see above). The mandatory inclusion of the self-employed in the public pension scheme was also discussed by expert commissions of both the Social Democrats and the CDU. Both argued that the need for protection for entrepreneurs could increase in the future, particularly in the case of intermittent careers. However they found significant legal and financial constraints, which make the inclusion of entrepreneurs too expensive for the social insurance scheme and too complex. The Social Democratic commission favoured mandatory contributions to private pension plans (BMGS 2003, p. 126; see also Betzelt 2004). The CDU commission was less specific (Herzog-Kommission 'Soziale Sicherheit' 2003, para. 59). Self-employed organizations do not favour compulsion.[16] Self-employed craftsmen do not see themselves in special need and therefore demand free choice over their investment in retirement savings instead of being temporarily compulsorily protected by the public pensions scheme (BWHT 2005; ZDH 2005, 2006).[17]

In summary there is a low likelihood that the framework for retirement provision of entrepreneurs will change substantially in the near future.[18] In the interviews conducted for this book the representatives of the employers' association, of the Federal Ministry of Social Affairs and the Social Democrats assessed the incentives for entrepreneurs for voluntary retirement provision as sufficient (see also Wirtschaftsministerkonferenz 2005).

CONCLUDING COMMENTS

Our simulations suggest that the German pension system is a system in transition, although its final destination remains open to debate (Lamping and Rüb 2004). The public pension system has been cut back, but still remains comparatively generous for those with reasonable attachment to the labour market and it protects some vulnerable groups such as carers. It lifts most of our biographies above the social assistance line and on average provides a pension that is generally comparable with the better public pensions provided by the countries included in this book, in particular those in the Netherlands and Switzerland. Like most of these countries, it is less successful for individuals who have weak attachments to the labour market.

The aim of the 2001 reform was gradually to supplement the generally solid public pension system. It was hoped that personal pensions subsidized by the state and more developed and systematic occupational provision for many workers would augment state provision. In this regard genuine efforts were made to try to open up access to occupational and personal pensions to women. With regard to the occupational pensions, progress has undoubtedly occurred. German corporatism has to some extent been able to incorporate new ways to solve social policy problems (Trampusch 2005; ZDH 2005, 2006). However so far our simulations suggest this development has not gone far enough to protect from social exclusion in retirement more than a minority of workers, those who were previously covered by collective agreements. Access to occupational pensions remains partial. If this does not change, many of our individuals would have to rely on private savings through the Riester pension. However the low take-up of these schemes suggests that in fact they will find themselves socially excluded in retirement.

Two potential future paths seem open in this regard. One is a path similar to that of the United Kingdom, where a largely voluntary framework with respect to occupational provision has led to significant variations in work-based pension coverage (Chapter 2). The other path is one similar to that of the Netherlands (Chapter 3), where state action to reinforce collective negotiations by the social partners has acted to increase occupational coverage substantially. At present, the former path seems more likely given the reluctance of the main policy actors to contemplate greater levels of state regulation over occupational pensions, but this could change if, for example, current workers focus more on the growing risks in the future of social exclusion in retirement. The shift in scheme administration to external providers might also be positive in this regard. Financial market institutions may profit from additional assets (Ebbinghaus 2000, p. 26), and therefore push to increase participation rates or even lobby for automatic enrolment into these schemes.

The third pillar, in contrast, appears much less promising as a means of supplementing state provision. Although Riester pensions promised a growing pension insurance market, the new products were much more regulated than the old ones and less attractive for the insurers. Some simplification has occurred but Riester pensions still have serious disadvantages. They are less generously subsidized than occupational pensions.[19] They are less easy to access and understand for the individual. The fact that the employers or trade unions select occupationally based investment products and that contributions are automatically deducted from the payroll significantly reduces the complexity of second pillar provision for employees.

In summary the German multi-pillared pension regime provides many opportunities and incentives for non-state retirement savings. However these opportunities are more available for those who benefit from collective actions by unions and employers. Who benefits and who does not is determined by structural factors like the sector of the economy and the size of the company one works in. Compared to the pre-reform period, when the public pension guaranteed a socially inclusive retirement to most citizens, inclusion has now become an objective for negotiation between many political actors operating in a fragmented policy field in relation both to state and non-state provision.

NOTES

1. Of course the contribution level was not unlimited and within the decade of the 1990s the pension benefit level was reduced.
2. For employees the total contributions including those made to private pension contracts will increase (Schmähl 2003, p. 9).
3. In 2001 only 2 per cent of all insured paid voluntary contributions, overwhelmingly with minimum contributions (VDR 2003b).
4. In 2006 the annual lower income ceiling was €4800.
5. These facilities were first introduced in 1985 and extended continually after that.
6. This is true for employers too, because they have to pay half of these contributions.
7. They may benefit indirectly if their spouse is eligible.
8. This limit increases from €12 000 to €20 000 in 2025.
9. The legal minimum rate of return of life insurances is 2.75 per cent only.
10. The retail worker's (bio 1b) pension is also increased by a small amount as the consequence of payments made by her former spouse after divorce.
11. The occupational pension schemes differ highly among the companies. BMW, Daimler-Chrysler and Ford operate more generous defined benefit schemes, for which detailed information is hardly available. In contrast Opel closed the occupational scheme for new employees in 1997. The scheme used for simulation therefore marks a lower limit for pension benefits in the car industry.
12. They argued for a minimum rate of return that equals inflation, but they wanted to exclude the obligation to adjust pension benefits after retirement.
13. This would only be the case if automatic enrolment would mean that the employer has to offer every employee the same scheme conditions. But this is not claimed by any political actor.
14. The form of the statement was: 'I do not trust the state or the government, because laws are changing too often'.
15. See above: subsidies are limited to employees who pay social insurance contributions, the unemployed and civil servants.
16. Apart from the self-employed, other employers' organizations did not issue written statements about this topic. Generally they argue against high social wages of employees; the issue of social protection of the self-employed remains untouched.
17. Temporarily for a period of 18 years.
18. The protection of the self-employed will improve by means of a draft law, which, in case of their bankruptcy, protects assets acquired in life insurances and private pension contracts (Deutscher Bundesrat 2005). The German Association of Skilled Crafts Confederations (ZDH) welcomed this initiative with open arms, but considered the level of protected assets as being too low (ZDH 2005).
19. This may change in 2009.

BIBLIOGRAPHY

Autogramm (2003), 'Keine Sorge um die Betriebsrente', 4 February.
BDA (2004), *Eingabe zum Alterseinkünftegesetz*, Berlin: Bundesvereinigung der Deutschen Arbeitgeberverbände.

BDA (2005), *Positionspapier zur Einführung verpflichtender Modelle der* *Entgeltumwandlung in der betrieblichen Altersvorsorge*, Berlin: Bundesvereinigung der Deutschen Arbeitgeberverbände.

BDA-Tarifabteilung (2006), *Tarifvertragliche Vereinbarungen zur betrieblichen Altersvorsorge auf der Basis des AVmG*, Berlin.

Beck, H. and Uttich, S. (2004), 'Altersvorsorge: "Die Rürup-Rente ist ein Rohrkrepierer". Interview mit Reinfried Pohl', *FAZ*, 9 November.

Bertelsmann Stiftung and Leinert, J. (2003), *Altersvorsorge 2003: Wer hat sie, wer will sie? Private und betriebliche Altersvorsorge der 30- bis 50-Jährigen in Deutschland*, 'Bertelsmann Stiftung Vorsorgestudien', Gütersloh.

Betzelt, S. (2004), *Konzeptvorschlag zur sozialen Altersabsicherung Selbstständiger. Gutachten im Auftrag des Projekts mediafon der Vereinten Dienstleistungsgewerkschaft (ver.di)*, Bremen: Zentrum für Sozialpolitik.

Blomeyer, W. and Otto, K. (2004), *Gesetz zur Verbesserung der betrieblichen Altersvorsorge: Kommentar*, München: Beck.

BMGS (Bundesministerium für Gesundheit und Soziale Sicherung) (2003), *Nachhaltigkeit in der Finanzierung der sozialen Sicherungssysteme. Bericht der Kommission*, Berlin.

Börsch-Supan, A. (2003), *What are NDC Pension Systems? What Do They Bring to Reform Strategies?*, MEA-Working Paper 42-2003, Mannheim.

Bundesregierung (2001), *Alterssicherungsbericht 2001*, Berlin.

Bundesregierung (2006), *Alterssicherungsbericht 2005*, Berlin.

Bündnis 90 / Die Grünen (2002), *Grundsatzprogramm – Die Zukunft ist grün*, Berlin.

Bündnis 90 / Die Grünen (2005), *Eines für alle: Das grüne Wahlprogramm 2005*, Berlin.

BVV Versicherungsverein des Bankgewerbes a.G. (2006), 'Fact Sheet'.

BWHT (2005), *Argumente zur generellen Problematik der Befreiung von der Sozialversicherung und Rückholung der zu Unrecht bezahlten Beiträge in der gesetzlichen Rentenversicherung*, Stuttgart (Baden-Württembergischer Handwerkstag e.V.).

CDU (2003), *Beschluss des 17. Parteitages der CDU Deutschlands 2003. Deutschland fair ändern*, Leipzig.

CDU/CSU – Bundestagsfraktion (Arbeitnehmergruppe) (2000), *Eckpunkte für eine Reform zur Stärkung der betrieblichen Alterssicherung*, Berlin.

Deutscher Bundesrat (2002), *Nationaler Strategiebericht Alterssicherung (NSB)*, BR–Drs. 501/1/02.

Deutscher Bundesrat (2005), *Gesetzentwurf der Bundesregierung zum Pfändungsschutz der Altersvorsorge und zur Anpassung des Rechts der Insolvenzanfechtung*, BR-Drs. 618/05.

Deutsches Institut für Altersvorsorge (2006), *Das DIA-Rentenbarometer 2006*, Berlin.

DGB (2005), *DGB-Diskussionspapier zur Fortentwicklung der Rente*, Berlin: Deutscher Gewerkschaftsbund.

Ebbinghaus, B. (2000), *Between State and Market: Occupational Pensions, Welfare Regimes and Labor Relations in Comparison*, Köln: Max Planck Institute for the Study of Societies.

Fachinger, U. (2002), *Sparfähigkeit und Vorsorge gegenüber sozialen Risiken bei Selbständigen: Einige Informationen auf der Basis der Einkommens- und Verbrauchsstichprobe 1998*, 'ZeS-Arbeitspapier 1/ 2002', Bremen.

FDP (2003), *Die Bürgerversicherung löst kein einziges Problem unserer Alterssicherungspolitik*, 'Liberale Argumente Nr. 12', Berlin.

FDP Bundestagsfraktion (2005), *Beschluss: Für eine generationengerechte und wachstumsfördernde liberale Rentenpolitik*, Berlin.

GDV (2004), *Stellungnahme zum Entwurf eines Gesetzes zut Neuordnung der einkommensteuerrechtlichen Behandlung von Altersvorsorgeaufwendungen und Altersbezügen*, Berlin: Gesamtverband der Deutschen Versicherungswirtschaft.

Herzog-Kommission 'Soziale Sicherheit' (2003), *Bericht zur Reform der sozialen Sicherungssysteme*, Berlin.

Karch, H. (2005), 'Altersversorgung unter Marktbedingungen. Das Versorgungswerk Metallrente', *Arbeitsrecht im Betrieb* (3), 165–9.

Kaufmann, F-X. (2003), *Varianten des Wohlfahrtsstaats. Der deutsche Sozialstaat im internationalen Vergleich*, Frankfurt am Main.

Koalitionsvertrag von CDU CSU und SPD (2005), *Gemeinsam für Deutschland. Mit Mut und Menschlichkeit*, Berlin.

Koch-Baumgarten, S. (1999), 'Vom 'Arbeitnehmerpatriarchat' zur Quotengewerkschaft? Ein Rückblick auf 50 Jahre Geschlechterverhältnisse in den Gewerkschaften der Bundesrepublik', *Femina Politica*, **8**(1), 36–48.

Lamping, W. and Rüb, F.W. (2004), 'From the Conservative welfare state to an "uncertain something else"', German pension politics in comparative perspective', *Policy and Politics*, **32**(2), 169–91.

Langelüddeke, A., Rabe, B. and Thiede, R. (1999), 'Flexible Anwartschaften und Anwartschaftszeiten. Ein Vorschlag zum Ausbau der eigenständigen Frauenalterssicherung und zur Anpassung der Rentenversicherung an den Wandel der Arbeit', *Die Angestelltenversicherung*, (1), 7–13.

Leinert, J. (2003), *Es geht auch ohne Zwang: Hohe Teilnahmequoten in der betrieblichen Altersvorsorge durch automatische Entgeltumwandlung*, 'Bertelsmann Stiftung Vorsorgestudien', Gütersloh.

Leinert, J. (2004), 'Freiwillige Altersvorsorge: Finanzielle Förderung ist nicht Alles', *Sozialer Fortschritt*, **53**(3/2004), 55–62.

Lindlar, L. and Scheremet, W. (1998), 'Germany's slump: explaining the unemployment crisis of the 1990s', Discussion Paper, Berlin: Deutsches Institut für Wirtschaftsforschung.

Metallrente (2006), *Press Release: Versorgungswerk weiter auf Wachstumskurs – Produktpalette erweitert*, Berlin.

Michaelis, K. and Thiede, R. (1999), 'Flexible Anwartschaften bei unstetigen Versicherungsverläufen', *Deutsche Rentenversicherung*, (8–9), 521–8.

Ruprecht, W. (2004), 'Automatische Entgeltumwandlung in der betrieblichen Altersversorgung – eine Replik', *Wirtschaftsdienst. Zeitschrift für Wirtschaftspolitik*, (10), 651–6.

Scheel, C. (2003), 'Private Vorsroge einfacher und flexibler gestalten. Eckpunkte für die Einführung von Altersvorsorgekonten', in Bündnis 90 / Die Grünen (ed.), *Sozial ist nicht egal. Reader zum Zukunftskongress von Bündnis 90 / Die Grünen*, (pp. 39–41), Berlin.

Schmähl, W. (2002), *The '2001 Pension reform' in Germany: A Paradigm Shift and its Effects*, 'ZeS-Arbeitspapier', Bremen: Zentrum für Sozialpolitik.

Schmähl, W. (2005), ''Generationengerechtigkeit' als Begründung für eine Strategie 'nachhaltiger' Alterssicherung in Deutschland', in G. Huber, H. Krämer and H.D. Kurz (eds), *Einkommensverteilung, technischer Fortschritt und struktureller Wandel*, (pp. 441–59), Marburg: Metropolis Verlag.

Schwind, J. (2005), 'Die Deckungsmittel der betrieblichen Altersversorgung 2003', *Betriebliche Altersversorgung* (4), 395.

Seeleib-Kaiser, M., van Dyk, S. and Roggenkamp, M. (2005), *What do parties want? An analysis of programmatic social policy aims in Austria, Germany, and the Netherlands*, 'ZeS-Arbeitspapier', Bremen.

Sozialbeirat (2001), *Sondergutachten zur Rentenreform*, Berlin.

Sozialbeirat (2006), *Gutachten des Sozialbeirats zum Rentenversicherungsbericht 2005 und zum Alterssicherungsbericht 2005*, Berlin.

Stanowski, J. and Tigges, U. (2004), 'Ein besseres Umfeld für die Altersvorsorge', *Zeitschrift für das gesamte Kreditwesen*, (4), 182–6.

Storm, A. (2005), 'Weitere Rentenreform in der nächsten Legislaturperiode unvermeidlich', *Betriebliche Altersversorgung*, (4), 311–12.

Taylor-Gooby, P. (ed.) (2005), *New Risks, New Welfare: The Transformation of the European Welfare State*, Oxford: Oxford University Press.

tns Infratest (2005), *Situation und Entwicklung der betrieblichen Altersversorung in Privatwirtschaft und öffentlichem Dienst 2001–2004. Endbericht*, München.

Trampusch, C. (2004), 'Vom Klassenkampf zur Riesterrente. Die Mitbestimmung und der Wandel der Interessen von Gewerkschaften und Arbeitgeberverbänden an der betrieblichen und tariflichen Sozialpolitik', *Zeitschrift für Sozialreform*, **50**(3/2004), 223–54.

Trampusch, C. (2005), 'Sequenzorientierte Policy-analyse: Warum die Rentenreform von Walter Riester nicht an Reformblockaden scheiterte', MPIfG Working Paper, Köln: Max-Planck-Institut für Gesellschaftsforschung.

TV TZR (2005), Tarifvertrag über eine Zusatzrente im Baugewerbe vom 15 Mai 2001 in der Fassung vom 31 März 2005.

ULA (2004), *Stellungnahme zum Entwurf eines Gesetzes zut Neuordnung der einkommensteuerrechtlichen Behandlung von Altersvorsorgeaufwendungen und Altersbezügen*, Berlin: Deutscher Führungskräfteverband.

VBL (2004), *75 Jahre VBL: Festschrift*, Karlsruhe: Versorgungsanstalt des Bundes und der Länder.

VDR (2003a), *Stellungnahme zum Entwurf eines 'Gesetzes zur Sicherung der nachhaltigen Finanzierungsgrundlagen der gesetzlichen Rentenversicherung'*, 'Ausschussdrucksache 0469', Berlin.

VDR (2003b), *Rentenversicherung in Zeitreihen*, Frankfurt am Main: DRV-Schriften.

VDR and BMA (1999), *Altersvorsorge in Deutschland 1996 (AVID 1996)*, München: Verband Deutscher Rentenversicherungsträger and Bundesministerium für Arbeit und Sozialordnung.

Verbraucherzentrale Bundesverband (2006), *Stellungnahme zur Situation und Entwicklung der betrieblichen und privaten Altersvorsorge*, Berlin.

Wirtschaftsministerkonferenz (2005), *Beschluss: Abschaffung der Handwerkerrentenversicherung*, Wörlitz.

ZDH (2005), *Stellungnahme zum Entwurf eines Gesetzes zum Pfändungsschutz der Altersvorsorge und der Anpassung des Rechts der Insolvenzanfechtung*, Berlin: Zentralverband des deutschen Handwerks.

ZDH (2006), 'GmbH-Chefs bleiben von Rentenversicherungspflicht befreit', Berlin: Zentralverband des deutschen Handwerks.

Primary Sources

Alterseinkünftegesetz–Gesetz zur Neuordnung der einkommensteuerrechtlichen Behandlung von Altersvorsorgeaufwendungen und Altersbezügen vom 5 July 2004 – Bundesgesetzblatt Teil I 2004 Nr.33 09.07.2004 S. 1427.

Altersvorsorgeverträge-Zertifizierungsgesetz (2004), vom 26. Juni 2001 (Bundes-gesetzblatt I S. 1310, 1322), zuletzt geändert durch Artikel 7 des Gesetzes vom 5. Juli 2004 (BGBI. I S. 1427).

Betriebsrentengesetz (2006), vom 19. Dezember 1974 (Bundesgesetzblatt I S. 3610), zuletzt geändert durch Artikel 1 des Gesetzes vom 2. Dezember 2006 (Bundesgesetzblatt I S. 2742).

BVV Versicherungsverein des Bankgewerbes a.G. and BVV Versorgungskasse des Bankgewerbes e.V. (2003), *BVV-Bedingungen, Tarifgemeinschaft N (Individualtarif)*, 'VA 51 – VU 2048 – 1/03', Berlin.

Deutscher Bundestag (2000), *Entwurf eines Gesetzes zur Reform der gesetzlichen Rentenversicherung und zur Förderung eines kapitalgedeckten Altersvermögens*, 'Drs. 14/4595', Berlin.

Rahmentarifvertrag zur Altersvorsorge im deutschen Bäckerhandwerk 18 December 2002.

Sozialgesetzbuch VI – Gesetzliche Rentenversicherung (2006), Artikel 1 des Gesetzes vom 18. Dezember 1989 (Bundesgesetzblatt I S. 2261, 1990 I S. 1337) in der Fassung der Bekanntmachung vom 19 Februar 2002 (Bundesgesetzblatt I S. 754, 1404, 3384), zuletzt geändert durch Artikel 2 Abs. 20 des Gesetzes vom 2 Dezember 2006 (Bundesgesetzblatt I S. 2748).

Tarifvertrag über die betriebliche Altersversorgung des öffentlichen Dienstes in der Fassung des Änderungsvertrages Nr. 2 vom 12. März 2003.

Tarifvertrag über eine Zusatzrente im Baugewerbe vom 15. Mai 2001 in der Fassung vom 31. März 2005.

Tarifvertrag über Rentenbeihilfen in Baugewerbe (TVR) vom 31. Oktober 2002.

Tarifvertrag über tarifliche Altersvorsorge in Hamburger Einzelhandel 20. Juli 2001.

6. The Italian pension system and social inclusion

Michele Raitano[1]

The Italian pension system used to be seen as very generous. It guaranteed high replacement rates and easy pathways into early retirement. The system guaranteed a minimum pension for all insured, and it offered a safety net for all poor elderly (Fracaro 2004). It also protected many unemployed citizens between 50 and retirement. It thus had a crucial role in preventing social exclusion in retirement, and also de facto took on roles that should have been carried out by other welfare state components (Pizzuti 2005). In this regard it compensated for the lack of a comprehensive unemployment benefit system in Italy and a means-tested safety net for everyone, independent of age.

However since 1992 Italy has undertaken a major pension reform process that has transformed the public sector and has sought to promote the private pillars. This brought with it significant cuts in the old system's generosity, the main objective being to ensure the financial sustainability of the public scheme. The old system had come under increasing pressure, partly through the constraints on public finances imposed by the convergence criteria of the single European currency and partly because of the huge expenditure increase expected in the next decades due to the very intensive population ageing process. The politicians responsible for the reforms pursued expenditure control through many reforms. These included an increase in the retirement age, a change of the indexation rule from wages to prices and the introduction of a new pension benefit formula – from defined benefit to notional defined contribution (NDC) – which links benefits to retirement age and to economic and demographic evolution in an actuarially consistent way.

On this basis it seems that the long-term sustainability of pension spending has in fact been placed on a firmer footing. While Italian pension spending is still higher than in the rest of the EU (Pizzuti 2005), after Austria Italy is the country with the lowest increase in the public gross pension spending to gross domestic product (GDP) ratio (EPC 2006); this ratio will increase from 14.2 per cent in 2004 to 14.7 per cent in 2050, while in the same period the EU15 average will increase from 10.6 per cent to 12.9 per cent (EPC 2006). However if the reforms might be judged effective in financial terms, they have also greatly reduced the projected replacement rates guaranteed by the public scheme (Pizzuti et al. 2006). In the future as the new NDC scheme is phased in, public pensions will be much lower than they used to be, especially for the early retired. In order to keep constant the old replacement rates and, for some, to avoid social exclusion risks, workers will have to work longer or pay additional contributions to supplementary private pension schemes, although the system will continue to provide a low means-tested minimum income to the poor elderly.

Italian policymakers, similarly to their German counterparts, are trying to encourage private pension schemes to compensate for public losses. These are collective, employer- or industry-based defined contribution schemes (*fondi chiusi*), or personal ones (*fondi aperti* and PIPs – *piani pensionistici individuali*). In addition there is the TFR (*trattamento di fine rapporto*), a kind of deferred wage retained by firms, which while not strictly a pension system is regarded by some policymakers as a potential foundation stone upon which greater private pension saving can be built (Covip 2006).

This chapter will show that for the most vulnerable Italian citizens this new pension framework does not look promising in terms of its capability of preventing social exclusion in retirement. Thus while after the reforms the Italian pension system is still overwhelmingly public and pay-as-you-go (Table 6.1), the substantial reduction of replacement rates since 1992, combined with the fact that the new NDC public scheme is almost completely redistributively neutral, means that it is less able to protect those with low wages or broken working-life biographies. With very low second pillar coverage, and little evidence that this is likely to improve despite government efforts, the Italian pension system will to a greater extent than before reproduce the inequalities and social risks present in the labour market and in society at large. Therefore the risk of social exclusion for pensioners has increased and future pensions may well be inadequate for many. In this regard, as will be seen, women are especially vulnerable, particularly given the comparatively low level of labour market activity among females in Italy (Table 1.2, Chapter 1). They remain overwhelmingly reliant on marriage as a means of avoiding social exclusion in retirement.

The chapter is organized in the following way: in the next section we will describe the main features of the Italian pension pillars, then we will discuss the social exclusion risks for our risk biographies; in the following section we will review the main themes of recent policy debates.

Table 6.1 The three pillars of the Italian pension system

	1st pillar		2nd pillar	3rd pillar
	Public pension	Social assistance (*assegno sociale*)	Occupational pension funds (*fondi pensione chiusi*)	Personal pension funds (*fondi pensione aperti*)
Principle	Universal	Universal	Occupational	Personal
Coverage	Compulsory for all workers (employees, self-employed and atypical workers)	Compulsory (means-tested) for all residents over 65 years old	Voluntary	Voluntary
Financing mechanism	Pay-as-you-go Wage related	General taxation	Funding Wage-related	Funding Wage-related
Contributions		–		
Benefits	Notional defined contribution	Income-tested	Defined contribution	Defined contribution
Objective	Income maintenance	Poverty prevention	Supplementary income maintenance (increase the public pension replacement rate, reduced by the 1990s reforms)	Supplementary income maintenance (increase the public pension replacement rate, reduced by the 1990s reforms)

THE ITALIAN PENSION SYSTEM

Since the 1990s the Italian pension system has been reformed many times, with the major changes, concerning both public and private schemes, approved in 1992, 1993, 1995, 1997, 2004 and 2005 (Franco 2002; Pizzuti 2005). The reforms were informed by the following views.

Many authors argued that, before the beginning of the reform process, the system showed three main problems: long-term financial unsustainability, distributive iniquity and significant microeconomic distortions, encouraging early retirement (Brugiavini and Peracchi 1999; Fornero and Castellino 2001; Franco and Marè 2002; Gronchi and Nisticò 2003). Moreover the shortcomings of a pension system based only on the public and compulsory first pillar was pointed out. Some authors argue that a mixed public and private system is better at protecting individuals against risks deriving from demographic, political, economic and financial changes, because the risks would be spread across schemes (Amato and Marè 2001; Fornero and Castellino 2001). In particular the 1995 'Dini reform' structurally changed the benefit calculation method of the public scheme, while maintaining the pay-as-you-go financing method. The traditional defined benefit scheme (called 'retributive'), that is an earnings-related formula, which also accounted for the number of contribution years, was replaced by a notional defined contribution method (called 'contributory'), in which pension benefits depend, in an actuarially consistent way, on the contributions paid during the whole working life and on the rate of return on such contributions, which is linked to GDP growth. Apart from the provision of an anti-poverty means-tested minimum income for the elderly, the pension amount in the new scheme depends only on contributions paid, so that benefit inequalities will mirror labour market inequalities and pension outcome differences will be the same as working-life differences.

However even though introduced in 1995, the NDC scheme will phase in over a very long transition period. Individuals who in 1995 had already worked for more than 18 years will continue to be included in the earnings-related scheme, while those with less than 18 years will have an earnings-related benefit for the contribution years up to 1995 and a contributory benefit afterwards. Only individuals who entered the labour market after 1995 will receive pensions entirely based on the new formula. This is true for the hypothetical individuals of this study, who all start work in 2003. The main regulations relevant for them are described in the next section.

The Public Pillar

Given the inextricable link between contributions and benefits in an NDC system, the level of contributions is a major component in determining pension outcomes. For employees the contribution rate is 33 per cent of gross wage, two-thirds of this is paid by employers, one-third by employees, while for the self-employed and atypical workers it will be 20 per cent (in 2005 it was about 18.5 per cent and will be gradually increasing). Individual contributions are accumulated into notional accounts. The NDC scheme therefore mimics funded systems; the main difference is that contributions are not invested in the capital market and are not subject to uncertain and risky market returns. Instead the return depends on the growth rate of nominal GDP. At retirement, accumulated capital is transformed in an annuity stream by a transformation coefficient depending on individual age and population life expectancy.[2] Using transformation coefficients for calculating annuities, the NDC method is actuarially fair and does not encourage early retirement. Pension benefits are price indexed and are taxed at the same personal income tax rates applying to workers. Because the NDC scheme offers all individuals the same rate of return on contributions it replaces the iniquities of the old final salary system, where rates of return were higher for individuals with a steep wage profile and where inequality also existed because of privileged regimes for some job categories.

But this kind of equity is not without costs. In the old earnings-related scheme replacement rates were between 70 per cent and 80 per cent of pensionable earnings after 35–40 years of contribution, usually amounting to an average of the last five years' wages, independent of age. In the new scheme, in 2040 a 64 per cent replacement rate will be reached only if people work much longer and do not retire before their 65th birthday; a worker retiring at 60 with 40 years of contributions will receive about 55 per cent of his final wage.

However atypical workers and the self-employed, whose contribution rate is 20 per cent, will achieve proportionally lower replacement rates and therefore face higher risks of social exclusion. For example a worker retiring in 2035 at age 65 with 40 years of contributions will receive a pension benefit lower than 40 per cent of his final wage (Pizzuti et al. 2006). Applying the same rate of return to every individual, the Italian NDC scheme has no redistributive features; it is merely the mirror of labour market outcomes.

The new system means particular losses for individuals working in the shadow economy, which is extensive especially in the south. Given that pensions will depend on the contributions paid during the whole regular working life, every year as an irregular worker, accruing no pension entitlements at all, will reduce the benefit. This is a substantial change compared to the old regime, where pensions were based only on a part of the individual's working life, and where irregular employment for a few years was less consequential for pension entitlement.

Only one limited form of redistribution exists in the new NDC scheme, and this favours women. The transformation coefficients formula is based on unisex average life expectancy, benefiting women who on average live longer. Moreover survivors' pensions worth 60 per cent of the deceased spouses' pension are provided; again they are usually paid to the longer-living widows. If the survivor has an independent income, this benefit is reduced by up to 50 per cent and it is nullified as soon as the survivor enters into a new marriage (INPS 2006). In case of divorce the stronger partner has to pay alimony to the weaker; this is paid for life, except when the weaker partner remarries. The amount of this allowance is not fixed by law, but it is decided on a case-by-case basis as part of the divorce settlement (http://cerp.unito.it). Consequently the pension system implicitly redistributes to women, but not in a substantial way.[3]

Contribution credits are paid to female employees for childcare, but not for care given to other members of the family, for example elderly parents. In case of maternity or illness of a child younger than three years the credit contribution amount is based on the last wage until six months of absence from work, after that the credit becomes means-tested. In case of illness of a three- to eight-year-old child the credit amount is usually much lower, because it is based on the means-tested social assistance, the *assegno sociale*.

The *assegno sociale* is also the benefit of last resort for the poorest elderly. It is granted independently of contribution records. This benefit is only income-tested, meaning that property is not taken into account. Therefore some limited redistribution exists at the bottom end of the income scale. However the benefit level is very low; individuals depending on it alone are at high risk of poverty, especially those who do not own their homes and have to pay rent, given the very low level of housing benefits in Italy.[4]

In terms of the three objectives – sustainability, adequacy and modernization – stated by the European Union in the open method of co-ordination regarding pensions (European Council 2003) the Italian public pension reforms have focused mainly on sustainability. They have increased modernization by assuring pension coverage also to atypical workers, albeit with a lower contribution rate, engendering a relevant social exclusion risk, but have clearly increased problems of adequacy of benefits. Consequently, as will become clearer in the policy section, given the strong decrease in replacement rates prompted by the 1995 reform, there is now a debate in Italy about how to increase such rates, and many economists and policymakers suggest developing a stronger privately funded second pillar and encouraging workers to enrol in it.

The Second and Third Pillar

After the 1993 reform that regulated the supply of private pensions, the private pillar is organized by means of three different kinds of pension funds: closed collective funds, open funds and personal pension plans (PIPs) (Fornero and Fugazza 2002; Forni 2003). Each of these is free to provide early retirement benefits and survivors' benefits. All three types are voluntary and fully funded, with benefits based on a defined contribution method, without any redistributive features. Contributions paid earn market return, depending on the kind of capital market investment chosen.

However before considering these three forms of private pension in detail, it is first important to consider another form of private benefit, the TFR, provided by employers. While not strictly a pension this is becoming increasingly important in efforts to stimulate private pension growth.

The TFR is a sort of deferred wage system, under which every year the employer retains 6.91 per cent of gross wages on which a fixed rate of return, 1.5 per cent plus three-quarters of the inflation rate, is guaranteed. This is compulsorily provided as a lump sum by firms to every employee when a job relationship ends because of firing, job dismissal or retirement. Moreover after eight years of an employment relationship, an employee can request 70 per cent of the capitalized TFR, if needed for buying a home or for medical and education expenses. Consequently the length of the average TFR accumulation does not exceed ten years (Castellino and Fornero 2000).

Firms are committed to the TFR because it provides a very cheap financing source: returns guaranteed to employees on the TFR stocks are usually much lower than the costs to be paid on bank credits, given the inefficiencies in the Italian financial markets, where very few companies are quoted and credit is often expensive and rationed (Onida 2004). However the TFR cannot be considered as a mandatory occupational private second pension pillar. Its main function is to solve liquidity constraints in some phases of life, such as at retirement or after having lost a job or for sustaining some relevant expenses, rather than to correct inadequacies in pension provision by ensuring an annuity stream during old age. It is mentioned here because the 2005 reform sought to use the TFR to foster pension fund development, the aim being to encourage workers to devolve the whole annual flows of TFR to closed, open or personal pension funds, rather than retaining them in the firms (see below).

With regard to these funds, the most common are the closed collective funds. These are the only occupational schemes. They are independent not-for-profit entities, which are set up within the frame of collective bargaining between employers and trade unions, whose representatives are members of the fund's board of directors (Cesari 2000). They can be created at several levels: company or group of companies, sectors and geographical areas. Self-employed associations can also organize a closed pension fund.

Closed funds are financed by employer and employee contributions, which are supplemented by a share of the TFR contribution rate for older workers and by the whole TFR for the so-called 'young' workers who, like our risk biographies, started to work after 1993. Only individuals working in a sector covered by a closed fund or with an employer managing such a fund can enrol in them. The levels of contributions are defined in the collective agreements. In 2005 the average employers' contribution rate was 1.17 per cent of gross wage, the employees' rate was 1.22 per cent and 2.39 percentage points of the TFR was paid to the funds, meaning that on average the total contribution rate to pension fund is about 5 per cent for 'old' and 10 per cent for 'young' workers (Covip 2006).

If a sector does not manage a closed fund, workers may decide, through collective bargaining, to invest their money in an open fund, to which employers contribute and into which TFR shares can be paid (Raitano 2006a). In contrast there are third pillar pensions, to which every individual, independently of his or her job status, can enrol, choosing an entirely flexible contribution rate. Employers do not contribute; and at present TFR shares cannot be devolved to them either, a situation which will change from 2008 (see below). These individualized insurance schemes are offered and managed by banks, and insurance and investment companies. They are for-profit entities (Covip 2006), which are governed by complex legislation that regulates the investment's risk profile. Moreover a supervisory public agency on pension funds, Covip, is responsible for controlling and authorizing their activities. The 2005 reform has increased public regulation on private schemes, improving transparency and information provided to potential members.

In 1993 fiscal incentives to encourage employees to enrol in pension funds were first introduced and they have been gradually increased since. Most recently the 2005 reform has substantially enlarged fiscal incentives for retirees' benefits. As a result of these initiatives, when fully phased in, benefits from private plans will be greatly favoured fiscally compared to the TFR and to the public scheme. However there are no such incentives provided to employers to offer pension funds (Giannini and Guerra 2006).

Yet despite tax incentives and the various new opportunities offered by the private sector, until now participation in the private pillar has been very low, as Table 6.2 shows.

In 2005 42 closed and 94 open pension funds were authorized. Enrolment in these was low; only 12.8 per cent of employees working in a sector or for an employer managing a closed fund are actually enrolled in

Table 6.2   Authorized Italian pension funds in 2005

	Number of funds	Members[1]	Potential members	Enrolment rate (%)[2]
Closed funds	42	1 091 698	12 846 000	n.a.
Addressed to employees	37	1 078 355	8 971 000	12.8
Sectoral and geographical funds	27	869 467	8 470 600	10.9
Companies funds	10	208 888	500 400	41.5
Addressed to self-employed	5	13 343	3 875 000	0.4
Open funds	94	393 208	n.a.	n.a.
Total new (open and closed) funds	136	1 484 906	n.a.	n.a.
Pre-existing funds	494	658 078	n.a.	n.a.
Personal pension plans (PIPs)	n.a.	735 417	n.a.	n.a.

Notes:
n.a.: not available.
[1] For PIPs the data refers to the number of issued policies.
[2] Given some duplications, the enrolment rate does not refer to the second and third columns ratio.

Source: Covip (2006).

it, while the figure for the self-employed is 0.4 per cent. The self-employed are more likely to enrol in an open fund but here too we only find less than 400 000 individuals (Covip 2006).

The enrolment rate to closed pension funds is higher at the company level than for sectoral funds because enrolment is seen as a form of fringe benefit included in the contract, and employers consider involvement in a fund as a way to increase employees' loyalty. In the sectoral funds the enrolment rate is high in the chemical and metal industries (more than 30 per cent) while it is very low in trade and services sectors and amongst the self-employed (less than 1 per cent). The establishment of occupational pension funds for the roughly 3 million public sector workers is still at an early stage (Covip 2006). Only those individuals who began to work after 2001 have access to the TFR and the first pension funds opened in 2004. Thus, very gradually, occupational pension funds will develop for public employees too.

However the biggest recent growth in non-state provision is in the personal savings schemes, PIPs. Despite the fact that they still cover fewer people, they have recently surged in popularity: between 2001 and 2005 more than 700 000 policies have been issued, maybe due to the fact that they have been strongly promoted by financial advisers (Covip 2006; Pizzuti 2005).

Enrolment rate differences can partly be explained by the different role played by trade unions in these sectors. Where occupational plans exist, trade unions usually try to persuade workers to become members, if only in order to safeguard their powerbase. Trade union strength increases with firms' size; therefore the likelihood of being a member of an occupational fund is also dependent on the size of a business (Covip 2006). In this sense Italy is no exception from other countries with occupational pension regimes. But in Italy the large majority of individuals work in small and medium-sized firms; 55 per cent of employees work in companies with less than 50 workers, while on average in the EU15 the figure is 35 per cent (Onida 2004). In addition and maybe more importantly, many individuals simply lack the available resources. Many authors state that a low participation rate to private pillars is explained by the high contribution rate paid to the public pillar, leaving little extra money that can be saved for old age consumption. In addition a deep-seated distrust in the performance of financial markets is widespread amongst Italians, increased by the recent scandals in important companies like Cirio and Parmalat (Cozzolino et al. 2006).

These factors affect the young generations in particular. Their enrolment rate to private schemes is very low even though their future replacement rates have been widely reduced by the 1995 reform (Pizzuti et al. 2006). Because of their limited resources they prefer the more liquid investment of the TFR to a pension fund investment (Cozzolino et al. 2006). Unless the young's view of the new pension regime changes, a high-growth potential for pension funds does not seem to exist, despite fiscal incentives.

The TFR and the 2005 Reform

Since December 2005 the more formal use of the TFR as a pension-saving vehicle has been envisaged. In this regard a reform to be phased in from January 2008 has introduced an auto-enrolment mechanism for the transfer of the TFR to pension funds. From then on, if the worker does not specify to which fund the TFR should be paid, it will be automatically transferred to the worker's closed or open fund, if such a fund is identified in the collective agreement. Thus the superiority of collective occupational provision has been retained, because trade unions and employers usually prefer that workers enrol in occupational funds. To gain companies' support for this measure, they have been granted lower taxation and easier access to credit markets when workers choose to devolve the TFR to pension funds (Pammolli and Salerno 2005).

Yet despite this reform it is far from certain that employees will wish to transfer TFR flows into pension funds. This is because TFR has a number

Table 6.3   Rates of return of pension funds and TFR in Italy

Period	1999–2004	2001–2004	2003–2004
Closed funds	15.4	6.7	4.7
Open funds	5.7	−0.4	4.6
TFR return	17.7	10.0	2.9

Source: Covip (2006).

of advantages for workers (Cozzolino et al. 2006). Firstly while at retirement the TFR pays a full lump sum capital amount, a worker can receive no more than half of the sum capitalized from a pension fund. Secondly while the TFR is similar to a defined benefit investment, offering a relatively safe return, pension funds operate on a defined contribution basis; thus while returns are potentially higher, they are less secure. Indeed, in the period 1999–2004 TFR rates of return were in fact much higher than the pension funds' average returns, although this was not true for 2003–04 (Table 6.3).

In addition to these advantages the TFR in firms also has important buffer stock features for the workers. For example when an employee is fired he or she will receive a much more certain sum from firms than from pension funds. In summary because TFR from firms is less risky and more liquid, this can therefore achieve objectives that the pension fund investment cannot achieve, such as unemployment protection, or alleviation of liquidity constraints. It thus covers risks not otherwise well covered by the Italian welfare system (Castellino and Fornero 2000).

For these reasons it is unsurprising that a recent survey based on an employee sample of about 2000 individuals (Cozzolino et al. 2006) shows that only 13 per cent of workers want to transfer the TFR to funds, in order to earn a bigger return, while the rest of the sample is split between those who still do not know what to do (41 per cent) and those 46 per cent who prefer to keep the TFR in firms. Thus at present it seems that the 2005 reform is not going to increase the pension fund participation rates by a large amount.[5]

THE SOCIAL INCLUSIVENESS OF THE ITALIAN PENSION SYSTEM FOR RISK BIOGRAPHIES

Methodological Assumptions and Caveats

In the next section we analyse how our risk biographies fare in the Italian pension system. These microsimulations only calculate the pension income assured by the public NDC pillar. We took this decision because private pillar participation is not compulsory, and as we have shown above, enrolment rates are still very low and slightly higher numbers can only be observed in large industrial businesses where the role of trade unions is stronger. Therefore voluntary enrolment is most likely for the illustrative individuals working in large companies of the industrial sector, for example our unqualified male worker (bio 4) and our worker in the chemical industry (bio 7). Yet under current conditions even they are unlikely to become scheme members. Against this background it seems methodologically more appropriate to calculate how much individuals would need to save in order to bridge their pension gaps than to assume arbitrarily that some of our illustrative workers are members of certain pension funds.

Moreover our simulations do not include the TFR as a mandatory second pillar pension. This is because the TFR's average length is less than ten years and, as has been seen, claimants use it for a plurality of objectives other than retirement income. In order to see how a private component could increase pension adequacy, we thus present savings calculations which measure a potential additional savings rate needed to reach a pension worth 40 per cent of average wages, our threshold for social inclusion. To judge whether such savings are possible we compare the necessary amount with the amount of savings made through the TFR (that is 6.91 per cent of gross wages).

However before interpreting the outcomes of the simulations it is important to discuss a number of features peculiar to the pension situation in Italy. First most of our hypothetical risk biographies work for more than 40 years. Under such conditions the Italian NDC scheme usually assures adequate pensions, provided employers and employees pay high contributions of 33 per cent. In reality there are few individuals in the Italian labour market for which this is true. Most workers retire after 35 years, very often encouraged by employers (Fornero and Castellino 2001). With regard to our typology this means that our small business entrepreneur (bio 6) and the incomplete resident with a short employment biography (bio 9) as well as the married carer and informal worker (bio 3) are most typical for the Italian situation. They are individuals with short working lives who pay much less contributions; therefore they are more at risk.

Another Italian peculiarity is the significant role of the self-employed and of atypical workers. Italy, together with Poland, is the country in this book with the highest share of self-employed by far (Table 1.2, Chapter 1). These citizens are at increased risk of social exclusion, because they pay a lower (20 per cent) pension contribution rate and because wages and job protection are lower (CeRP 2003; Pizzuti and Raitano 2005). Atypical workers interrupt their jobs more frequently, without having the right to claim unemployment or other benefits. Moreover there is no closed fund for atypical workers, whose contract also does not provide for the TFR. After recent labour market reforms, making it easier for employers to offer flexible contracts, the number of atypical workers has grown from about 840 000 in 1996 to 1 750 000 in 2004 (Raitano 2006b). Our married carer and informal worker (bio 3), the small business entrepreneur (bio 6) and the intermittent construction worker (bio 5) illustrate these social risks best.

Finally Italy is characterized by great geographic disparities. Wages are usually lower and unemployment rates much higher in the south than in the north (Rossi 2005). Moreover the black economy is stronger in the south and as a consequence the risk of not being covered by the pension system is larger (Roma 2001). Last but not least there is less formal provision of long-term care in the south (Gabriele et al. 2006), leaving many women little choice but to look after dependants in need. Again these characteristics point towards the married carer and informal worker, the small business entrepreneur and the intermittent worker as most typical for the situation in the south. Overall all of these workers are more suited for the Italian situation than our classic 'Fordist' workers in the car or retail industry (bio 1, 4) or our middle manager (bio 8). Remembering these caveats, we can describe the microsimulations' results and analyse how the pension schemes reduce exposure to the different risks considered.

Protection of Individuals

Given the actuarial neutrality of the NDC scheme, one would expect a direct causal relationship between the employment careers and lifetime earnings of our biographies and their risk of social exclusion after retirement. Table 1.2 in Chapter 1 shows that those biographies with the lowest wages in the group are characterized by periods of part-time work and employment interruptions and are predominantly female. The carer and informal worker earns the least throughout her lifetime (bio 3), closely followed by the mother and unqualified retail worker and the mother and qualified worker in the welfare sector who both retire early (bio 1a, 2a). The only man with an income below half the average is the incomplete resident (bio 9). Conversely the only woman with an income higher than 50 per cent of the average is the qualified welfare worker with a longer spell of full-time work (bio 2b).

These income differences are indeed reflected by our simulations of pensions. Figure 6.1 shows the mother and carer (bio 3a) at the bottom of the pension hierarchy, with entitlements below the social assistance line, rendering her dependent on her husband. Moreover in line with their lower incomes, all biographies with pensions just above this poverty line are

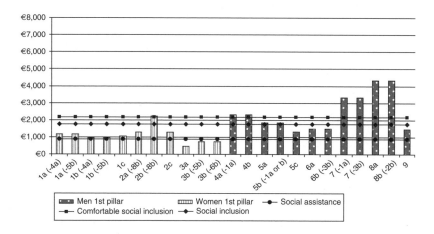

Notes: Social assistance = Social assistance for individuals if person is single on retirement; married individuals get double the amount; Social inclusion: 40% average wage; Comfortable social inclusion = 50% average wage. See Appendix 1.2, Chapter 1 for details.

Figure 6.1 Projected real monthly compulsory pension levels from the first pillar for Italian men and women in 2050

women. Only the mother and qualified part-time worker in the welfare sector with a higher lifetime income and a longer spell of full-time work is much better protected (bio 2b). She is the only woman who reaches the comfortable inclusion line.

The same relationship between lifetime income and pensions can be found amongst the men. Generally the males' pension levels reflect their status in the earnings hierarchy. The incomplete resident (bio 9) has the lowest lifetime income and consequently receives a pension below the social inclusion line. The middle manager (bio 8) and the divorce provider (bio 7) have the highest earnings and both receive pensions substantially above the level of comfortable social inclusion. The notable exception in the male group is the small business entrepreneur (bio 6). Despite his earning of 84 per cent of the average, his pension level is below social inclusion, illustrating that the self-employed are at a high risk of poverty because they pay lower contributions into the first pillar. The same risk arises for intermittent workers (bio 5) who spend a large part of their working life as self-employed, consequently paying a lower pension contribution rate of 20 per cent, although some variants of this individual nevertheless surpass the social inclusion threshold (bio 5a, b).

The discussion above demonstrated that lifetime income is by far the strongest factor influencing pension levels in Italy. However it is not the only one. The case of our small business entrepreneur exemplifies that the self-employed suffer a comparative disadvantage because of their lower contributions. Paying 20 rather than 33 per cent of gross wages into the NDC scheme during someone's working life will reduce their pension by more than one-third. This is particularly significant when we consider the important role self-employment plays in the Italian labour market (see above). In our simulations we have assumed a lower contribution rate for the small business entrepreneur (bio 6), for the intermittent worker (bio 5a, b) when he is self-employed and for the homemaker (bio 3) while she is in the family business; all other biographies are more likely to receive a normal contract.

In conclusion it is apparent that all of our hypothetical individuals with interrupted or weaker ties to the labour market or with lower social insurance contributions due to self-employment will not be comfortable in retirement, unless supported by other means of income. We argued earlier that less-established labour market links are typical for many Italian citizens and that therefore certain individuals in our typology represent the Italian situation better than others: the incomplete resident (bio 9), the married carer (bio 3), the small business entrepreneur (bio 6) and the intermittent worker (bio 5). The discussion has shown that within our typology these are amongst the individuals most at risk of becoming poor pensioners. The only exception is the intermittent worker, who is better off because he has a higher wage than the women and because he paid the higher level of pension contributions for the early part of his working life.

Savings

How much would these individuals need to save in order to make up for the shortfall in their first pillar pension? Figure 6.2 shows that most individuals at risk would need to save between 1.5 per cent (bio 6a) and 7 per cent (bio 1a) of lifetime income to secure a pension that lifts them above the inclusion threshold. A higher savings rate of 11.4 per cent, depending also on her lower contribution rate in the periods spent as atypical, characterize the carer and informal worker who divorces and who is on the second-lowest income in the group (bio 3b), while the married carer and informal worker (3a), whose life is built on the assumption that she will be dependent on her husband, would need to save about 24 per cent to make her independent.

How likely is such saving? Above we have argued that citizens distrust financial markets and that many believe that an overall public pension contribution rate of 33 per cent already decreases their income significantly. Moreover every employee apart from the self-employed and those on

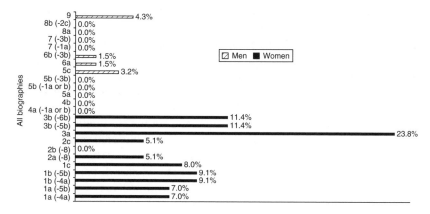

Notes: Each individual linked to another individual receives or pays contributions to divorced partner. Assumptions for private savings: Appendix 1.2, Chapter 1.

Figure 6.2 Third pillar savings from lifetime income required of Italian men and women to reach social inclusion line of 40% average wage in 2050

atypical contracts pays an additional 6.9 per cent of their wages for the TFR, further reducing their capacity to save for private pensions. Against this background many people will not be prepared to save even a fairly small additional sum. Could the situation change because of the devolution of the TFR to pension schemes from 2008? Those individuals who, in addition to the compulsory contribution to the public pillar, choose to give up the TFR as a financing tool for other events in their lives and to invest it for retirement benefits, paying it into the private pillar, in principle could save a sufficient amount for a pension.

Given our assumptions on the real return earned in the private pension sector, the incomplete resident (bio 9) and the worker in the welfare sector (bio 2a, c) would achieve pensions above the 40 per cent threshold if they allowed for the TFR payments to devolve into pension funds. However as we have shown above the TFR plays an important role for citizens' financial planning and they value it for other reasons than security after retirement. It is improbable that this function of the TFR will change quickly, and therefore many citizens are unlikely to give up the TFR for a pension easily. The poverty risk for such individuals is therefore likely to remain until they change their attitude towards the TFR. However even if they give up the TFR in favour of pension funds they might merely be reducing their poverty risk when old, by increasing their risk exposure when young, for example to unemployment.

On the other hand the small business entrepreneur, the intermittent worker with a disability and the carer (bio 6, 5c, 3a, b) do not pay into the TFR and thus do not have available TFR contributions as a tool to decrease poverty risks when old. However because the entrepreneur and the intermittent worker have a fairly high income and pay lower social insurance contributions, it would be comparatively easy for them to save the required amount of, respectively, 1.5 and 3.2 per cent during their lifetime, in order to achieve the 40 per cent average wage threshold. The situation is rather different for the carer; she would need very high additional savings – 11.4 per cent of lifetime income in the case of the divorced carer (bio 3b) and 23.8 per cent for the one who stays married (bio 3a) – in order for her to achieve the social inclusion threshold when old. Such amounts are highly unlikely given her low income.

Protection of Couples

In our savings simulations above we have adopted an individualistic stance, in that we assessed what an individual could do to avoid poverty. However many pensioners are part of a couple and live together pooling their pensions.[6] To what extent can sharing a household be a protection from poverty for those individuals most at risk from exclusion?

In line with the situation for individuals, what can be noted first is that none of the couples receive a pension lower than the social assistance benefit. However even if we apply the higher inclusion line of 40 per cent average wages, most couples are protected. For the male partners this means no real improvement compared with their inclusion status as individuals. For the females, sharing a household means better protection. Italy is peculiar in our group because redistributive measures that significantly acknowledge care responsibilities are absent. Thus women normally have much lower pensions than men (Figure 6.1) and are therefore more dependent on them for additional protection than women in other countries of our study. Figure 6.3 illustrates this dependency. It shows that sharing a home with a partner ends the materially insecure situation of all our individually precarious women, and it can mean significant improvements. The mother and unqualified worker's (bio 1) pension moves from below the social inclusion line above the comfortable social inclusion threshold in two cases and above the social inclusion line in two more cases; even the variant who is married to the disabled construction worker (bio 1c and bio 5c) improves her situation through marriage, coming close to social inclusion.

Still more pronounced is the difference the partner makes for the qualified worker in the welfare sector who retires early (bio 2c and 8a).

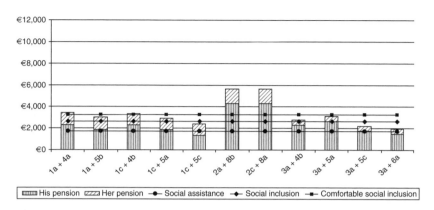

Notes: Social assistance line = 2×Social assistance line for individuals; Social inclusion line for couples: 1.5×40% average wage; Comfortable social inclusion = 1.5×50% average wage.

Figure 6.3   Projected real monthly pension levels of Italian couples in 2050

Her relationship lifts her income from below the social inclusion line to a joint pension worth 179 per cent of comfortable inclusion. By the same logic, precariousness can be enforced, if both male and female have low first pillar pensions. This is true with regard to the carer and the small business entrepreneur (bio 3a and 6a). However as we argued above he could fairly easily save towards a higher pension, while the same is unlikely for her.

Considering the important role male pensions play in Italy, it is fair to say that the system enforces the male breadwinner model. Given the low female employment rate – with 45 per cent in 2005 Italy had the lowest of the countries included in this study (Table 1.2, Chapter 1) – taking into account also the gender wage gap and also considering that women often have to provide informal long-term assistance to their parents, since care by the state is not formally provided, marriage very often represents an insurance against poverty for women. From this point of view, divorced women and single parents are often exposed to higher risks than couples.

How does the breadwinner role affect the relative position of males with regard to our inclusion lines? For most hypothetical men pension-sharing with a partner on a lower income leaves their relative position with regard to our inclusion lines unchanged. Only the unqualified car worker married to a carer (bio 3a and 4b) moves from comfortable inclusion to social inclusion, because the female pension is too low to make a real difference to household income.

In conclusion our simulations show that public pension benefits are usually sufficient to live above the means-tested absolute poverty threshold, but if we apply the inclusion line, women and atypical workers are at risk, because the pension system does not have a redistributive impact, as in other countries studied in this book, but mimics labour market differences. For the self-employed, savings may address this risk but many other atypical workers are at risk of exclusion. For women, marriage is still the most robust insurance against poverty.

THE REFORM DEBATE IN ITALY

Despite many recent reforms pensions are still at the centre of the political debate in Italy and all political parties and social partners continue to discuss them and to propose further changes.[7] Therefore the Italian pension reform process has been defined as never-ending (Franco 2002).

Our simulations show that from the point of view of our risk biographies there are good reasons to continue with the reform debate. Above we identified three main factors that put our illustrative biographies most at risk: employment interruptions, for example because of care responsibilities, low income and atypical contracts. This means firstly that women are threatened by poverty more than men and that the regime enforces their dependency on a breadwinner. Secondly because of the lack of redistributive elements the system leaves class differences untouched, putting people with low qualifications and low wages at particular risk; this is especially true for the increased number of workers on atypical contracts. Thirdly by implication this means that current regulations do not address the geographical divide: southern Italians are more at risk than people from the north.

In the political debate the acknowledgement of these 'adequacy of pensions' problems seems to be growing. This is especially the case regarding the effects on pensions that derive from the lower contribution rate for self-employed and mostly atypical workers (Raitano 2006b). The redistributive neutrality of the NDC scheme is less debated. The main measures proposed can be divided according to public or private schemes.

From 2001 to 2006 pension policy of the right-wing government coalition has focused mainly on issues of spending and sustainability, not least in order to fulfil the constraints on public finances imposed by the EU. After the 1995 Dini reform was approved by a broad coalition between government and trade unions, attempts have been made to reduce expenditure during the NDC's very long transition period, mainly through the tightening of early retirement rules. Reforms in this regard were introduced in 1997 and 2004 and discussions about further reform is ongoing between Government and social partners.[8]

In order to reduce pension expenditure further during the transition phase, it is currently being debated whether to raise the retirement age for women to that of men, that is from 60 to 65. Whether such a reform would have a desirable or detrimental impact on women's pension rights is not a subject of this debate. Likewise the extended recognition of care periods is not seriously considered by the mainstream politicians. Therefore one of the strongest risks that our simulations identified, that of women with care responsibilities, is not acknowledged in the political debate.

However questions of pension adequacy are not absent from reform discussions. Anticipating the big reductions in expected replacement rates caused by the 1995 reform, the attention of centre-left politicians and trade unions is now beginning to turn towards the looming insufficiency of pension benefits, and the view is gaining ground that better benefits are needed to protect individuals at risk, despite difficult public finances and even though individuals substantially affected by the new NDC regulations will only begin to retire around 2015 (RGS 2006). As a consequence there are proposals to make the first pillar more protective. For example some left-wing policymakers and the main trade unions have demanded an increase of the minimum pension level and a parametric change of the notional defined contribution (NDC) public scheme, especially for the most vulnerable workers. This proposal suggests indexing pension benefits to nominal wages instead of prices, at least until some income threshold is reached (Unione 2006).

Moreover growing attention is dedicated to the expected living standard of atypical workers. Atypical contracts had been designed to ease entry into the labour market through granting flexibility to employers. However for many individuals working under atypical conditions – on lower wages, with lower contribution rates and excluded from the TFR – has instead become a permanent status, exposing them to risks of social exclusion after retirement (Benetti 2006). Centre-left-wing politicians are now debating how to reduce the precariousness of atypical workers and how to increase pension benefits for individuals who have worked under these conditions for many years. In the recent debate on the 2007 Financial Law the government has increased from 20 per cent to 23 per cent the atypical workers' contribution rate, although there are doubts whether such rate is enough to prevent poverty risks when old (Raitano 2006b). In order to improve their prospects, many argue that the present contribution of 1 per cent of gross wages paid by the state has to be increased (Pizzuti et al. 2006). In addition others state that additional public pension contributions for atypical workers payable during periods of unemployment and maternity care have to be substantially increased, so that these individuals could start to receive some kind of unemployment or care-related benefits (Muehlberger and Pasqua 2006). In this context it has also been proposed to increase employers' contribution rate on atypical contracts to the level paid for dependent workers, in order to get rid of the perverse incentive for employers, who, with the aim of reducing labour costs, have substituted permanent with fixed-term atypical contracts (Di Nicola 2006). Should such reform plans be implemented, they would help to protect better those risk biographies most typical for the Italian situation: the married carer and informal worker (bio 3), the small business entrepreneur (bio 6) and the intermittent construction worker (bio 5). They would thus also help women, even though their special circumstances are not explicitly recognized. Moreover bearing in mind that such biographies are more concentrated in southern Italy, the changes would also help to mitigate the concentration of pensioner poverty in the south.

A more radical reform plan was reported by leading newspapers at the beginning of 2006 (Pizzuti et al. 2006). According to this, some influential centre-left politicians are considering a new structural pension reform. In order to reduce labour costs for firms and to boost their price competition, this includes a contribution rate rebate to the NDC scheme for employees and employers of about five percentage points. To address the current poverty risks of the system, the contribution rates for atypical workers and the self-employed would be increased to the level of the employees' rate. This would be coupled with a new, tax-financed, universal anti-poverty flat rate benefit for every elderly person (Pizzuti et al. 2006). This reform would increase the pension replacement rates and it would address some of the main risks our microsimulations have identified, these being the insufficient protection of non-standard workers and of women and carers. However the introduction of such a reform would be very costly and, in view of the difficult Italian public finances, its introduction seems unlikely at present.

Apart from these proposals directed at public pillar reform, in the last decade a debate has also taken place about the very low enrolment rate to the widely accessible private pensions and about how to create incentives for increased participation in such schemes in order to address the under-savings problem. As described above, the reform of the TFR payments into pension funds will become the default option for workers from 2008, and therefore coverage through private pensions looks set to increase. However growth is likely to be limited because up to now pension funds have not been very attractive for individuals, who pay high public scheme contributions and thus have little extra money to spare, who like the TFR's potential to address immediate liquidity constraints and, besides, who usually distrust financial markets.

Thus policymakers are challenged to consider how to convince workers to enrol in private pension schemes. This could be achieved, for example, by improving trust in financial markets through better regulation, or by increasing further the tax-deductibility of pension fund contributions. The TFR would also lose some of its attractiveness as a bridge during times of income loss if adequate unemployment and other benefits were available which could induce workers to invest the money into pension funds instead (Unione 2006). The reform of the TFR has been a very controversial piece of legislation and some of its aspects are still being debated. In the 2007 Financial Law the government has advanced the starting date from 2008 to 2007. In particular the non-portability of the employers' contributions for workers choosing to pay the TFR to personal schemes is still contested. According to the 2005 reform a worker can freely choose the private pension scheme to which he or she will devolve the TFR. However all additional employer and employee contributions fixed by collective agreements can only be paid into the closed funds. This advantage granted to companies is strongly criticized by insurance companies and right-wing politicians who argue that it limits individuals' freedom of choice and efficient competition in the private pension market.

In response employers' associations and trade unions argue that this legislation in favour of occupational funds is needed, because unless employees' investments are safeguarded by collective agreements individuals are in danger of making wrong choices, because they lack perfect information on the different funds and risks, as for example the British mis-selling scandal illustrated. Moreover it is pointed out that personal plans are often characterized by higher, often regressive and non-transparent administrative costs (Pizzuti and Raitano 2006).

Another controversial point of the recent reform between the two main political coalitions concerns the fiscal incentives to pension fund membership (Unione 2006). The reform has changed the tax rates on benefits from a progressive income tax with marginal rates usually higher than 30 per cent, to a low and proportionate one of between 9 per cent and 15 per cent, depending on the length of pension fund enrolment. However these incentives can be criticized both on equity and efficiency grounds. They favour the better-off and they do not seem able to increase the participation rate of individuals at risk whose problems are essentially liquidity constraints. In addition, fiscal incentives mainly provided in the phase of benefit payment could appear unreliable to individuals who might fear that in the future policymakers may change the fiscal rules and therefore decide not to enrol in private schemes but to retain the TFR in firms. Apart from the future costs of such tax expenditure, many authors show the fundamental incoherence between a public scheme which taxes benefits progressively and a private one which taxes them less and in a substantially regressive way, given that the probability of access to private schemes increases with income. Consequently such tax rates differences could induce in the long run a strong demand by the better-off to reduce the contribution to the public system in order to increase private pension savings (Pizzuti and Raitano 2006).

In conclusion, despite massive changes in the Italian pension regime, social inclusion for many and particularly for our risk biographies continues to depend on state provision, and for many women it will continue to be mixed with dependency on a partner, given their lower wages which in a redistributively neutral system means lower pensions. However relations and partnerships between public and private agents – employers, trade unions, banks and insurances – are still in an emergent state. In the future more robust arrangements may materialize, based mainly on the TFR devolution. Should occupational and personal schemes indeed achieve broader membership, they could contribute to social inclusion in a significant way, as our savings calculations have shown. However current evidence suggests that Italian private pensions do not mean social inclusion.

NOTES

1. This chapter has been prepared under the scientific supervision of Paolo Calza Bini. The simulations presented in section 3 have been calculated together with Stefano Leoni (INPS). The author thanks Marco Accorinti, Paolo Calza Bini, Stefano Leoni and Sandro Turcio for their useful suggestions.
2. In order to neutralize the pension system from demographic risk, transformation coefficients are updated every ten years in line with life expectancy evolution.
3. At the same time the annuity provision is regressive because well-off people live longer (thus they will receive annuities for a longer period of time).
4. In 2005, the annual amount was €4785. It is entirely paid to individuals at least 65 years old who have no other income, and it is proportionally reduced until the threshold of €4785 yearly income is reached. For a couple the threshold is doubled to €9750 (for a couple only the total income is taken into account, independently of its distribution). For example, if a couple's total yearly earnings amount to €8500 a yearly benefit of €1250 is paid (INPS 2006).
5. Ferrera and Jessoula (2007, p. 442) have a more optimistic opinion of the future improvement of the second pillar coverage.
6. Although as was suggested in Chapter 2, it cannot be assumed that equal pooling between marriage partners always occurs.
7. The ideas of the two main political coalitions (centre-left and centre-right) concerning public and private pension schemes are reported in Unione (2006) and Brugiavini (2006).
8. At the time of writing (June 2007) the government is analysing a new public pension reform in order to change the retirement age established by the 2004 reform and the calculation method for the individuals still retiring, at least partly, by the old retributive scheme. This reform, focusing on the individuals retiring in the next years, should not concern our individuals who will retire with a pension based entirely on the NDC method.

BIBLIOGRAPHY

Amato, G. and Marè, M. (2001), *Le pensioni: il pilastro mancante*, Bologna: Il Mulino.

Benetti, M. (2006), 'Pensioni, i problemi nascosti sotto il tappeto', www.eguaglianzaeliberta.it.

Brugiavini, A. (2006), 'Pensioni, contributi e sostegni agli anziani nei programmi elettorali', www.lavoce.info.

Brugiavini, A. and Peracchi, F. (1999), 'Reforming Italian social security: should we switch from PAYG to fully funded?', mimeo.

Castellino, O. and Fornero, E. (2000), 'Il TFR: una coperta troppo stretta', *Rivista di Politica Economica*, **90**(9), 107–26.

CeRP (2003), *La previdenza dei parasubordinati: situazione attuale e prospettive*, Turin: CeRP Report.

Cesari, R. (2000), *I fondi pensione*, Bologna: Il Mulino.

Covip (2006), *Relazione per l'anno 2005*, Rome: Commissione di Vigilanza sui Fondi Pensione, www.covip.it.

Cozzolino, M., Di Nicola, F. and Raitano, M. (2006), 'Il futuro dei fondi pensione: opportunità e scelte sulla destinazione del TFR', ISAE Working Paper n. 64, Rome.

Di Nicola, F. (2006), 'Alla previdenza serve un'altra riforma', www.eguaglianzaeliberta.it.

EPC (2006), *Age-Related Public Expenditure Projections for the EU25 Member States up to 2050*, Brussels: Economic Policy Committee.

European Council (2003), *Joint Report by the Commission and the Council on Adequate and Sustainable Pensions*, Brussels.

Ferrera, M. and Jessoula, M. (2007), 'Italy: a narrow gate for path-shift', in E.M. Immergut, K.M. Anderson and I. Schulze (eds), *Handbook of West European Pension Politics* (pp. 396–498), Oxford: Oxford University Press.

Fornero, E. and Castellino, O. (2001), *La riforma del sistema previdenziale italiano*, Bologna: Il Mulino.

Fornero, E. and Fugazza, C. (2002), 'Un mercato troppo segmentato? Uniformità e differenze nel mercato previdenziale italiano', Working Paper MEFOP n. 4/2002.

Forni, L. (2003), *Alcune considerazioni sui provvedimenti recenti e sul dibattito in corso in tema di previdenza complementare*, Argomenti di Discussione CeRP, n. 3/03.

Fracaro, M. (2004), 'Le nuove pensioni', *Corriere della Sera Editions*, Milan: ETAS.

Franco, D. (2002), 'Italy: a never-ending pension reform', in M. Feldstein and H. Siebert (eds), *Coping with the Pension Crisis: Where Does Europe Stand?*, Chicago, IL: Chicago University Press, pp. 211–62.

Franco, D. and Marè, M. (2002), 'Le pensioni: l'economia e la politica delle riforme', *Rivista di politica economica*, **92**(7–8), pp. 197–276.

Gabriele, S., Cislaghi, C., Costantini, F., Innocenti, F., Lepore, V., Tediosi, F., Valerio, M. and Zocchetti, C. (2006), 'Demographic factors and health expenditure profiles by age: the case of Italy', Enepri Research Report, n. 18.

Giannini, S. and Guerra, M.C. (2006), 'Alla ricerca di una disciplina fiscale per la previdenza complementare', in M. Messori (ed.), *La previdenza complementare in Italia*, Bologna: Il Mulino, pp. 473–520.

Gronchi, S. and Nisticò, S. (2003), 'Sistemi a ripartizione equi e sostenibili: modelli teorici e realizzazioni pratiche', CNEL Working Paper, n. 27.

INPS (2006), *TuttoInps*, Istituto Nazionale Previdenza Sociale, www.inps.it.
Muehlberger, U. and Pasqua, S. (2006), 'The continuous collaborators in Italy: hybrids between employment and self-employment?', ChilD Working Papers n. 10/2006.
Onida, F. (2004), *Se il piccolo non cresce*, Bologna: Il Mulino.
Pammolli, F. and Salerno, N.C. (2005), *Le imprese e il finanziamento del pilastro privato*, Nota CERM n.8/05.
Pizzuti, F.R. (2005), *Rapporto annuale sullo stato sociale*, Anno 2005, Turin: Utet.
Pizzuti, F.R. and Raitano, M. (2005), 'La copertura pensionistica delle diverse figure di lavoratori', in F.R. Pizzuti (ed.), *Rapporto annuale sullo stato sociale. Anno 2005*, Turin: Utet, pp. 293–301.
Pizzuti, F.R. and Raitano, M. (2006), 'La politica previdenziale del governo Berlusconi', in F.R. Pizzuti (ed.), *Rapporto annuale sullo stato sociale. Anno 2006*, Turin: Utet, pp. 258–84.
Pizzuti, F.R., Raitano, M. and Tancioni, M. (2006), 'Le principali questioni che si pongono in campo previdenziale: alcune proposte e la simulazione dei loro effetti', in F.R. Pizzuti (ed.), *Rapporto annuale sullo stato sociale. Anno 2006*, Turin: Utet, pp. 317–47.
Raitano, M. (2006a), 'La previdenza complementare', in F.R. Pizzuti (ed.), *Rapporto annuale sullo stato sociale. Anno 2006*, Turin: Utet, pp. 249–57.
Raitano, M. (2006b), 'I lavoratori parasubordinati: dimensioni, caratteristiche e rischi', *ISAE Rapporto Trimestrale Finanza Pubblica e Redistribuzione*, Rome, pp. 133–59.
RGS (2006), *Le tendenze di medio-lungo periodo del sistema pensionistico e sanitario – Le previsioni della Ragioneria Generale dello Stato aggiornate al 2005*, 'Rapporto n. 7', Rome: Ragioneria Generale dello Stato.
Roma, R. (2001), *L'economia sommersa*, 'Editori Laterza', Bari.
Rossi, N. (2005), *Mediterraneo del Nord. Un'altra idea del Mezzogiorno*, 'Editori Laterza', Bari.
Unione (2006), *Per il bene dell'Italia*, 'Government Programme 2006–2011', Centre-Left Wing Coalition.

7. The Polish pension system and social inclusion

Marek Benio and Joanna Ratajczak-Tuchołka[1]

The Polish pension system before 1999 was dominated by a state pay-as-you-go scheme that had both Bismarckian and Beveridgean features (Żukowski 1994). It was Bismarckian in the sense that provision was calculated according to an earnings-related defined benefit formula. In addition there were early retirement privileges for some occupational groups, for example miners, steel workers, railway workers and teachers, and separate pension provision existed for farmers, soldiers, police, judges and prosecutors. The system was indebted to the Beveridgean ideal because a fixed social amount was added to all provision.

Pension reforms started at the beginning of the 1990s after the transition from communism, with new arrangements coming into operation in 1999. Change was prompted, as in other mature systems in developed industrial democracies, by concerns that demographic change would lead to increased costs. However there were also other reasons for reform specific to Poland and other previously communist countries. Firstly the costs of the system were inflated by the fact that it had been used as a buffer for an otherwise even higher unemployment rate, with universal access to early retirement schemes granted in 1992 as a reaction to growing unemployment. Secondly acceptance of the system in society was low because it was subject to political manipulation, especially during elections. For instance, benefit indexation was not automatically price or wage growth related, but subject to political decision. Thirdly without any funded pillar the system was unable to contribute to the development of the Polish capital market.

The 1999 reform was broadly consistent with the recommendations made by the World Bank. It involved the establishment of a three pillar system (Table 7.1) similar in design to the general framework recommended by the World Bank in *Averting the Old Age Crisis* (1994). The most important difference was the construction of the first pillar, which in Poland is based on two methods of financing: notional accounts and funded accounts. The first of these is a mandatory, universal, pay-as-you-go scheme, legislated and administered by the State Social Insurance Institution (Zakład Ubezpieczeń

Table 7.1   The three pillars of the Polish pension system

	1st pillar NDC Notional account	1st pillar FDC Funded account	2nd pillar PPE Employees Pension Schemes	3rd pillar IKE Individual Pension Accounts
Principle	Employment-related	Employment-related	Occupational	Individual
Coverage	Universal, mandatory	Universal, mandatory	Voluntary	Voluntary
Financing mechanism	Pay-as-you-go	Funded	Funded	Funded
Contributions	Earnings-related, shared with employer	Earnings-related, shared with employer	Individual, shared with employer	Individual
	Defined contribution schemes, benefits related to life expectancy			
Benefits	Notional account of indexed contributions	Value of invested contributions	Value of invested contributions	Value of invested contributions
Objective	Basic income maintenance	Basic income maintenance	Complementary individual needs	Complementary individual needs

Społecznych).[2] The latter is also mandatory but is financed on a funded basis through individual accounts. The second pillar, which in Poland is called the third, is voluntary and funded.

The goals of the pension reform declared by the government in 1999 were 'to create a transparent pension system that would resist demographic and macroeconomic pressures, while at the same time ensuring the highest possible level of benefits for future generations' (Chłoń-Domińczak 2002, p. 109). As is well known, important social and economic advantages have been claimed for such a multi-pillar approach (World Bank 1994). However from the social inclusion point of view no explicit declaration regarding the target level of pension provision was made. On the contrary individual responsibility for future pension incomes was emphasized. Stronger connections between contribution and benefit as well as substantial reduction of redistribution were implemented. Apart from the guarantee of a minimum pension (see below), which is subject to a minimum insurance record, little direct financial support by the state was granted. Thus on a prima facie basis the new pension scheme appears to be seeking to guarantee future financial viability at the expense of the goal of the adequacy of pension provision.

This chapter will assess the accuracy of this impression. It will show that Poland has gone the furthest of our six countries in moving away from pay-as-you-go financed state provision, with prefunded pensions expected to play a major role in the prevention of poverty; that overall the system offers a mandatory pension which leaves most of our hypothetical biographies at considerable risk of social exclusion; and that contrary to a general trend throughout the industrialized world, the new Polish system involves a strengthening of the male breadwinner model, with women dependent to a large extent on a married partner for an income in retirement close to or above the social inclusion line.

THE POLISH PENSION REGIME

First Pillar: Notional Account Defined Contribution

The most important change in the mandatory and universal state pay-as-you-go element of the Polish pension system, when compared to the old single pillar system, is that a much closer and more transparent relationship now exists between contributions and benefits. In common with Italy (Chapter 6) and Sweden (Anderson and Meyer 2003, p. 44) for example, Poland has moved to a system of notional defined contributions (NDC) in its pay-as-you-go pillar. Thus pensions are calculated according to an actuarial formula, considering the length of the insurance record and the indexed value of notional assets accumulated in an individual pension account. This guarantees that the pension level reflects individual lifetime earnings. As will be seen, the latter creates particular problems for women because, despite initial proposals to the contrary, the pension age for men and women remains different, 65 and 60 respectively.

The first pillar notional account is financed by earnings-related contributions that also finance the first pillar funded account. The total contribution is equally split between the employer and employee and amounts to 19.52 per cent of the gross wage; 12.22 per cent goes to the first pillar notional account, while 7.3 per cent goes to the first pillar funded account. There is a ceiling on contributions to the mandatory pillars, which means that contributions are not collected on income exceeding 2.5 times the average salary.[3] The self-employed and small business entrepreneurs pay a much lower contribution. Thus a self-employed person may declare his or her income as the basis for social insurance contribution at a minimum level of 60 per cent of the national average wage (Law on the Social Insurance System 1998).

The contribution and benefit indexation method of the first pillar notional account plays an important role in influencing the future level of pension provision. When the reform was introduced the indexation of the virtual assets of individuals in the first pillar notional account was based on 75 per cent real growth of the total contribution base (wage bill). The decision not to base indexation on 100 per cent of real wage growth was designed to save some financial resources to cover the transition costs of the reform and to reduce the contribution rate. It was also justified by the relatively better economic position of the older generation in comparison to workers. However this stipulation has recently been amended, with indexation based since 2005 on 100 per cent of real wage bill growth. With regard to the indexing of pensions in payment, a price inflation increase of 20 per cent of real wage growth was prescribed when the reform was introduced. In 2005 it was changed to conform only to the inflation rate. This will mean that the value of the first pillar pension is set to fall gradually in relation to average wages (see below).

First Pillar: Funded Account Defined Contribution

The other component of the Polish first pillar, the funded account, is called the second pillar in the Polish literature but it is very different from the second pillars of the other countries included in this study. It is not occupationally based and, given the comparatively small scale of the first pillar notional account, it has a poverty-prevention rather than income-replacement role in the overall system.[4] For comparative reasons therefore it will be referred to as the first pillar funded account. Like the Polish first pillar notional account, the first pillar funded account is also mandatory and universal for all employees; it differs in that it is a fully funded scheme. It is regulated and supervised by the state,[5] but administered by 16 Pension Fund Societies (Powszechne Towarzystwa Emerytalne) that operate as joint stock companies. The State Social Insurance Institution (Zakład Ubezpieczeń Społecznych) that administers the first pillar notional account is also responsible for collecting and transferring contributions to the first pillar funded account. All employees and employers, irrespective of the type of company or sector of the economy, have to pay the same share of wages as contributions. Individual accounts are located in one of the 16 Open Pension Funds (Otwarte Fundusze Emerytalne), that are managed by the above-mentioned legally independent Pension Fund Societies. In the draft law on payment of pensions from the first pillar funded account, four types of annuities were proposed to be paid by specialized private pension companies: individual and marital, both with or without a guaranteed payment period (see below).

Pensions from the reformed first pillar are not due until 2009 and precise operation of the funded account pension payments is yet to be finalized. Nevertheless some declared framework rules have been established for paying out pensions. The scheme basically operates as a defined contribution scheme with some state protection of individuals against investment risk. Thus while benefits depend on the pension fund's performance, the state regulates asset management and minimum rates of return in an attempt to assure the security of assets. With regard to the former, investment portfolio limitations have been introduced, such that Pension Fund Societies may invest only up to 40 per cent of assets in shares of listed stock exchange companies. The rest must be located in state bonds and obligations. Foreign investments are limited to 5 per cent of assets and investments in real estate are prohibited. With regard to the rate of return, a minimum standard has been set: whenever in a given Open Pension Fund the rate of return from a half-year period falls under 50 per cent of average rate of return of all funds, the Pension Fund Society responsible for that fund transfers their own assets to cover the difference. This prevents a single fund from poor performance against other funds, but does not prevent poor performance by all funds due to a stock exchange crash, for example. In practice, so far, a higher net return rate in comparison to benchmarks on the capital market has been achieved (*Gazeta Wyborcza* 2005; *Rzeczpospolita* 2005) and this is reflected in the simulations detailed below. There are also limitations on commission and asset management charges for all the Pension Fund Societies.

Pension Schemes For Privileged Workers

There are also other state-supported systems for privileged workers, which were largely unchanged by the 1999 reform. Thus a social insurance scheme for farm workers is over 95 per cent financed by the state budget (Ministry of Social Policy 2005, p. 16). It is financed and administered on a different basis from the universal scheme for employees. The contribution is lower, collected quarterly and related to the average national wage, not to the farmer's actual earnings. Benefits are not earnings-related but are dependent on years of insurance only. There are separate schemes for the military, police judges and prosecutors which are state financed, defined benefit and far more generous than the system that caters for workers and the self-employed.

Protection of Social Risks in the Mandatory Pillars

From the perspective of social inclusion the first pillar provides almost universal coverage, because both elements are compulsory for all types of workers and the self-employed, other than those covered by the pension schemes for privileged workers. A minimum pension from this pillar is guaranteed by the state, such that if the sum of pension benefits from both components does not reach a minimum threshold upon retirement which is set in nominal terms and indexed as other benefits, the state budget will make up the difference. In order to qualify for this benefit citizens must have reached the statutory pension age of 60 years for women and 65 for men and have a minimum contribution record of 20 years for women and 25 for men. This requirement may lead to the exclusion from the pension insurance system of long-time carers or housewives (see below) who must then claim a social assistance-type benefit, that is a means-tested minimum.

Indeed women and any person who is inactive in the labour market are vulnerable in the Polish system. In most countries where the pension level is related to the work record or to the contribution record and years of service or years of insurance, the state has acted to compensate women for the loss of contribution during child-rearing periods. In Poland, in contrast, carers' pension rights have been systematically reduced since 1999, with only some minor exceptions.[6] This situation is reflected in an underdeveloped credit system which disadvantages all those who experience non-working periods. By and large, where credits are available, they are fixed on a much lower base than earnings-related contributions. Only in the case of maternity benefit is the contribution fully replaced by the state budget. In the case of parental leave the basis for contribution is a nursing benefit. This is flat rate (€105 a month in 2006) so the contribution is not earnings-related, and is more than six times lower than average monthly earnings (€660 in 2006). In the case of care for a disabled family member the base for contribution is the income threshold for social assistance. This is also the case when a person is claiming social assistance allowance. Credits for unemployment are also low. They are paid by the Labour Fund on the basis of the unemployment benefit level and only for as long as the benefit entitlement period of usually six months, which leads to exclusion of the long-term unemployed. All these situations, so characteristic for our biographies, lower substantially their future pension entitlements.[7]

Instead of a credit system for women with children, a mechanism of income redistribution from men to women in the pension system has been introduced in the first pillar notional account pension formula. The average life expectancy upon retirement used for actuarial calculation of the pension is assumed to be the same for both genders. This assumption is intentionally false, as women live on retirement for approximately 11 years longer than men. On average they retire five years earlier and die six years later. But such a mechanism only compensates for different pension ages and longer female life expectancy. It does not compensate for non-contributory periods or reduced contribution due to childcare obligations.

If a partner dies before retirement, their first pillar notional account pension rights are non-transferable; his or her individual account is cancelled. The only possible transfer of entitlements is through a survivor's benefit.[8] In contrast, the funded account first pillar assets are transferable, to an open pension fund account of a previously specified beneficiary.

In the case of divorce, both before and after retirement, the first pillar notional account provides no compensation or pension credits transfer whatsoever, unless the former spouse was entitled to alimony benefit. In the first pillar funded account, assets acquired during marriage are treated as common marital assets and are divided according to the court's ruling, that is, two individual accounts are split in halves and the halves are exchanged between the divorced, naturally only for pension purposes. Assuming husbands' higher income, the funded mandatory pillar assets will thus be partly transferred from men to women. Again, such a transfer is marriage related, and does not provide a general systemic income redistribution from all the better-off, usually men, to all the worse-off, usually women.

Voluntary Pension Schemes

There are various forms of voluntary pension provision in Poland. Two of these are 'qualified' forms, meaning they are supported by the state: Employees Pension Schemes (Pracownicze Programy Emerytalne – PPE),[9] and Individual Pension Accounts (Indywidualne Konta Emerytalne – IKE).

State support for these schemes involves tax exemptions on the revenue accrued from invested assets, as well as state supervision over the financial institutions providing pension investments services. In relation to the other countries of this study, some elements of the PPE are similar to second pillar occupational schemes, although they are far less developed. IKEs are more consistent with broader understandings of the term 'third pillar'.[10]

In Employees Pension Schemes (PPE) contributions may consist of two parts: basic and additional contributions. Once a scheme is provided, the basic contribution is obligatory and covered by the employer. It cannot exceed 7 per cent of the individual gross employee wage and is excluded from the base contribution to the social insurance. The costs of setting up and running the PPE are considered business operation costs, so they may be deducted from the income tax base of the employer. Additional contributions to the PPE are voluntarily declared and paid by an employee from his or her net income. Schemes must by law be accessible to at least 50 per cent of employees. Depending on the form of the scheme the employer has higher or lower influence on its administration. In the case of Employees Pension Fund, the investment decisions are taken by the fund's board appointed by the employer. In the case of group life investment insurance and investment funds, the administration is in the hands of the insurance company and the investment society, accordingly. In the latter two cases, the employer concludes an agreement on locating the contribution in the insurance or investment fund, accordingly.

The annual contribution to Individual Pension Accounts is also capped: it may not exceed 1.5 times average monthly earnings. The assets are managed by private asset management companies, banks, insurance companies or by employer-established employee pension funds. All qualified forms of pension provision are defined contribution schemes, sometimes linked with group or individual life insurance. There is no minimum pension guarantee for these schemes, nor the possibility of asset transfer unless otherwise specified in the contract.

At the end of September 2006 there were only 954 active Employees Pension Schemes (PPE) out of 1053 registered (KNUiFE 2006). The schemes are established in small and big companies, but are most common in the big ones employing over 100 employees. In the first three years after the reform PPE were offered mainly in the financial, energy and telecommunications sectors, the latter due to a practical monopolist – TP SA – which created 64 schemes in 2001 alone. The undeveloped nature of PPE schemes is mainly explained by their expense. Although a contribution to them does not really constitute additional labour costs for an employer, because they receive an equivalent deduction from the first pillar pension contribution base, the cost of launching a pension scheme is high. Compared to the few advantages the scheme brings, this cost may prevent an employer from offering the scheme at all.

The IKE, introduced in September 2004 as a state protected option of individual voluntary savings, has been opened only by about 430 000 people up to December 2005. There are two main reasons for this. Firstly no voluntary pension tier existed under the centrally planned economy before 1989 and as a result no tradition developed of individual or occupational responsibility for living standards in old age. People used to rely only on state protection to deliver the appropriate level of pension provision. After 15 years of a market economy in Poland this attitude has not changed to a large extent, either among individuals or employers (Liberda 2005). The second reason for the low popularity of personal savings is inadequate financial support from the state. While IKEs are supported by the state through tax exemptions for income from investment up to the defined level of contributions (150 per cent of a forecasted average monthly national salary), pension experts regard this as insufficient (Broda 2005).

THE SOCIAL INCLUSIVENESS OF THE POLISH PENSION SYSTEM FOR RISK BIOGRAPHIES

In summary the outline provided above of the new Polish pension system highlights the important differences in the approach taken to social protection in Poland when compared with the other five countries included in this study. These differences relate particularly to the nature and role of the notional account and funded account components of the mandatory pillar. Poland's lack of a developed occupational sphere, and thus the reliance on voluntary protection, is also different from the veteran countries – the Netherlands, Switzerland and the UK – but similar in some respects to Germany and Italy.

The simulations detailed in this section outline the effect of the Polish system on our risk biographies (Figure 7.1). They only include the outcomes of mandatory provision for each individual given the undeveloped nature of occupational provision. The simulations show that by itself, the state pay-as-you-go pillar (notional accounts) in Poland is the least generous of any of the countries included in this study, guaranteeing very few of our biographies an income in retirement above the social assistance line. However the intention of the policymakers who constructed the reform was that the two components of the mandatory scheme should operate in combination. Judged on this basis, the first pillar of the Polish system fulfils a similar quantitative role to that played by the first pillar elsewhere, although to a greater extent than in our other countries first pillar outcomes are

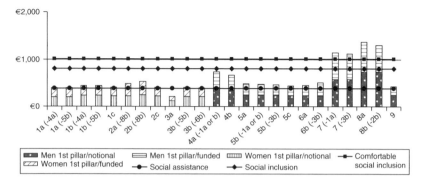

Notes: Social assistance=Social assistance for individuals if person is single on retirement; for married individuals: 50% of couples' social assistance; Social inclusion: 40% average wage; Comfortable social inclusion=50% average wage.

Second pillars include divorce payments for divorcees; see Appendix 2, Chapter 1 for details.

Please note that the scaling of the y-axis in the Polish case is different from the otherwise standard scale used in all other countries. This is because Polish pensions and wages are much lower in comparison and using identical scales would have made reading this figure difficult.

Figure 7.1 Projected real monthly pension levels from the notional and funded component of the first pillar for Polish men and women in 2050

dependent on the rate of return achieved on investments. Moreover, given the almost total absence of redistribution between income groups and the close relationship between pension rights and labour market participation in the first pillar, our biographies are particularly vulnerable in the Polish system: the majority receive a mandatory pension income in retirement of less than 50 per cent of the social inclusion line. The extremely undeveloped nature of the occupational sphere means that substantial levels of personal saving are required by these individuals to provide them with a pension free from social exclusion.

The following sections explain these general conclusions using the simulations of our risk biographies. We will then consider how likely it is that our individuals will save sufficient amounts to fill the gaps between their mandatory provision and the social inclusion threshold. In this regard, we have divided our biographies into three groups. These groupings illustrate the importance in the Polish system of labour market attachment and life-time income for the distribution of post-retirement pension with those individuals who experience longer periods out of the workforce, work part-time and/or have lower wages, particularly vulnerable to social exclusion in retirement.

Social Inclusion of Typical Long-Term Insured Workers

The first group consists of all long-term insured workers, that is, biographies of persons who work full-time and are employed throughout all, or most, of their productive age. Such a biography is traditionally typical of the male breadwinner. This group includes the unqualified worker in the car industry (bio 4), the divorced provider in the chemical industry (bio 7) and the middle manager in financial services (bio 8).

This group of workers is protected best of all our risk biographies by the Polish pension system. None of the typical long-term insured workers receives a provision below the social assistance line (Figure 7.1), however the pensions differ across the biographies between around 170 per cent of the social assistance threshold for the car worker who became unemployed four years before retirement (bio 4b), and 301 per cent of social assistance for the best-performing middle manager (bio 8).

Nevertheless our simulations also show that all of the unqualified car workers (bio 4) are threatened by social exclusion in old age because all variants fail to cross the 40 per cent average income threshold. These variations can be explained by differences in lifetime income due to varying spells of unemployment. As a result, the unqualified worker in the car industry is reliant on third pillar protection to avoid a socially excluded retirement.

Protection of Mothers

The second group incorporates biographies involved in child upbringing or looking after relatives, who consequently experience employment breaks, periods of part-time work, and/or forced labour market absence. Separating these biographies as a single group shows how the important task of caring reduces pension outcomes in comparison to the long-term insured workers. This group includes the mother and unqualified part-time worker in the retail sector (bio 1), the mother and qualified part-time worker working in the welfare sector (bio 2), the married carer and informal worker (bio 3).

In comparison with the long-term, full-time insured men, mothers and carers fare significantly worse. The average pension provision in the second group amounts to 42 per cent of the average provision of the first group. Thus while most of our female biographies cross the poverty threshold, one does not, and those that do only do so by a very small margin. The worst performers in this regard are the carer and informal worker married to the intermittent worker or the small business entrepreneur (bio 3a). They both fall considerably short of the social assistance line. In contrast the best female performers, variants of the mother and qualified part-time worker (bio 2a, b) exceed the social assistance line by 83 per cent and 42 per cent respectively. Nevertheless even they are not within 25 percentage points of the social inclusion line. Overall this is the worst performance for women of any country included in this study.

Nevertheless, while our women as a whole do badly in the Polish system, some do better than others. These variations are explained to a significant extent by differences in lifetime income and labour market attachment. Thus it is mainly on this basis that the three variants of the mother and qualified part-time worker (bio 2), who have the highest life-time income of our women biographies (Figure 1.1, Chapter 1), achieve the highest pension outcome, with the lowest-paid biography, the married carer and informal worker (bio 3a), receiving the lowest pension income in retirement.

Protection of Short-Term Insured Employed Biographies

To the third group belong biographies who also differ from the long-term employed, but for reasons other than their social care role. This group consists of the intermittent worker in the construction industry with long periods of self-employment (bio 5), the small business entrepreneur (bio 6) and the incomplete resident (bio 9).

Although the average pension outcome of both the second and third groups is almost equal, the latter group's wages are generally much higher than those of the mothers, with the only exception of the incomplete resident (bio 9), who earns less than the mother in the welfare sector (bio 2b; Figure 1.1, Chapter 1). This is because of the way their different life-course experiences, especially self-employment or entrepreneurship, interact with the pension regime. The incomplete resident was included in this group as well, because of the shorter coverage under the compulsory pension system. The pension levels of all these biographies are above the social assistance line, but far below the social inclusion line (Figure 7.1). A high poverty risk exists for the intermittent worker with long periods of self-employment (bio 5a, b) and disability (bio 5c) and the small business entrepreneur (bio 6), despite being amongst the highest earners in the sample. This is explained by the fact that they paid the lowest possible amount of social insurance contributions, based on 60 per cent of the average wage, which is almost always declared during periods of self-employment. The reason for the low pension of the incomplete resident is a rather short time of insurance (25 years), which plays a substantial role in reducing pension outcomes in the defined contribution system in Poland.

Savings

As has been seen, the low overall level of first pillar provision and the almost total absence of occupational provision means that most of our biographies require some form of additional saving to achieve a pension income on retirement above the social inclusion threshold (Figure 7.2).

The amount each individual requires to save varies quite substantially, from a low of 4 per cent of average gross income for a variant of the unqualified male worker (bio 4a) to a high of 45 per cent of gross income for a variant of the married carer and informal worker (bio 3a). These variations generally reflect differences of lifetime earnings which as has been seen are reproduced in the Polish first pillar.

For some workers it is clear that the savings rates they require are not feasible: they simply would not be able to afford to save at the levels required. This is the case for all of the women biographies (bio 1, 2, 3), whose incomes are low, particularly given the comparatively high cost of living for carers. It is even unlikely that the married carer (bio 3) would save the 6 per cent of gross income our calculations suggest she requires to avoid poverty.

The situation is not quite so clear-cut for those of our biographies who experience prolonged periods of self-employment (bio 5, 6). Both need to put away between 7 and 10 per cent of their annual gross wage, which might be possible given that they are better paid than the female biographies.

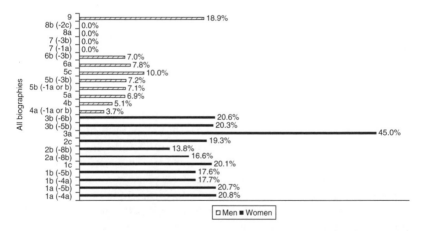

Notes: Each individual linked to another individual receives or pays contributions to divorced partner. Assumptions for private savings: Appendix 1.2, Chapter 1.

Figure 7.2   *Third pillar savings from lifetime income required of Polish men and women to reach social inclusion line of 40% average wage in 2050*

However, as was seen in the first section, there is little evidence that saving at this level is taking place. Figures for 2005 suggest that only about 43 per cent of self-employed workers had any savings (Czapiński and Panek 2005, p. 36).

The individual who is in the most promising situation with regard to a possible role for voluntary savings is the unqualified male worker (bio 4). According to our simulations, he requires personal savings amounting to no higher than 5 per cent of the average annual gross income to avoid social exclusion. Theoretically this should be possible even though his earnings are not high. However without a contribution from an employer and given the slow development of the Polish personal savings market it is unlikely that even this individual would save sufficient over his working life to lift his pension income on retirement above the social inclusion threshold.

Protection of Couples

There are no special provisions for couples in the Polish pension system. Initially in the draft law of the 1999 reform there were plans to introduce a joint marriage pension as a default pension provision from the first pillar funded account scheme for couples. This idea, involving a mechanism of income redistribution from husbands to wives, has been abandoned. A couple's pension income is made up of the sum of each individual's entitlement. On this basis, as the simulations show, all couples have a pension income above the social assistance threshold (Figure 7.3). The situation is least favourable for couples where both partners have short histories of social insurance contributions. This is particularly true for families consisting of a carer and informal worker and an intermittent worker with long periods of self-employment (bio 3 and 5) or the small business entrepreneur (bio 3 and 6). Their pension income lies at the relevant social assistance line. The financial situation for couples with at least one long-term insured partner is much better, but only two couples exceed the social inclusion line, those that include the middle-level manager in the financial services and the highest earner in the female group (bio 2 and 8). Other couples receive a pension income below this line, which indicates that by itself long-term insurance connected with full-time employment of one partner is not enough to avoid social exclusion, as the case of the married unqualified car worker (bio 4) shows. Rather, the requirements are both long-term coverage under the compulsory system and high wages.

In terms of the partners' contribution to the couple's pension income, women's contribution is much lower than men's. Generally speaking the disparities between the partners reflect the different employment biographies

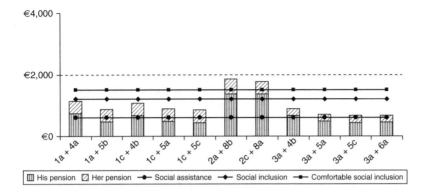

| His pension | Her pension | Social assistance | Social inclusion | Comfortable social inclusion |

Notes: Social assistance line = Social assistance line for couples;
Social inclusion line for couples: 1.5 × 40% average wage; Comfortable social inclusion =
1.5 × 50% average wage.
    Please note that the scaling of the y-axis in the Polish case is different from the otherwise
standard scale used in all other countries. This is because Polish pensions and wages are
much lower in comparison and using identical scales would have made reading this figure
difficult.

Figure 7.3   Projected real monthly pension levels of Polish couples in 2050

and salaries of both sexes which impact on their pension provision levels in both components of the first pillar.

With regard to divorce, as explained above there is no mechanism in the first pillar notional account scheme to ensure the sharing on retirement of pension rights built up by either partner during marriage, unless the alimony was granted by court, but the latter case is not reflected in our simulations. However pension sharing is possible in the funded part of the first pillar, with pension entitlements built up during marriage divided between the spouses. Where this arrangement is applied our simulations suggest it is sufficient to ensure that divorced women are not disadvantaged in relation to their married equivalents. In fact a comparison between the married and divorced variants of the unqualified mother and part-time worker (bio 1c, b), who otherwise have very similar biographies and identical lifetime incomes, shows that the divorcee receives a slightly higher pension than the married woman.

The Polish Pension System and Social Exclusion

The main conclusions from the analysis of the simulations can be divided into two parts: the first relates to the contribution of each part of the pension system to social inclusion and the second to the protection against the risk of poverty and/or social exclusion of individuals and couples.

Firstly both compulsory schemes, the notional and the funded accounts, contribute to a similar extent to individual pension provision, although, as explained at the beginning of this chapter, the pension contribution for the notional account is nearly twice as high as in the funded account. The better outcomes from the latter are linked to the higher net return rate than in the pay-as-you-go financed part of the first pillar.[11] This is also caused by the dividing of pension entitlements in the funded part of the first pillar in case of divorce.

However the overall level of mandatory provision for our risk biographies is very low, particularly for those with more unstable employment biographies and/or lower income levels. This makes second and third pillar saving extremely important. Yet so far the role of the voluntary pillars has been insignificant (Ministry of Social Policy 2005, p. 12). In December 2005 only 260 000 were covered by occupational schemes (PPE), constituting 2.6 per cent of total employees in the fourth quarter, and only 430 000 people invested in state-supported Individual Pension Accounts (IKE). Other forms of personal saving, like life insurance, are also not popular, especially among low-income workers.

Secondly because of the strong link between contributions and pension level, benefits reflect wage position during working life. Both components of the compulsory pillar provide, on the one hand, universal coverage. On the other hand, they do not offer sufficient protection to those without long-term social insurance as part of a full-time job. Only well-paid, long-term, full-time insured workers will be protected against both poverty and social exclusion, and even those biographies are unlikely to be able to maintain their previous living standard, which is partly the result of the ceiling on contributions to both components. The self-employed receive a pension above the poverty line, but below social inclusion. This protection against poverty is ensured because of the legally prescribed minimum contribution base, and therefore contributions level, for both obligatory components of the first pillar for the self-employed.

The worst situation in regard to social inclusion concerns women involved in raising children or caring for other adults. Some of them, especially full-time carers and informal workers, are threatened by poverty in old age. The reasons for this are the significant reduction of redistribution in the pension system after the pension reform of 1999 and the lower female retirement age. Poland has instead adopted a strong male breadwinner approach to the social protection of women that increases personal dependency on men (Lewis 1992). Thus the distribution of pension income among spouses in case of divorce plays some role in protecting against poverty. A split of pension assets upon divorce increases in significance for the 'weaker' employment biography the greater the working time and earnings level differences between the spouses. Yet, as has been seen, this route is problematic as a means of protecting women, not least because it is only open to divorcees, and not to unmarried mothers, for example.

THE REFORM DEBATE IN POLAND

Overall Poland has the most individualized pension scheme of the six countries included in this study involving the smallest amount of pay-as-you-go financing. On the basis of the simulations it is clear that three interrelated features of this system put vulnerable citizens at risk of experiencing social exclusion in retirement. These are: the low level of mandatory provision and its close relationship to working time income and/or regular labour market attachment; the lack of protection afforded to women independent of marriage; and the almost complete absence of an occupational pension sector.

However despite the existence of this high social exclusion risk, consideration by political actors of the types of reforms required to address the problem is largely absent. Instead concern is focused on the budgetary pressures created by existing pensions awarded under the old regime. This concern has grown stronger since the 1999 reform because the transition costs to the new system turned out to be higher than expected, exacerbating current financing problems, a situation made worse by increased fears about demographic change (Twoja emerytura 1998).[12] Indeed some recent reforms have involved a further tightening of the mandatory system. In 2005 the indexation of pension provision from the first pillar notional account was reduced, so that it now conforms only to the inflation rate. In the case of stable real wage growth, this will lead to the gradual decrease of the real value of pensions, a situation that will be worse the older a pensioner is and the higher real growth.

In this context it is felt that dealing with future problems of social exclusion now will merely raise present costs and force savings in other policy areas. Reliance is placed instead on future state budget supplements to minimum pensions and social assistance to cover the future problem of social exclusion. The problem is being put off until at least 2009 when pension payments from the new system start to be provided. At the beginning these costs will be relatively low because of the quite big role of pension entitlement awarded in the old system (so-called initial capital) and the temporary regulations for old–new mixed pensions for women in the years 2009–2013 (Góra 2003, p. 200). Nevertheless they will grow with time.

Some arguments for reform on the basis of concerns about social exclusion do exist nevertheless. The next section will summarize the proposals made to reform the Polish system with regard to each of the three features identified above and indicate the obstacles that currently exist in the way of these reforms.

Changes in the Compulsory Pension Schemes

Given the domination of financial concerns, only relatively minor issues have surfaced in current Polish debates with respect to the question of social inclusion and the mandatory pension system. These relate to the minimum pension guarantee, the indexation of funded first pillar pensions and self-employment.

Minimum pension guarantee

In Poland, the minimum pension is not universally available but is subject to a minimum insurance record, which limits its accessibility for part-time and intermittent workers. It is not even called a 'minimum pension', but a 'social part of the pension'. The state guarantees a minimum pension from mandatory schemes so long as citizens have worked for 20 or 25 years respectively for women and men. These requirements were adopted from the old system and only the source of financing was changed, from the contributions of other insurers to the state budget. However because of the new economic circumstances, with long-term unemployment becoming a more common feature, this approach is being reviewed. There are concerns that more citizens will not fulfil the necessary requirements, putting greater pressure on social assistance. On the other hand, some commentators fear that mitigating the employment-based requirements for pension provision will weaken the motivation to work and the intended strong contribution–benefit linkage. A non-stigmatizing solution was put forward in 2006 by Robert Gwiazdowski, the President of the State Social Insurance Institution Supervisory Board (Omachel 2005), who suggested that the notional part of the first pillar should be transformed into a flat rate social minimum, while its funded part, as well as the second and third pillar pensions, would reflect lifetime earnings. The contribution to the first pillar would remain earnings-related, thus reintroducing a strong element of income redistribution from the better-off to the poorer.[13] However there is very little public support for such a proposal and it thus seems unlikely to be implemented.

Changing the indexation for funded first pillar pensions

Indexing regulation changes are also a way of improving pension income. The level of indexation during accumulation in the funded part of the first pillar, for example, can be influenced indirectly by setting the minimum rate of return, limiting various kinds of investments or limiting the commission level. As we discussed above, some steps were taken in this regard when the new system was introduced. In 2004 various changes were made that aim to provide higher funded account outcomes. Firstly the calculation of the legally set minimum rate of return of the 16 open pension funds was changed and the influence of the biggest of these funds on that weighted average index was restricted. Secondly the maximum level of both contribution and management commission, that most influence an individual's capital accumulation, was also reduced and unified. However further steps in this direction are unlikely because such steps reduce competition on the open pension fund market and lead to homogenization. The Pension Fund Societies lobby will probably not let it happen. It should also be noted that the Polish funded part of the mandatory pillar already has the lowest fees compared to similar schemes in Europe and Latin America.

Changing the contribution base for self-employment
As explained earlier, self-employed and small business entrepreneurs pay a much lower, practically flat rate contribution in comparison with ordinary employees. In a pension system built on individual insurance contribution records this leads to a lower pension. The reason why such a solution was implemented was not that the self-employed were considered likely to invest in their firm to provide them with the required additional income upon retirement; rather it was the product of weak state control over self-employed income. In 2003 the Ministry of Economy, Labour and Social Policy issued a proposal for changing the contribution base for the self-employed (Ministry of Economy, Labour and Social Policy 2003). The contribution would depend on real income and not on declared minimum income. However because of the lack of agreement on how the individual contribution base should be calculated, and strong opposition from the small business lobby, no further steps were undertaken. The main argument of the small business lobby was that a higher social contribution would lead to higher costs of operation and they would have to dismiss employees and even liquidate their businesses. Higher contributions would also jeopardize their international competitive advantage. The argument of low pension entitlements was dismissed by the lobby with the argument that there is no better pension investment than in their own company, which could be sold upon retirement. This argument is not always true and obviously has nothing to do with insurance.

Improving pension protection for women
In contrast to other Western countries, Poland's 1999 reform involved reductions in the compensation mechanisms for scheme participants who

bring up children and look after other dependants. As our simulations have shown, this is likely to leave many women dependent on the retirement income of a spouse or former spouse, through divorce pension-sharing arrangements, to escape poverty in retirement. It also means that unmarried women with children are extremely vulnerable. In the longer term there are also concerns that not compensating for parental leave will lead to lower fertility and a higher burden on future generations to finance the future pension system (Kotowska 2006, p. 14).

Introducing or widening credit arrangements for women would not require a change in system construction, but only the introduction of state budget contribution paid on behalf of the carer during the legally defined child-rearing period. Taxes would not have to be raised significantly and assets could be shifted from other social expenditure, such as state support for schemes for privileged workers (see below). In the future such state 'investment' would bring the benefit of a lower subsidy to the minimum pension.

However a reform of this type seems unlikely in the short term. No strong political party is willing to put forward the argument, especially after elections, that non-contributory periods can have a broader social value and that consequently there must be a mechanism of income redistribution from those who continue paying contributions to those who for a socially valuable reason cannot. The Law and Justice Party from the right (Prawo i Sprawiedliwość), that won the parliamentary election in September 2005, proposed during the campaign increasing pension contributions for mothers, but there are no law drafts in progress in this matter. Indeed, overall, the problem of insignificant recognition of motherhood or parenthood and care is hardly discussed. This is firstly because the new pension system and its outcomes are little known in society in general. With the first female pension from the three pillar system not due until 2009, political pressure is low and problems are ignored. Secondly the additional costs that would have to be paid by the state budget are inconsistent with the general desire to limit state subsidies and control the budget deficit, notwithstanding the possible methods for funding such a reform from cuts in other forms of expenditure. Thirdly women are overall weakly represented in public debate and a lack of co-operation among female organizations means they have been unable to set up common goals and consequently fight for their achievement (Fultz and Silberstein 2003, p. 10). Finally a traditional, quite paternalistic, family model of the male breadwinner and the female taking care of children has reasserted itself in Poland. This model was formally denied during the communist regime and is now going through a revival. Right-wing parties opt for traditional role-splitting between spouses. The steps undertaken by them, like prolonging maternity leave and abolishing the Government Plenipotentiary for Equal Status of Women and Men, a former minister, are aimed rather at maintaining the weaker socio-economic position of women. Left-wing parties formally support improvements in women's position, but little was done during their period of government (Nowakowska and Piwnik 2003, p. 85 and following).

However, paradoxically, with respect to the pension system, the most important reason for gender inequality is women's resistance to an equal pension age. Given the design of the pension system – defined contribution based mainly on the length and type of work or service – early retirement results in a lower pension. Less capital is accumulated, fictitious and real, to serve a longer life expectancy. The five-year difference in the legal retirement age of women and men explains therefore to some extent the disproportion in the level of pensions of both sexes. When the 1999 reform was proposed an equal retirement age of 62 was recommended, which meant a decrease from 65 to 62 for men and an increase from 60 to 62 for women. However since the lower retirement age for women was perceived as a privilege in Polish society, the proposition was rejected. Four years later, in the above-mentioned report of the Ministry of Economy, Labour and Social Policy, an increase of women's retirement age up to 65 years beginning from 2010 with changes of six months a year was suggested. At the same time a proposal concerning the flexible retirement age for all insurers at the age of 62 and a part pension provision only from the notional part of the first pillar was put forward. During the debate in parliament both solutions were rejected in the face of strong pressure from trade unions, who were concerned about the effect of reform on unemployment and who perceive earlier retirement of women as a just solution (CBOS 2005, pp. 1, 2). This was despite the fact that the population's acceptance for increasing the retirement age, especially among young women, rose significantly (CBOS 2005, p. 4). In the Strategy of Social Policy for the years 2007–2013 a flexible retirement age was once more announced. The proposal concerned the possibility of a part-time pension two years before legal retirement age (from 2009) for people who are working or looking after family members (Ministerstwo Polityki Społecznej 2005, p. 34).

Unequal treatment of men and women was ruled out in other EU countries by the European Court of Justice. Moreover on 5 July 2006 the European Parliament and the Council adopted a Directive on the implementation of the principle of equal opportunities and equal treatment of men and women in matters of employment and occupation (Directive 2006/54/EU). This obliges member states to introduce an equal statutory pension age for men and women by October 2008. Thus no matter what political arguments are put forward, the legal obligation will force Poland to introduce an equal pension age.

One additional argument should be mentioned when discussing reasons why an increase in the female retirement age is currently resisted. Grandmothers in Poland are the predominant carers of children and older relatives, for example parents or parents-in-law. Involving older women in the labour market would prevent grandmothers from leaving employment to take personal care of their grandchildren. This would mean a loss or reduction of those unpaid resources, and increase pressure on the state to take over care-related tasks, leading to additional public expense, for which there is little support.

Reforming the pension schemes of privileged workers

As has been seen, the problem of scarce financial resources comes up in every discussion about new compensation mechanisms in the mandatory pillar, or increasing financial incentives in the voluntary pillars (see below), particularly given the deficit that has developed due to the underestimation of the costs of the transition to the new system in 1999. One method for freeing up scarce resources to assist the more vulnerable citizens, such as our risk biographies, is reform of other state-supported pension schemes, such as those for farm workers, judges, lawyers and the military. With regard to farmers, the *Green Book* report recommended in 2003 a change from a flat rate to an income-related contribution base to bring the scheme into line with the main state scheme (Ministry of Economy, Labour and Social Policy 2003), and there is agreement among experts that such a reform is unavoidable (Góra 2003, p. 205). However this proposal was rejected just before the 2005 parliamentary elections. With regard to the schemes for judges, lawyers and for the military service an attempt was made in 1999 to shift these occupational groups into workers' and self-employed pension systems. However because of strong lobbying from both the legal profession and the military, this proposed reform has been abandoned. With the problems of creating a clear parliamentary majority and with the threat of social unease, the current government is very unlikely to implement these reforms.

Changing the voluntary pension schemes

As our simulations showed, the mandatory pillars by themselves leave the large majority of our biographies well short of a socially inclusive income in retirement. However so far the voluntary pillar has not played any significant role in delivering pension provision in old age. Thus while the number of registered Employees Pension Schemes increased from 342 in December 2004 to 995 in December 2005, much of this increase was due to a change in the regulation of existing non-qualified schemes in 2005. Employers had to convert their existing provision to qualified schemes or lose the exemption from the mandatory social security contribution they gained from paying contributions to these schemes (see the beginning of this chapter).

With regard to Employees Pension Schemes, three main reasons are suggested to explain why developments have not been greater (Broda 2005). Firstly the depressed state of the Polish labour market gives employers few incentives to establish schemes for reasons of human resource management. They are made even less attractive because, as explained above, by Polish law each scheme must be accessible to at least half of the employees and therefore employers cannot use them selectively to retain and attract desired workers only. Secondly our interviews with trade union leaders suggest there is little pressure from them to develop occupational pensions. This is because trade unions in Poland are much weaker than in other former communist countries (Golinowska 2005, p. 47). Moreover the necessity of securing existing jobs in a high-unemployment labour market is so strong that it prevents trade unions from even negotiating the possibilities of launching Employees Pension Schemes, particularly given that the average employee does not realize the role of personal, additional pension savings for his or her income in old age. The final reason relates to the limited nature of state support. In the circumstances just described, employer voluntarism is only likely to occur in response to significant state support with the costs of launching a pension scheme, but so far there has been little assistance in this regard.

With regard to Individual Pension Accounts (IKE) the main explanation provided for their slow development is inadequate state support. The current tax exemptions for income from investment up to the defined level of contributions (150 per cent of a forecasted average monthly national salary) are considered insufficient by expert opinion. They suggest strong financial state support such as income tax exemption (Broda 2005). In this regard, the Law and Justice Party has recently announced the liquidation of the tax on investment return and promised income tax exemptions in exchange, but no detailed proposals have been made up until now and the particular problems of women in undertaking private personal saving are not considered at all (see Political Programmme of Law and Justice 2005). A further problem is that the wage level in Poland is relatively low in comparison to the cost of living, making additional personal savings very difficult for citizens. Moreover, as can be seen from the example of the other five countries in this study, there is no guarantee that direct tax subsidies would be much more successful in inducing citizens to save.

Increasing the public knowledge of the pension scheme
As has been suggested, because pensions from the new system are not to be paid before 2009, the question of lower pension provision from both compulsory pillars in comparison to the old regime is not a public issue. Moreover discussion about future pension outcomes and possible steps anticipating the problem of increasing poverty, like postponing retirement, is limited to experts and not a matter of public debate. Awareness of these issues is only likely to rise if there is an intelligible, honest informational campaign about the new pension rules, involving the State Social Insurance Institution and the 16 Pension Fund Societies. The promotion of the latter at the end of the 1990s was one-sided and led people to become convinced that the pre-funded pension would ensure a luxurious standard of living. Before the reform started and during its initial stages, the government conducted an information campaign (Chłoń 2000). Yet it was limited in time and therefore information on and promotion of private pension schemes is currently insufficient.

Increasing labour market activity and wage levels
Given that currently significant change to the strong labour market basis of the Polish pension system is unlikely, efforts to ensure appropriate conditions for individuals to achieve a decent pension income through labour market participation become crucial in the fight against poverty in old age. Poland and Italy have the lowest employment rates in our group (Table 1.2, Chapter 1) and there is a need to increase them both for men and women (Ministry of Social Policy 2005, p. 20 and following). To this end, the reconciliation of employment and childcare must be made much easier through affordable services; it is necessary to develop employment opportunities for older people; and investment in lifelong learning needs to be expanded. Currently there is no appetite for reforms in these areas.

In summary we can therefore say that the main poverty risks identified by our simulations – lack of protection because of low general pension levels and strict equivalence of pensions and earnings for socially insured workers only – are not sufficiently addressed in current debates. The future of the public pension system is still closely associated with the right way to contain spending, and relevant actors outside the state seem to be either content with the situation or unable to push for change. Large employers have no interest in offering occupational schemes, trade unions are too weak to change this position, and the medium-term economic interests of the one-third of the employed population in self-employment (Table 1.2, Chapter 1) run counter to ensuring their security in retirement. This leaves private citizens, of whom women are most affected by the looming risks due to care responsibilities; however they have no political voice strong enough to question public spending priorities or to make trade unions recognize their interests. Thus, after decades of state socialism, and a fairly sudden shift towards the market, neither is a return to a more generous public system for the protection of older people on the horizon, nor the emergence of strong private agents who could ensure improved collective provision outside the first pillar. So far in Poland 'private pensions' mainly mean mimicry of the market by a retrenched public scheme. There is no sign yet that alternative forms of private pensions could make a relevant contribution to social inclusion.

NOTES

1. The authors would like to thank Agnieszka Chłoń-Domińczak, Ministry of Labour and Social Policy, Poland for her helpful comments on a previous draft of this chapter.
2. This is a public entity supervised by the Ministry of Labour and Social Policy. Apart from the Old Age Fund, it administers three other Social Insurance Funds. These are: Disability and Survival Fund, Work Injury Fund and Sickness and Maternity Fund. All four funds constitute the Social Insurance Fund (Fundusz Ubezpieczeń Społecznych).
3. Every year when the basis for contribution (individual gross earnings) exceeds 30 times the average national monthly salary the contribution is not collected on the exceeding income in the given calendar year.
4. With regard to poverty prevention, the only similar system is the UK state second pension, although this operates as a back-up to an occupational system and is not pre-funded.
5. The institutions in the first pillar funded account and the voluntary pillar are supervised by the Financial Supervisory Commission, which in 2006 replaced the Commission for Insurance and Pension Funds Supervision (Komisja Nadzoru Ubezpieczeń i Funduszy Emerytalnych).
6. The only positive change in the 1999 reform, in both notional and funded components of the first pillar, was cancelling the previous limitation of years of parental leave, which applied in the pension system before 1999, as so called non-contributory years.
7. Of course, in the second voluntary pillar all these periods would remain non-contributory, unless it is otherwise specified in the group or individual life insurance contract.
8. Another insurance benefit paid from the mandatory pillar in case of death is funeral benefit. The latter however can hardly be called a transfer of benefits.
9. Non-qualified group life insurance schemes have been offered on a voluntary basis to employees in many companies since 1990.
10. In the Polish literature all voluntary schemes are numbered as the third pillar due to the fact that two components of the mandatory scheme NDC (notional defined contribution) and FDC (funded defined contribution) are numbered as pillars one and two. For comparative reasons, we have labelled both mandatory elements as the first pillar pension.
11. The assumptions made in the simulations can influence the contribution of pension provisions from the two respective schemes of the mandatory pillar to the total pension, of course. It should be highlighted that the exact role of both components of the compulsory pillar could change according to the real gross return rate and cost of accumulating pension capital, which differ between the open pension funds (although both minimum return rate and maximal commissions are legally prescribed). Moreover the rules of providing the annuities are not precisely known and the cost of paying out the pension are difficult to assess, especially because the appropriate law concerning the payment of pension from the funded first pillar has not been passed so far.

12. See Góra (2003), Chapter: Redukcja długu (Reducing the deficit), p. 199.
13. It is worth mentioning that Mr Gwiazdowski was presenting his own opinion and not the views of the State Social Security Agency.

BIBLIOGRAPHY

Anderson, K.M. and Meyer, T. (2003), 'Social democracy, unions, and pension politics in Germany and Sweden', *Journal of Public Policy*, **23**(1), 23–55.

Broda, M. (2005), *PPE Konsultanci*, Warsaw: Ogma.

CBOS (2005), *O wieku emerytalnym kobiet i mężczyzn raz jeszcze*, 'Raport z badań Centrum Badania Opinii Publicznej'.

Chłoń, A. (2000), *Pension Reform and Public Information in Poland*, WB Pension Primer series, Washington, DC: World Bank.

Chłoń–Domińczak, A. (2002), 'The Polish pension reform of 1999', in E. Fultz (ed.), *Pension Reform in Central and Eastern Europe, Vol. 1: Restructuring with Privatization: Case Studies of Hungary and Poland*, pp. 98–205, Budapest: International Labour Office.

Czapiński, J. and Panek, P. (2005), 'Diagnoza społeczna 2005', *Warunki i jakość życia Polaków*, Annex 1.

Directive 2006/54/EU *Official Journal of the European Union*, L 204/24. 2006.

Fultz, E. and Silberstein, S. (2003), 'Reformy systemu zabezpieczenia społecznego w okresie transformacji a sytuacja kobiet i mężczyzn (na przykładzie Republiki Czeskiej, Węgier i Polski)', in B. Balcerzak-Paradowska (ed.), *Kobiety i mężczyźni w reformach systemu zabezpieczenia społecznego w Polsce, Instytut Badań nad Gospodarką Rynkową we współpracy z Międzynarodową Organizacją Pracy i Przedstawicielstwem Fundacji Heinricha Bölla w Polsce*, Warszawa, pp. 7–43.

Gazeta Wyborcza (2005), 'Konkurs na najlepszy fundusz emerytalny rozstrzygnięty'.

Golinowska, S. (2005), 'Social change and social policy during the transformation period', in S. Golinowska (ed.), *The Social Report Poland 2005*, pp. 29–54, Warsaw: Friedrich Ebert Foundation.

Góra, M. (2003), *System emerytalny*, PWN Warszawa.

KNUiFE–Komisja Nadzoru Ubezpieczeń i Funduszy Emerytalnych (2006), *Rejestr PPE*, Warszawa.

Kotowska, I. (2006), *Podstawowe informacje o rozwoju demograficznym Polski do 2004 r. Materials from XXIII Symposium on Contemporary Public Economy and Administration*.

Law on the Social Insurance System (1998), *Journal od Laws nr. 137, item 887, with later amendments*.

Lewis, J. (1992), 'Gender and the development of welfare regimes', *Journal of European Social Policy*, **2**(3), 159–73.

Liberda, B. (2005), *Savings in Poland in the Year of the EU Accession*, in Foreign Trade Research Institute Annual Report, Polish Foreign Trade and the Economy, Warsaw: Foreign Trade Research Institute.

Ministerstwo Polityki Społecznej (2005), *Strategia Polityki Społecznej 2007–2013: dokument przyjęty przez Radę Ministrów 13 września 2005*, Warszawa.

Ministry of Economy, Labour and Social Policy (2003), *Report about Rationalization of Social Expenditures – The Green Book*, Warsaw.

Ministry of Social Policy (2005), *Poland: National Strategy Report on Adequate and Sustainable Pensions*, Warsaw.

Nowakowska, U. and Piwnik, E. (2003), 'Kobiety w rodzinie', *Kobiety w Polsce – 2003 (2003), Raport Centrum Praw Kobiet, Fundacja Centrum Praw Kobiet*, Warszawa, pp. 49–90.

Omachel, R. (2005), *Emerytura równa dla wszystkich*, Dziennik.

Political Programmme of Law and Justice (2005), *Prawo i Sprawiedliwość*, Warsaw.

Rzeczpospolita (2005), 'Moje Pieniądze', *Różnice są dość duże, Suplement*, 13 October.

Twoja emerytura (Your Pension) (1998), *Biuro Pełnomocnika Rządu ds Reformy Systemu Ubezpieczeń Społecznych*, Warszawa.

World Bank (1994), *Averting the Old Age Crisis*, Oxford: Oxford University Press.

Żukowski, M. (1994), 'Pensions policy in Poland after 1945: between "Bismarck" and "Beveridge" ', in J. Hills, J. Ditch and H. Glennerster (eds), *Beveridge and Social Security: An International Retrospective*, Oxford: Oxford University Press.

PART IV

Conclusion

8. Private pensions versus social inclusion? Three patterns of provision and their impact

Paul Bridgen and Traute Meyer

We started this book with the observation that a shift away from public provision and an increase in private forms has taken place across the industrialized world. On the basis of the preceding six chapters we can now say to what extent this trend is evident in the countries included in this study, what patterns of public and private provision these changes have created, and what their outcome is for citizens at risk.

Thus this chapter seeks to answer from a comparative perspective the central question at the heart of the book: are private pensions fundamentally incompatible with social inclusion or are there circumstances in which they can play a more positive role?

In the following a similar structure to that of the country chapters will be used. First we will consider our six country regimes and identify the most important shared features and differences with regard to each pillar. In the following section we will assess the overall results and make clear connections between the performance of all risk biographies and the different types of pension system design. The final part of the chapter will identify the design features most useful in helping to secure retirement incomes above the social inclusion threshold in the new pensions policy paradigm, and discuss the likelihood of the adoption of such features in those countries where they are not already in existence. Overall this chapter argues that policymakers should be worried about the future implications of current pension systems in relation to social exclusion.

PASSIVE PRIVATIZATION

In the literature the term 'passive privatization' (Bonoli et al. 2000) has been used to describe an increased need for citizens to find alternative provision in the face of reductions in the pension levels previously guaranteed by the state. The country studies in this book show that 'passive privatization' is a dominant trend. However this trend is experienced by citizens not only through public, but also through corporate retrenchment. In recent times entitlements in all collective schemes, public or occupational, have been reduced in all our countries and the direct relationship between individual earnings and pension outcome has been tightened. Insurance against social risks is therefore increasingly individualized, making personal savings schemes more important.

Passive Privatization Through First Pillar Retrenchment: The Newcomers

In Germany, Italy and Poland the decision to turn towards multi-pillar systems meant that politicians have taken steps to reduce entitlements in their hitherto dominant first pillars. This has been done in different ways. In Germany the new demographic factor that was added to the basic formula used to calculate first pillar pensions depresses the pension level for all, but the overall formula was not changed fundamentally. The redistributive elements of the first pillar remain, specifically with regard to care responsibilities. In Italy the change in the benefits formula induced a more fundamental switch from earnings-related to notional defined contribution principles; here the main aim was to strengthen the relationship between individual contributions and pension outcome, and redistributive elements are almost entirely absent from this first pillar. Similarly after the Polish reform of its first pillar which introduced strict defined contribution principles for individualized pension accounts, compensation for time spent out of the labour market is minimal. The performance of the funded second tier depends entirely on the amount of contributions paid for each individual and their long-term performance on the market.

In all three countries the changes in the first were accompanied by increased support for second and third pillars, but crucially participation in such schemes is entirely voluntary. Tax and/or social insurance contribution exemptions are in place for employers and employees setting up occupational schemes, and there is state support for personal savings accounts. Italy has moved the furthest from the voluntary path with the introduction of a more encompassing form of private saving using an existing occupational benefit, the *trattamento di fine rapporto* (TFR).

Coverage of occupational provision is thus patchy at best. In Poland social actors and citizens have been least likely to use these opportunities. In Italy we see some growth in occupational and some in personal pensions, but it reaches comparatively few citizens.[1] Expansion in Germany has been strongest, especially with regard to occupational welfare, as trade unions sought the opportunity to include pensions in the collective bargaining process; take-up of personal schemes remains much weaker.

We conclude that generally 'privatization' for all three countries was 'passive' because cuts in the public sector were not compensated for by the more effective encouragement of alternative provision. In addition some public pillars have adopted a private face. In Poland rates of return in the pre-funded scheme depend on market performance, and in both Italy and Poland a very close relationship between contributions and earnings has been established, while the sensitivity for social risks is minimal. In contrast the mimicry of market rules by the state has not increased in Germany, where redistribution in favour of people facing certain social risks continues to be recognized as an important function of the public pillar.

Passive Privatization Through Second Pillar Retrenchment: The Veterans

In Britain, the Netherlands and Switzerland retrenchment in recent years has predominantly taken the form of cuts in occupational pensions. These were the result of government action to an important extent, although in Britain occupational retrenchment was never a policy intention. In the Netherlands government pushed the social partners towards a new occupational pension settlement based on average wage schemes and reduced early retirement in order to cut costs and increase employment participation. Likewise a reduction of spending was the motive of the Swiss government when it decreased the legally set interest and conversion rates for occupational pension assets in recent years; however it also lowered the access threshold to the second pillar for lower incomes, broadening its scope. The British government was less directive in comparison. The withdrawal in 1997 of the possibility for pension funds to claim a refund for the 20 per cent Advance Corporation Tax they paid on funds' share dividends was believed by many to have triggered the massive closure of defined benefit schemes since the late 1990s, but this was not the intention of the reform, and even after its passage British corporate actors still had much more room for manoeuvre than their Dutch and Swiss counterparts (Bridgen and Meyer 2005). Therefore in Britain retrenchment in occupational schemes has occurred to a significantly greater extent than elsewhere as the result of the decision of large employers to close their more generous schemes to new members. However employer decisions play some role in the Swiss case as well. Businesses have increasingly reduced their contributions to second pillar schemes to the minimum level prescribed by the state, the Obligatorium.

In summary changes to the public pillar in the veteran countries have been less far-reaching during the same time period. The universal, highly redistributive and therefore socially inclusive public schemes continue to play a crucial role for poverty prevention in the Netherlands and in Switzerland; the Swiss level remains slightly below the old age social assistance line, but this is very high in comparative terms. In Britain, the public pillar has remained sensitive to various types of social risks, and redistributive for citizens on low income, yet entitlements for many continue to be below the poverty line. In all three countries incentives exist to induce voluntary third pillar savings. However with the exception of Swiss small business entrepreneurs, our risk biographies are unlikely to make such savings. For the three veterans we conclude that 'passive privatization' has taken the shape of second pillar retrenchment, which was not compensated for by increased individual saving.

Three Patterns of Collective Provision

Overall the country studies show three patterns of collective provision. The first is evident in the Netherlands and Switzerland and consists of an inclusive first pillar and a compulsory second pillar. In the Netherlands, a residency-based first pillar protects against all social risks by guaranteeing a flat rate pension at the poverty threshold; this is supplemented by a quasi-compulsory second pillar with broad coverage which is also sensitive to risks such as part-time work or divorce.

The Swiss system is also based on a universal, redistributive and risk-sensitive first pillar, albeit one that does not aim to guarantee pensions above the poverty threshold. Second pillar coverage is far-reaching, compulsory and sensitive to some risks.

The second configuration is characteristic for Germany and Britain. Here we find a risk-sensitive first pillar, not unlike the Swiss, which acknowledges care responsibilities in particular, but which does not have a poverty threshold. This is complemented by a second pillar system based on voluntarism; coverage is patchy, but particularly good in the public sector.

Finally, in Italy and Poland the first pillars are largely insensitive towards social risks, and instead apply actuarial equivalence and bank on economic prosperity. As in Germany and Britain, second pillars are based on voluntarism, and coverage is weak but growing in Italy and infinitesimal in Poland.

PENSION SYSTEM DESIGN AND SOCIAL INCLUSION: A BROAD OVERVIEW

What is the relationship between the patterns summarized above and pension outcomes? Before we go into more detail a broad overview is given below.

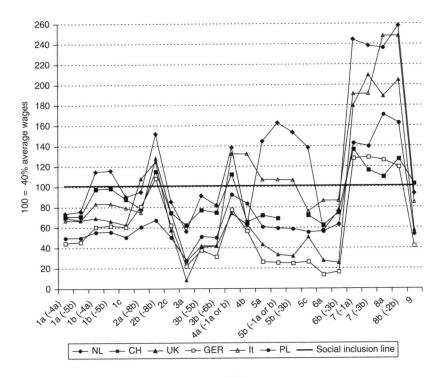

Note: Data for the Swiss bio 5b-3b is not available.

Figure 8.1 Projected pension levels from first and second pillar of all individuals as percentage of social inclusion line, 2050

Figure 8.1 shows all projected pensions for all individuals from first and second pillars for Britain, the Netherlands, Switzerland and Germany and for the first pillars only for Italy and Poland. The data are expressed as percentage of the social inclusion line and therefore illustrate who is likely to be vulnerable and who is not.

Overall results are not encouraging. Should the pensions systems currently operating in the six countries covered in this study remain unchanged, the results suggest that vulnerable citizens who started work in 2003 are at serious risk of social exclusion when they retire in 2050. In all countries except the Netherlands the majority of our 24 hypothetical individuals fail to surpass the national social inclusion threshold when they become pensioners. It must also be remembered in considering these figures that the pension income simulated for each individual is likely to represent the maximum income they will achieve during their retirement relative to the social inclusion threshold. This is because the income our biographies receive on the day of their retirement is likely to lose value thereafter because, while it is generally indexed to prices, the social inclusion threshold is linked to average wages. Thus those of our individuals who marginally surpass the poverty and/or social inclusion thresholds at retirement age are likely to sink below later in their life.

As we argued in the introduction, few studies have assessed the distributive consequences of current pension regimes, while governments have presented reforms as consistent with social inclusion objectives. Our results throw considerable doubt on the legitimacy of these claims. The simulations suggest that the focus in recent reforms on fiscal sustainability has occurred at the expense of the protective potential of the pensions systems, creating significant risks of greater social exclusion in retirement in the future than has been experienced in recent years. Even when reasonably optimistic assumptions are made about the coverage of occupational provision, rates of return for defined contribution occupational pensions and pension-sharing after divorce, the potential of non-state provision, particularly for less-advantaged individuals, has significant limitations. Non-state provision will have to develop much more than it has so far if it is indeed to play the role governments want it to play.

Pension System Design and Social Inclusion: A More Detailed Picture

On the basis of these broad results, it might be concluded that the privatization of pensions systems is simply inconsistent with the objective of a socially inclusive retirement for all citizens with incomes above the social inclusion line during their working life. However such a general conclusion is not satisfactory because, firstly, there are significant differences in overall system generosity between countries. Secondly in all countries excluding Poland some of our risks biographies achieve a pension income above the social inclusion threshold. These better-performing individuals experience significant social risks and are not always the best paid of our group; they show that in certain circumstances non-state provision can offer some vulnerable individuals a pension income above the social inclusion threshold. Thirdly the individual results shown in Figure 8.1 do not include private savings; the assessment of three pillar regimes is therefore incomplete. Finally the figure says nothing about the potential of marriage to protect individuals against exclusion.

Against this background the following sections will assess the performance of our country regimes in a more disaggregated way. We will take three steps. In the first the focus will be on collective provision for individuals only, that is on the first and second pillars. Our evaluation of the relative

Table 8.1   Comparative country performance in relation to social inclusion

	Number of individuals above social inclusion	Median pension as % of social inclusion	Median first pillar as % of social inclusion	Median second pillar as % of social inclusion
NL	12	104	48	47
CH	7	78	63	23
UK	6	62	27	29
GER	5	51	45	3
IT	9	86	86	0
POL	4	57	51	0

Note: Social inclusion line=40% average wages.

Table 8.2   Comparative country performance in relation to social inclusion by gender

	Lower paid men above the social inclusion line	Male median pension as a % of social inclusion line	Women above the social inclusion line	Female median pension as a % of social inclusion line
NL	5	139	3	90
CH	1	73	1	77
UK	0	50	2	66
GER	0	26	1	60
IT	4	106	1	61
POL	0	60	0	50

Note: Social inclusion line = 40% average wages; Male biographies exclude bio 8.

performance of individuals in this part is based on Figure 8.1. In addition to gauge comparative generosity of the overall regimes we counted for all countries the number of all individuals and of all men and women above the social inclusion line; moreover we calculated the median pension in relation to the social inclusion threshold for the respective national groups and for their males and females (Tables 8.1, 8.2).[2] To assess levels of inequality between individuals we also calculated the range of outcomes for our biographies (Table 8.3). In a second step we assess median savings rates necessary in each country to surpass the inclusion thresholds (Table 8.4), and in a third we evaluate the possible role of marriage for the protection

Table 8.3   Comparative range of pension outcomes for individuals

	Range
IT	222
UK	201
NL	182
POL	143
GER	115
CH	74

Note: Range = highest pension as % of social inclusion minus lowest pension as % of social inclusion.

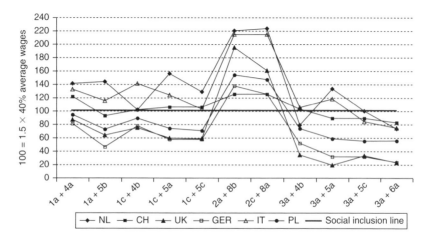

Note: For Italy and Poland only the first pillar is included.

Figure 8.2   Projected pension levels from first and second pillar of all couples as percentage of social inclusion line

of individuals, by comparing the pension income of all couples with the inclusion line for couples in each country (Figure 8.2).

Three Patterns of Collective Provision and Social Inclusion of Individuals

Inclusive first, compulsory second pillar: the Netherlands and Switzerland
The best-performing country is the Netherlands. Here 12 individuals receive pensions above the social inclusion threshold and another three are within ten percentage points of it. The Dutch median pension for all of our

individuals lies above the social inclusion line, and it is 18 percentage points higher than the next-best performer, Italy (Table 8.1). In addition the Netherlands also comes first in terms of the number of females who surpass the social inclusion line: three women achieve pensions above this level and another two are within 10 per cent. Among the individuals who have pensions above the social inclusion line some experience a range of social risks, and eight have lifetime wages below the national average (Figure 8.1). This is true, for example, for the divorced mother and part-time retail worker who interrupts her employment to care and retires early (bio 1b) and earns only 47 per cent of the average during her lifetime, least in this group (Table 1.1, Chapter 1). Members of this group also represent a variety of sectors and types of employment. Even so, there are limits to the inclusiveness of the Dutch system. Below a certain level of wages, inclusiveness declines, and employment sector can also affect pension outcome in a negative way. Thus of the 12 individuals with lifetime earnings below about 45 per cent of the average, ten do not achieve a pension above the social inclusion threshold. The other two individuals (bio 6a, b) who fail to exceed the social inclusion threshold are self-employed, a group that is less well protected by second pillar provision. This problem would similarly affect those individuals who fall through the 'white gaps' in the Dutch second pillar.

Overall, however, the public–private mix evident in the Netherlands is clearly the most successful with regard to social inclusion of our countries. The risk sensitivity and scope of both pillars, the second being regulated by the state and negotiated between the social partners as part of broader corporatist arrangements, has guaranteed high-quality pensions and protected citizens from unilateral interventions by employers and/or the state. In this regard the findings fully bear out the characterization of the Dutch welfare state as a social democratic regime (Goodin et al. 1999).

As suggested above, the Swiss pension system is similar to the Dutch in many ways: a redistributive and risk-sensitive first pillar which however does not always guarantee pensions above the comparatively high poverty threshold, and a compulsory second pillar sensitive to some risks. Given these similarities, one might expect similar outcomes. This expectation is partly borne out: seven individuals achieve pensions above the social inclusion line and another two are within 3 per cent, and the overall median pension in relation to the social inclusion line is the third-highest of the six countries (Table 8.1). As in the Netherlands, individuals who experience a range of social risks including low pay and detachment from the labour market are included among the better-performing workers and women are generally well served: while only one (bio 2b) is above the social inclusion threshold, the two individuals within 3 per cent of this level are both women (bio 1b and 4a, 1b and 5b), and the median pension level for women at 77 per cent of the social inclusion threshold is the best of our six countries (Table 8.2). Women benefit, as they do in the Netherlands, from an inclusive first pillar, and are also protected by the Swiss contribution-sharing mechanism.[3]

Nevertheless the Swiss system is clearly not quite as successful as the Dutch: fewer individuals surpass the social inclusion threshold and the overall median pension is lower. The reason for this difference is a lower second pillar. Indeed the Swiss first pillar performs better than the Dutch; it provides our individuals with a median pension of 63 per cent of the social inclusion line, compared to only 48 per cent in the Netherlands (Table 8.1). In contrast the Swiss second pillar is significantly less generous than its Dutch equivalent. This is partially a product of Bertozzi and Bonoli's decision (see Chapter 4) to use the state-set minimum standard, the Obligatorium, as the basis for their simulations. However this decision was taken in light of the clear retrenching trend evident in the occupational sphere in Switzerland. This trend reveals an important difference between the public–private mix in the two countries. In Switzerland, the state and employers have had more latitude than in the Netherlands to curtail the level of provision in the second pillar in line with concerns about financial sustainability. Thus while non-state provision in both countries takes place in a collective context with the state acting as regulator and promoter of occupational provision, the Swiss system is not entrenched within broader corporatist arrangements, making it easier for Swiss businesses to drop pension levels. However, the up-side of this situation is that levels of inequality are lower among our Swiss low-paid biographies. The range of pension outcomes among our risk biographies is significantly lower in Switzerland than in the Netherlands (Table 8.3).

Risk-sensitive first, patchy voluntarist second pillar: Britain and Germany

State pensions in Britain and Germany are meant to provide the foundation for a multi-pillar system and both have largely voluntary second pillars, with the state's role confined to fiscal encouragement and financial regulation. Consequently coverage is patchy in both countries. The German first pillar remains significantly more generous than the universal state system in the United Kingdom, while British occupational provision is much more developed, although there are definite indications that the German second pillar is beginning to grow.

How does the more voluntary, less collective context in these countries affect pension outcomes for our risk biographies? First, it is clear that neither country performs particularly well. In Britain only two of our lower-paid individuals, variants of the mother and qualified part-time worker (bio 2), achieve a pension above the social inclusion threshold, with no other individuals within 26 percentage points of this line (Figure 8.1). Overall

Britain has only the fourth-highest median pension for our individuals (Table 8.1). In Germany, the results are even worse: only one of the lower-paid individuals (bio 2b) surpasses the social inclusion threshold and no one else is even within 20 percentage points. In fact, the German median pension for our individuals is the lowest of our six countries. The comparative result for women is slightly better. Britain produces the third-highest female median pension and Germany the fifth-highest.

The main reason for these results is slightly different in the two countries. In Britain, the first pillar is the biggest problem: it provides on average the lowest amount by far to our risk biographies in relation to the social inclusion threshold (Table 8.1). In Germany, in contrast, the first pillar is only slightly less generous overall than the highly inclusive Dutch first pillar, and actually provides a higher pension in relation to the social inclusion line to some of the lower-paid individuals (bio 1c, 2a, 4a, b, 9. Figure 3.1, Chapter 3 and Figure 5.1, Chapter 5). The main problem in Germany is the second pillar, which in relation to the social inclusion threshold contributes an income of only 5 per cent or less to 17 of the risk biographies (Figure 5.1, Chapter 5). In Britain, in contrast, even most of the lower-paid individuals receive occupational provision equivalent to at least 23 per cent of the social inclusion threshold (Figure 2.1, Chapter 2).

While for Britain these findings are entirely in line with expectations of the liberal welfare regime, they question whether it is still appropriate to count the German pension system among the constitutive elements of the conservative welfare state (Esping-Andersen 1990). German pensions remain earnings-related but because of the cuts in the first pillar and the weakness of the second, status preservation above the inclusion line is threatened even for employees with lifelong work histories. Thus with regard to pensions, Germany has moved closer to the liberal model.

Despite these generally disappointing results in Britain and Germany, some of our individuals do reasonably well. It is a typical feature of systems where occupational provision is voluntary that some of the lower-paid are privileged with regard to occupational provision because of their sector of employment, or their employer.

To illustrate this feature let us focus first on the lower-paid woman who exceeds the social inclusion threshold in both countries – the divorced variant of the mother and part-time worker who is employed in the welfare sector (bio 2b). She faces a number of risks throughout her life including periods of labour market detachment and part-time work (Table 1.1, Chapter 1). Yet despite these risks, her income in retirement is higher in both countries than that of some other biographies who earn more than she does. The reason is that she receives a comparatively generous public sector pension. Public sector membership thus helps boost women's pensions in particular, given that in both Britain and Germany female employment is disproportionately located in this area.

Significant differences of outcome are not just confined to the sectoral level – they can also take place within sectors, where the quality of pension schemes can vary by employer. Our unqualified worker in the car industry (bio 4a) is an illustration. In Britain this individual's final pension does not surpass the social inclusion threshold but he is nevertheless one of the better performers. His employment at Rover and Vauxhall – typical large, Fordist companies with an interest in retaining workers – gives him an advantage over those 40 per cent of workers in the car industry who, despite identical employment careers, work for firms which do not engage in occupational welfare and who therefore end up with a much lower pension (Table 2.2, Chapter 2).

In Germany this situation is less marked at present. Occupational provision is less developed and as a result our unqualified male worker is not as fortunate: his Volkswagen pension adds to his state provision a supplement which is only equivalent to 5 per cent of the national social inclusion threshold (Table 5.1, Chapter 5). However Germany's decision to adopt a largely voluntary attitude to the occupational sector does run the risk of creating the same type of inter-sector and intra-sector variability evident in Britain. This is a clear feature of public–private mixes based on the type of approach adopted in both countries. Where it is most developed it can create high levels of inequality, as is illustrated by the fact that Britain has the second-highest range of outcomes of our six countries (Table 8.3).

To summarize while in Britain and Germany some lower-paid citizens have a pension income above the social inclusion line because of non-state provision, this is by no means true for all. Moreover the criteria which determine who benefits and who does not among this group are largely arbitrary (Meyer and Bridgen forthcoming 2008). The implications of this situation for those that lose out are currently worse in Britain than Germany given the lower level of state provision. However only greater collective action in both countries, similar to that undertaken in the Netherlands or Switzerland, can address this variation, although as Bannink and De Vroom show in Chapter 3, some degree of arbitrariness and inequality continues in the Netherlands, as the necessary outcome of the flexibility the social partners have to negotiate scheme details.

Strictly income-related first, patchy voluntarist second pillar: Italy and Poland

In contrast to the other four countries in this study, in Italy and Poland occupational pension providers remain very much junior partners in the public–private mix. State provision has been significantly retrenched in both countries, yet the state's role remains substantial. In Italy the median first pillar pension in relation to the inclusion line for our biographies is substantially greater than anywhere else and it is third-highest in Poland (Table 8.1). Despite strong efforts in Italy to extend occupational provision and the involvement in Poland of non-state actors in delivering the new funded part of the first pillar, the development of a multi-pillar system still seems some way off. Overall then, as was suggested above, privatization has been passive, involving a reduction and individualization of the still dominant first pillar.

These individualized state systems are in theory capable of providing good-sized pensions to individuals at risk. Thus in Italy five of our lower-paid biographies receive pensions above the social inclusion threshold (bio 2b, 4a, b, 5a, b) and the median pension for our individuals, at 86 per cent of the social inclusion threshold, is the second-best of the six countries (Table 8.1). The results for Poland are not as good: indeed it is the only one of our countries where no lower-paid individuals surpass the social inclusion line. However two (bio 4a, b) receive pensions within 17 per cent of this threshold, only one remains below the social assistance line, and overall the Polish system performs better for our risk biographies than the German system (Figure 7.1, Chapter 7).

Given the individualized nature of the new regimes in Italy and Poland the dominant determinant of which individuals do well is lifetime income, and this advantages men (Table 8.2). Thus in Italy, of the five lower-paid individuals who surpass the social inclusion threshold, four are male and all have lifetime incomes above half the national average. The only woman who crosses this line is a variant of the welfare worker and mother (bio 2b) who is the best paid among our females. Overall the gap between the male median pension and the female median pension in Italy is the greatest of all six countries (Table 8.2). This is also the reason why the range of pension outcomes in Italy is the highest of our six countries (Table 8.3). This result might be somewhat misleading given the large number of male atypical workers in Italy whose biographies in terms of labour market detachment and pension contribution rates are more consistent with those of our individuals who fare less well. Thus the high levels of gender inequality shown by our results also indicate high levels of inequality between standard and atypical workers. In Poland there is also a disparity between the pensions of men and women, a situation which is exacerbated by the earlier female retirement age but which is likely to become less stark given the EU's 2006 directive imposing equalised pension ages. No Polish female gets within even 30 per cent of the social inclusion threshold, while some lower-paid males come much closer (bio 4a, b) (Figure 8.1).

The only real disruption to this strict equivalence between earnings and pensions in both countries is self-employment, which reduces the pension of some of the higher-paid male biographies.

The gender disparities in Italy and Poland also lead to significant differences in the comparative performance of the two systems for men and women. Thus, while the Italian males receive the second highest median pension across our sample, the Italian women receive the fourth highest. Similarly while Polish men receive the fourth highest median pension, Polish women receive the lowest. In relation to our assessment of different forms of public–private mix these results suggest that particularly for women an individualized state pillar in a system lacking additional provision can be more problematic than a system with a much smaller first pillar, but greater access to good second pillar schemes. For example British women do better overall than the Italian women, despite the fact that first pillar provision is much lower, because some have access to generous second pillar pensions as employees of public sector organizations.

The Impact of Private Savings on Pension Income

Personal savings schemes are part of multi-pillar systems and the country chapters have shown that current policymakers in all countries have strongly favoured them as a potential means for covering some of the gaps in first and second pillar provision. In the following we will consider the extent to which private saving does indeed provide the means for filling the gaps identified above in the various types of public–private pension system.

Our results give few reasons to be optimistic. First we have seen that despite significant efforts in each country to encourage greater personal private saving, there is little indication that these have been successful, particularly with regard to those on incomes below the national average. Take-up has been universally poor amongst this group. However even if it were greater, the level of savings our simulations suggest would be required by many vulnerable citizens to lift them above the social inclusion threshold seems at best to be unlikely. For those with levels of pay below the social inclusion line, like our married carer and informal worker (bio 3), any savings are unfeasible. For other biographies the situation varies across the six countries. As one would expect, required savings rates are highest in Poland, Germany and Britain where collective provision is smaller, and lower in Switzerland, Italy and the Netherlands. By the same logic women in all countries but Germany have to save more than men (Table 8.4).

Therefore the levels of savings required to reach the social inclusion line seem most feasible, particularly for men, in our least-individualized countries. Where private saving is most required because collective provision is

Table 8.4   *Median required saving rates and current tax rates*

	Savings rates			Tax rates*
	All	Women	Men	
CH	4	7	3	27
NL	2	4	0	50
UK	8	10	8	33
GER	10	10	10	51
IT	4	8	0	37
POL	16	17	7	35

Notes:
Assumptions: See Appendix 1.2, Chapter 1.
* Average personal income tax and social security contribution rates for a single person without dependant at 67% of the average wage.
OECD Tax Database, 2006.

low it seems least likely to occur, certainly at the levels necessary for it to be successful as a means of reducing social exclusion.

A counter-argument to this conclusion might be that private saving is more feasible in the less-collective countries because lower levels of compulsory provision mean lower pension contributions. Certainly individual pension contributions are in general significantly lower in Britain, Germany and Poland than they are in the Netherlands and Switzerland (Table 8.4), although Italian rates are more comparable due to comparatively high employer contributions. Yet because of the broader tax environment in each country there are good reasons to doubt whether this situation makes private saving more likely in our more individualized countries. In one of the more individualized countries – Germany – overall individual tax rates of 51 per cent for employed workers on 67 per cent of average earnings would seem to make any additional saving unlikely for those on lower levels of pay let alone savings at the levels indicated by our simulations. But even in Britain and Poland where tax rates are lower, savings at the levels indicated by our simulations would mean that overall our lower-paid employed individuals would be losing on a regular basis about half or more of their gross income. This reduction in individuals' disposable income might be possible if it occurs compulsorily as part of the welfare system, but it is highly improbable to take place on a voluntary basis (Rowlingson 2002). For the same reason, it is doubtful that many of those mainly female individuals who are required to save voluntarily in our more collective countries will do so. In the Netherlands in particular the scope for third pillar savings seems extremely limited, given its tax rate for employed individuals of 50 per cent. Swiss taxation is lower, which perhaps explains why this country has seen the most promising third pillar developments of our six case-studies. For our self-employed individuals saving might be more feasible where it is required, because their pay is higher. However as our country studies have shown, there is in fact little indication that most self-employed workers save at all, let alone at the levels indicated as necessary by our simulations.

Patterns of Collective Provision and Social Inclusion of Couples

So far no allowance has been made for marriage. In many post-war pension systems marriage to a male breadwinner was regarded by policymakers as a standard form of protection for women, as a compensation for insufficient independent pension rights (for example Lewis 1992; Lewis and Ostner 1994). However an individualization of social rights has taken place in European countries, and explicit strong breadwinner models have been changed as a consequence (for example Lewis 2001; Meyer and Pfau-Effinger 2006). This trend was also observed in our country chapters. However modernization notwithstanding, many public pension systems assume that married couples share their resources and therefore treat them differently from individuals. Couples have a joint first pillar account in Poland, and they receive a joint pension in the Netherlands and Switzerland, which is lower than the double of an individual's pension. British spouses without independent pension rights are entitled to derived rights through their partners. In Germany and Italy a survivor's pension exists, but there are no other pension rights within marriage. In addition of course, marriage breakdown often leads to a redistribution of resources. On the basis of such legislation, a realistic assessment of pension entitlements must include marriage. In addition many people live as couples and indeed pool their resources.

Our following account of the comparative performance of couples therefore follows policymakers' assumption that married partners share their pensions. This assumption means overall outcomes may be based on economic dependency of one partner, normally the woman, on the other.

Below we will first consider whether the general performance of our systems is better when viewed on the basis of couples rather than individuals. We will then compare the pattern of support within couples to assess the extent to which men are playing a breadwinner role in relation to women. Throughout the course of this analysis we will relate our results to the differences outlined above in the public–private pension mix in the six countries.

Comparing Figure 8.1 and Table 8.5 we can see very little difference in the performance of couples in relation to individuals. The Netherlands is

Table 8.5   Comparative country performance of couples

	Median pension for all couples as a % of social inclusion	Number of couples below social inclusion	Women lifted above social exclusion threshold by marriage	Men lifted above social exclusion threshold by marriage
NL	133	2	7	0
CH	102	4	7	3
UK	60	11	1	0
GER	57	11	2	0
IT	115	3	8	0
POL	74	11	2	0

Note: Social inclusion line = 1.5 times the individuals' social inclusion line i.e. 40% average wages.

again the most successful, lifting nine out of 11 couples above the social inclusion line. It also provides the largest median pension for couples (Table 8.5). Likewise Germany remains the worst performer, with all but two couples receiving an income below the social inclusion line on retirement and a median pension for our couples, which is lower than in the other five countries.

However this ranking masks the fact that in all systems at least one individual is lifted above the household social inclusion line as a consequence of marriage. Marriage has the strongest effect in Switzerland, Italy and the Netherlands.[4] Thus in Switzerland ten of those who as individuals would receive a pension income below the social inclusion line are lifted above it through marriage. In Italy this is the case for eight individuals, in the Netherlands there are seven. In contrast, the same is only true for two biographies in Germany and Poland and for one in Britain.

Obviously the larger the inequalities within marriage, the more the spouse with the lower income can benefit. Strongest disparities are evident in Italy, where those individuals who are lifted above the household social inclusion line as part of a couple were on average 38 per cent below the social inclusion threshold as individuals. In Switzerland they were 26 per cent below and in the Netherlands 21 per cent.[5]

The smaller difference in the Dutch and Swiss cases is explained by the good-sized independent pension income that both systems provide even to those individuals below the social inclusion line. In Italy these same individuals are more dependent on their spouse, and dependence is highly gendered. The man's contribution to the household's pension is higher than the woman's for all 11 Italian couples and all individuals who are lifted out of social exclusion as part of a couple are women (Figure 6.3, Chapter 6). In the Netherlands men's pensions also provide the bulk of the income in the large majority of marriages, but here the relative contribution of women is greater (Figure 3.4, Chapter 3). In Switzerland, the pensions of women are greater in four couples and the average relative contribution by gender is close to parity (Figure 4.2, Chapter 4). Viewed in the context of the three forms of public–private pension mix discussed above, the Italian example shows that for women in particular passive privatization in the form of individualized first pillar provision leads to increased dependence on their spouses. A similar situation is evident in Poland, although to a lesser extent. Here too the man's pension contributes more to the joint income than the woman's, but because of the lower overall level of provision, only two women are pulled above the household social inclusion line by their partners as a result. In the Netherlands and Switzerland, in contrast, women's independence is greater, notwithstanding the greater role for non-state provision, because of the highly inclusive first pillar and the wide coverage of the second.

In Britain and Germany, a couple's effect is less evident. Generally speaking, if a biography's pension is below social inclusion in these two countries, it is also below social inclusion as one part of a couple. Nevertheless the situation in Britain and Germany is unusual in the six countries because overall women's pensions play a greater relative role. They are dominant in four couples (bios 1a and 5b, 1c and 4b, 1c and 5a, 1c and 5c), more than in all of the other countries other than Switzerland. Moreover, women's pensions can make a far greater contribution to the couple's income than anywhere else. For example in Switzerland the lowest contribution made by a man to a couple's joint income equates to 43 per cent of the total pension (Figure 4.2, Chapter 4). In Britain the lowest male pension is 24 per cent (Figure 2.2, Chapter 2). In Germany the male con-tribution in four couples is below 40 per cent of the total pension (Figure 5.2, Chapter 5).

This situation is a product of the low levels of state provision in these countries for self-employed workers and in Britain of the variation produced by a voluntarist second pillar. Overall because men's pensions are compara-tively low, particularly when second pillar provision is unavailable, they are less able to play the type of breadwinner role they perform elsewhere.

Divorce

The important role marriage continues to play in protecting otherwise vul-nerable citizens in most of our countries gives added significance to the risk of divorce. As has been seen, governments have recognized this risk with

Table 8.6   Comparative household pension of mother and unqualified part-time worker as percentage of social inclusion by marital status and partner

	Divorced from the unqualified male worker (bio 1b and 4a)	Divorced from the intermittent worker (bio 1b and 5b)	Married to the unqualified male worker (bio1c and 4b)	Married to the intermittent worker (bio 1c and 5a)	Married to the disabled intermittent worker (bio 1c and 5c)
CH	97	98	102	106	106
NL	114	116	102	156	106
UK	69	66	75	60	59
GER	60	61	78	57	57
POL	55	56	89	74	70

Notes:
Household pension = individual pension for divorced variant and total pension of couple for married variant.
    Social inclusion = 40% average wages for divorced variants and 60% of average wages for married variants.

new legislation to protect those disadvantaged by a marriage break-up in all six countries except Italy. Our results suggest that where these are in place, they can protect some women if we make optimistic assumptions about the take-up of new pension-sharing mechanisms, but not all. The best illustration is a comparison of two variants of our mother and unqualified part-time worker (bio 1b, c), whose biographies differ only to the extent that while one (bio 1b) divorces, the other (bio 1c) does not (Figure 8.1).

To assess the success of the divorce arrangements we compared the position of the divorced variant in relation to the inclusion line for individuals with that of the married variant's household pension in relation to that line for couples. On that basis, how does pension-splitting compare with marriage as a means of protection against social exclusion? The answer is, not very well (Table 8.6). Divorce only has no real negative impact in the Netherlands where both variants are above the social inclusion line.

In contrast, in Switzerland her access to her spouse's pension and the reduced costs of living in a couple protect her more successfully than pension-sharing after divorce. As a consequence she is only above the social inclusion threshold as a married woman (with bio 4b, 5a, c).

In Britain, Germany and Poland, both married women and divorcees are below the inclusion line, but most of the former are better off in relation to this line than the latter. In the few cases where divorcees do better, the low level of pensions for the self-employed is responsible. Because her partner's benefit in Britain and Germany is so low, she is worse off in relation to the (higher) inclusion line for couples than with a divorcee's pension in relation to the (lower) inclusion line for individuals.

Thus, overall, pension-sharing after divorce is far less successful than marriage in compensating women for their absence from the labour market due to caring. Given that generally the trend for divorce rates in our six countries is upwards (see Table 1.4, Chapter 1), this situation emphasizes the importance for women of more individualized protective arrangements in the first pillar. The residency-based first pillar pension in the Netherlands is a good example of such protection and an important reason why the Dutch divorced biographies do comparatively well.

SUMMARY: FEATURES OF SOCIALLY INCLUSIVE PENSION SYSTEMS

Above we have shown that the focus in recent reforms on fiscal sustainability involving the passive privatization and/or individualization of existing pension systems has occurred at the expense of the protective potential of these systems, increasing risks of social exclusion in the future. However the chapter also demonstrated that in certain circumstances a role for non-state provision is consistent with social protection: it is possible to identify design features of multi-pillar pension systems that can secure retirement incomes above the social inclusion threshold. First a non-means-tested, inclusive public pillar which provides a sound base, especially for citizens at risk, is indispensable. This is an important part of the regime in the Netherlands and Switzerland, where it guarantees a non-stigmatized minimum level of income for those who inevitably fall through the gaps in non-state provision. This role is also played to some extent by the first pillars of Italy and Germany. Of these the German first pillar is the most redistributive and inclusive, but neither currently reaches the standard set in the Netherlands and Switzerland.

However given that protection through the state alone is no longer a public policy aim anywhere, to achieve a more inclusive system the public pillar needs to be complemented by second pillar schemes with broad coverage. Our findings suggest that this can only be ensured through state compulsion or social partner enforcement or both, as evident in the Netherlands and Switzerland. We put much greater weight on the second pillar because our results show that personal savings schemes have done little in all countries to protect vulnerable citizens. It is neither reasonable nor realistic to ask lower-paid individuals to fill by themselves the gaps left by the decline of collective provision.

This is not to say that more voluntary patterns of collective provision cannot provide good pensions to vulnerable individuals. Britain's occupational sector leads to comparatively high pensions for some. However the system is unequal, it leaves many unprotected and outcomes are arbitrary to some extent. In Germany social partners have taken the firmest steps towards developing a multi-pillar regime in the newcomer group, but similar features to the British system are emerging and the dominant effect so far has been a 'privatization of risks'. Italy has produced fairly good overall results, too, but they are generated by the public pillar exclusively and because of their strict earnings-related nature they favour established male workers and promote the male breadwinner model. In a similar vein, the Polish public pension grants higher benefits than the German, but men profit more than women. Moreover, Polish second and third pillars have hardly expanded; the existing public incentives seem to be ineffective.

Against this background the final discussion will focus on two questions. First, what is the likelihood of more encompassing, collective second pillar provision emerging in the four countries where they are lacking so far? Secondly, given that in all countries the majority of our risk biographies remain below the social inclusion line, what chance is there on the basis of the national reform debates that these looming problems are going to be addressed?

Prospects for Increased Collective Provision in the Voluntarist Countries

Britain, Germany, Italy and Poland have in common their essentially voluntarist framework for non-state provision. Under these conditions it is unlikely that regimes will develop whose inclusiveness is comparable to the Netherlands or Switzerland because there is no homogeneous interest of non-state actors to initiate such provision voluntarily. The literature on occupational pensions has shown that substantial collective provision on a voluntary basis rests on the support of large employers (see Chapter 1). For reasons of human resource management they have an interest in pensions and their size ensures the resources to realize it. The state can create incentives for business to offer occupational welfare, or through regulation increase their costs. Likewise trade unions can have a role in promoting occupational pensions. Yet even if business interest in occupational welfare is supported in different ways, employers will take a range of positions with regard to occupational welfare, depending on sector, macroeconomic conditions and individual performance of the company. For small employers occupational welfare generally appears as costly and they tend to resist state intervention. Heterogeneity and selectivism are therefore inherent traces of voluntarism. This is confirmed by our case-studies. We have seen larger employers act as social policy players in all our voluntarist countries but Poland.

In Britain their engagement has led to occupational coverage for about half of private and 80 per cent of public sector workers, also bringing with it inequality in provision and arbitrariness in outcome. Moreover, in recent years employers have retrenched collective provision, giving much the same reason as public policymakers: the need to ensure financial sustainability.

In Germany the social partners have used the incentives introduced by the state to develop new occupational schemes, and as Riedmüller and Willert show in Chapter 5, there is still much potential for further growth, yet already inequalities are emerging across sectors.

The increase in Italian occupational welfare, where it does take place, is based on similar motives by large employers and trade unions, but, as Raitano argues in Chapter 6, it is stifled by high social insurance contributions towards the first pillar, and a reluctance of individual workers. However the policy that will auto-enrol employees for occupational pensions from 2008, at the expense of contributions to the long-established occupational savings scheme the TFR, may support future second pillar expansion, even though Raitano is sceptical whether the Italians will relinquish the current options the TFR offers them (see also Ferrera 2006). Poland is the only country in our group where employers have so far not shown any interest in developing independent schemes at all. Benio and Ratajczak-Tuchołka argue in Chapter 7 that businesses have no recruitment and retention problems under current economic conditions, and therefore are not inclined to invest in additional occupational welfare.

With regard to small employers, they indeed are not in favour of occupational pensions. In fact their resistance against compulsion has borne fruit in all of our countries, not only in the second pillar but also the first. The self-employed are exempted from social insurance payments in Germany and their contributions are lower in Italy and Poland; in Switzerland and the Netherlands they do not have to participate in the second pillar; and in Britain they are excluded from the State Second Pension. Our findings suggest that their role as officially accepted risk-takers leaves them largely unprotected, which is particularly problematic in Italy and Poland where a substantial share of the population is self-employed. We therefore conclude that voluntarism has still some way to go in our newcomer countries, but there is no empirical evidence and no theoretical reason to expect that coverage will become as broad and substantial as it is in Switzerland or the Netherlands, unless more compulsion is introduced. Against this background, what are the chances of the voluntarist regimes becoming more compulsory? Currently there is no reason to expect such a development in Poland. In Germany the trade unions would like to instate auto-enrolment in occupational schemes, but employers and insurers oppose this plan and there are no signs that labour will prevail.

In contrast in Britain and Italy developments towards stricter regulations can be observed, albeit for different reasons. British voluntarism could indeed be entering a more regulated phase. We argued in Chapter 2 that in 2007 a broad societal spectrum, including employers, insurers and the Conservative Party, favours an increase in the universal state provision, which amounts to an important policy change in the United Kingdom. In addition a pension reform now seems likely that will introduce auto-enrolment in pension schemes for workers not sufficiently covered otherwise, including compulsory employer contributions. There may be general lessons to be drawn from this development about the limits of voluntarism. The turn now likely in Britain towards employer compulsion reveals a dilemma for policymakers that is not uniquely British. Retrenchment in collective provision – no matter whether in the first or second pillar – can easily lead to an increase in dependency on means-tested benefits for those on lower incomes and therefore obstruct the development of further private provision. Citizens are less inclined to save privately, in second or third pillar schemes, if they fear that their savings might not secure a pension above means-tested assistance and could therefore have been in vain. This puts governments in a quandary: if they want to encourage citizens to save, they need to curb the role of means-tested pensions for retirement income and this can only be done through re-collectivization, by either raising the level of the first pillar or increasing the scope of the second. In Britain we see something of both. Bertozzi and Bonoli discuss a similar problem for Switzerland in Chapter 4, where savings incentives are diminishing due to second pillar retrenchment and a high level of means-tested benefits for older people. They argue that this trend could well undermine the trust Swiss citizens have in the second pillar. Benio and Ratajczak-Tucholka report concerns that the drop in the level of the first pillar will put pressure on social assistance in Poland.

The government most determined in the voluntarist group to introduce tighter regulation in order to ensure broader second pillar coverage has been the Italian one. As Raitano shows, from 2008 the contributions towards the established occupational benefit, the TFR, will be automatically used for occupational pension schemes covered by collective agreements, unless workers opt out. This was possible because Italian governments had the TFR, an existing occupational benefit to which workers and employers already paid contributions, as an institutional advantage over their colleagues in the other voluntarist countries who also wanted to reduce the first and expand the second pillar (Ferrera and Jessoula 2007, p. 443–5). Whereas in the other countries the introduction of auto-enrolment in occupational schemes would generally have involved a sudden increase in expenses for employers, employees and the state, the TFR in Italy provided an ' "institutional gate" for policy change' which some commentators suggest makes probable the establishment of a multi-pillar system in Italy (Ferrera and Jessoula 2007). In Chapter 6 Raitano expresses more scepticism about the medium-term effect of this change and argues that opting out could become the norm, simply because workers value the TFR. Indeed the fairly low transfer of TFR contributions to pension funds so far could be an indicator that government has opened an 'institutional gate', through which unions, employers and workers are reluctant to go because they still have a strong stake in the previous system. Whatever the future will bring, in the Italian case more directive state intervention with regard to the second pillar happened because government had the option to reappropriate existing resources.

Awareness of Poverty Risks in Reform Debates: The Voluntarist Countries

Given that the political current is not likely to bring in compulsory multi-pillar systems in Poland, Germany, Britain and Italy, despite the considerable social risks their systems present for more vulnerable citizens, how are these risks addressed in national debates? The general answer is that this issue is not high up the political agenda in any of our countries. Concern about fiscal sustainability continues to exert a predominant influence in most, and to the extent that the potential plight of future cohorts of pensioners is considered at all, the solutions being proposed are based on the type of approach to private savings our research suggests is inadequate to deal with the scale of the impending problem.

Thus in Germany, which as we illustrated above is facing the highest risk of exclusion in our group, financial sustainability was the main driver behind the landmark reform of 2001, and individual responsibility is now an underlying principle of welfare reform, supported by all the main political parties. As Riedmüller and Willert show there are no plans to improve public pensions and reliance continues to be placed on the largely voluntarist policy framework with regard to the other pillars. German decision-makers are aware of gaps in the system, but do not want to take distinctive steps to address them.

Britain is also faced with high poverty risks. However here the pension situation is more dynamic with consideration of reforms affecting all three pillars. Yet while pensioner poverty has featured strongly in this debate, it is the poverty of today's retired citizens that has had the most impact on policy, through the introduction of the means-tested Pension Credit. This has undoubtedly lifted the income of some of today's pensioners, but as was suggested above this has occurred at the expense of policy coherence in the longer term. Most of the policy proposals currently being debated are designed to address this issue rather than future concerns about rising social exclusion: increasing voluntary private personal saving remains an important goal. British policymakers are still resistant to a more significant increase in state provision, despite facing the most favourable projections for fiscal sustainability of our six countries, and largely as a result, at least a third of pensioners are predicted to be below the social assistance line in 2050 even if current proposals are implemented in full (DWP 2006; Pensions Commission 2005; PPI 2006).

In Italy poverty risks are particularly high for informal workers, part-time employees, many of whom are female carers, and the self-employed; the regime performs fairly well for the higher earners in our group. However Raitano argues that some of these least-protected Italian biographies (bio 3, 5, 6) are more indicative of the system as a whole because they represent the many Italians in atypical and informal employment. This notwithstanding, the ongoing debate about pension reforms is more concerned with the TFR than with the social risks of those more vulnerable workers without access to that benefit. There is growing awareness of the long-term poverty risks of atypical workers but none of the proposed solutions to this problem affecting either the first or second pillar are likely to be implemented. Instead governments are strictly committed to the financial sustainability of the first pillar.

Poverty risks are also high in Poland, especially for women, due to a strictly earnings-related public scheme and the absence of voluntary schemes, but they are generally ignored in the public debate. Benio and Ratajczak-Tuchołka describe how generally, significant political mobilization in favour of proposals to increase the system's sensitivity for social risks is lacking and in its absence, a political establishment dedicated to cost containment has further tightened the public pillar, and gives little support to voluntary occupational and personal savings schemes.

Awareness of Poverty Risks in Reform Debates: The Regulated Countries

As we have shown the prognosis for Switzerland and the Netherlands is less stark. Both offer significantly better protection against poverty risks for our individuals, despite some retrenchment of their second pillars in recent years. This notwithstanding, both countries also have certain shortcomings that leave some biographies exposed to risks of exclusion.

In the Swiss regime fewer of our individuals surpass the social inclusion line than in the Dutch, because its second pillar is less generous and its scope is less broad. As Chapter 4 shows, the trade unions and the Socialist Party recognized the poverty risks of those on lower wages and very low-paid workers, and have been strong promoters of more inclusive second and higher first pillar pensions. Yet their success has been mixed and as Bertozzi and Bonoli argue most other reform options which have the potential to increase the inclusiveness of the system are unlikely to be realized in the medium term. We can therefore say that in 2007 the left in Switzerland has been most aware of and most ready to address the risks to social inclusion of the pension regime, but the centre-right government was not prepared to accede to their proposals. In the Netherlands no policies are being discussed that would move more of our individuals above the social inclusion line than there are currently. A rise in the level of the second pillar or the mitigation of heterogeneous, sector-specific outcomes are not political issues. This is not surprising considering that the government showed significant determination in containing costs, against considerable resistance of the social partners (Anderson 2007). The pressure on the first pillar has also been to make it less generous rather than more so. Yet while no improvements in the system's generosity can be expected, the status quo, particularly of the first pillar, is protected by a strong coalition. Bannink and de Vroom show that the indexing of the public pension to contract wages could mean a gradual decline in the inclusiveness of the first pillar, but that pensioners are currently compensated for this gap by government, and that a typically Dutch constellation of actors, including employers, unions and organizations for the elderly ensures that this support will continue (see also Anderson and Immergut 2007, p. 34–5; Anderson 2007). The Dutch system therefore continues to protect its citizens who in turn continue to protect the system.

RECALLING THE MAIN QUESTION OF THIS BOOK

Overall, then, are private pensions and social inclusion reconcilable? This study suggests that much depends on the type of private pension and the overall regime framework in which they are placed. It has demonstrated that where private occupational pensions form part of an essentially collective system, non-state pension provision need not be generally inconsistent with social inclusion; where the state provides an inclusive and generous first pillar and employers are subject to compulsion the results, even for citizens at most risk, can be good.

The problem with this model as a guide for policymakers is that its existence is likely to be the product of particular historical and institutional circumstances. Historically, its development was founded on the voluntary provision by employers of occupational pensions in socio-economic circumstances in the middle part of the last century which most commentators believe no longer apply: national economies with large Fordist organizations less influenced by shareholder interests, who wanted to retain experienced workers, and a less mobile qualified workforce in which levels of unionization were greater (Sass 1997, 2006; Clark 2006; Clark et al. 2007, pp. 18–20; Whiteside 2006). In today's climate, where cost constraints are driving public and corporate social policy actors, the general odds are against flourishing collective protection of any type. Institutionally, the extension of voluntary provision to all or almost all citizens owed much in the Netherlands to corporatism and in Switzerland to its constitutionally entrenched system of referenda (Anderson and Immergut 2007, pp. 26–7; 34–5; Bonoli 2004).

Thus, while in retrenching their public pillars, the 'newcomers' in our study have all to a greater or lesser extent sought to promote occupational provision as a means of mitigating the consequences of retrenchment, there are severe obstacles in the way of the development of the type of system operating in the Netherlands and Switzerland. Employers are reluctant, unions are divided and unsure whether to focus their attention on defending state provision or encouraging occupational provision, and consequently politicians, as has been seen, are not taking a firm lead. Promising developments are evident in Italy and Germany but in general there seems little reason to be optimistic that occupational provision will grow dramatically where it is not already an entrenched feature of pension systems.

For those who fall through the gaps, the other form of private provision – individual personal saving – is the only possible supplement to state provisions. However, while governments continue to promote these instruments, our study has found little evidence to suggest that they can be relied upon in any major way as a component of a pension system designed to secure outcomes consistent with social inclusion. This means that, for many, state pensions will continue to be their only source of retirement income. However, where we see a trend towards market mimicry in this sector even state protection for the types of individuals included in this study is becoming more unreliable.

NOTES

1. Ferrera and Jessoula (2007) argue that considering the unfavourable conditions for second pillar expansion in Italy the growth has actually been good. However, Raitano's account shows that in relation to those not covered only a small minority have access to such schemes.
2. In the gender-specific tables the middle manager (bio 8) is excluded because this individual on a higher wage was only included in our study to provide a partner for the qualified mother and part-time worker (bio 2) (Chapter 1).

3. The absence of a mechanism similar to the Dutch franchise system means that part-time women are less well protected in Switzerland. However, all of our female biographies earn wages above the threshold for compulsory occupational provision so this does not show up in our simulations.
4. This positive result reflects in part the generally accepted view that household income does not need to increase proportionately with each extra person because of 'economies of scale'. Thus, the couple's social inclusion line is only 1.5 times the individuals' social inclusion line, which automatically increases the relative worth of our married individuals' pensions.
5. The figures are based on the results shown in the figures for individuals and for couples in the respective country chapters.

BIBLIOGRAPHY

Anderson, K.M. (2007), 'The Netherlands: political competition in proportional system', in E.M. Immergut, K.M. Anderson and I. Schulze (eds), *Handbook of West European Pension Politics* (pp. 713–57), Oxford: Oxford University Press.

Anderson, K.M. and Immergut, E.M. (2007), 'Editors' introduction: the dynamics of pension politics', in E.M. Immergut, K.M. Anderson and I. Schulze (eds), *Handbook of West European Pension Politics* (pp. 1–48), Oxford: Oxford University Press.

Bonoli, G. (2004), 'The institutionalisation of the Swiss multipillar pension system', in M. Rein and W. Schmähl (eds), *Rethinking the Welfare State: The Political Economy of Pension Reform* (pp. 102–21), Cheltenham, UK and Northampton, MA, USA: Edward Elgar.

Bonoli, G., George, V. and Taylor Gooby, P. (2000), *European Welfare Futures: Towards a Theory of Retrenchment*, Cambridge: Policy Press.

Bridgen, P. and Meyer, T. (2005), 'When do benevolent capitalists change their mind? Explaining the retrenchment of defined benefit schemes in Britain', *Social Policy and Administration*, **39**(4), 764–85.

Clark, G. (2006), 'The UK occupational pension system in crisis', in H. Pemberton, P. Thane and N. Whiteside (eds), *Britain's Pension Crisis: History and Policy* (pp. 145–68), Oxford: Oxford University Press.

Clark, G., Munnell, A. and Orszag, M. (2007), 'Pensions and retirement income in a global environment', in G. Clark, A. Munnell and M. Orszag (eds), *The Oxford Handbook of Pensions and Retirement Income* (pp. 10–28), Oxford: Oxford University Press.

DWP (2006), 'Security in retirement: towards a new pensions system', London: DWP, available online at http://www.dwp.gov.uk/pensionsreform/pdfs/white_paper_complete.pdf, accessed October 2006.

Esping-Andersen, G. (1990), *The Three Worlds of Welfare Capitalism*, Princeton, NJ: Princeton University Press.

Ferrera, M. (2006), 'Pension reforms in Southern Europe: the Italian experience', in H. Pemberton, P. Thane and N. Whiteside (eds), *Britain's Pension Crisis* (pp. 208–22), Oxford: Oxford University Press.

Ferrera, M. and Jessoula, M. (2007), 'Italy: a narrow gate for path-shift', in E.M. Immergut, K.M. Anderson and I. Schulze (eds), *Handbook of West European Pension Politics* (pp. 396–498), Oxford: Oxford University Press.

Goodin, R.E., Headey, B., Muffels, R. and Dirven, H-J. (1999), *The Real Worlds of Welfare Capitalism*, Cambridge: Cambridge University Press.

Lewis, J. (1992), 'Gender and the development of welfare regimes', *Journal of European Social Policy*, **2**(3), 159–73.

Lewis, J. (2001), 'The decline of the male breadwinner model: implications for work and care', *Social Politics*, **8**(2), 152–70.

Lewis, J. and Ostner, I. (1994), 'Gender and the evolution of European social policy', in S. Leibfried and P. Pierson (eds), *European Social Policy*, Washington, DC: Brookings Institute.

Meyer, T. and Bridgen, P. (forthcoming 2008), 'Class, gender and chance: the social division of welfare and British occupational pensions', *Ageing and Society*.

Meyer, T. and Pfau-Effinger, B. (2006), 'Gender arrangements and pension systems in Britain and Germany: tracing change over five decades', *International Journal of Ageing and Later Life*, **1**(2), 67–110, http://www.ep.liu.se/ej/ijal/.

Pensions Commission (2005), 'A new pensions settlement for the twenty-first century. The second report of the pensions commission', London: The Stationery Office, available online at http://www.pensionscommission.org.uk/publications/2005/annrep/annrep-index.asp, accessed November 2006.

PPI (2006), 'An evaluation of the White Paper state pension reform proposals', London: Pensions Policy Institute, available online at http://www.pensionspolicyinstitute.org.uk/uploadeddocuments/Nuffield/PPI_evaluation_of_WP_state_pension_reforms_20_July_2006.pdf, accessed October 2006.

Rowlingson, K. (2002), 'Private pension planning: the rhetoric of responsibility, the reality of insecurity', *Journal of Social Policy*, **31**(4), 623–42.

Sass, S. (1997), *The Promise of Private Pensions: The First Hundred Years*, Cambridge, MA: Harvard University Press.

Sass, S. (2006), 'Anglo-Saxon occupational pensions in international perspective', in H. Pemberton, P. Thane and N. Whiteside (eds), *Britain's Pension Crisis: History and Policy* (pp. 191–207), Oxford: Oxford University Press.

Whiteside, N. (2006), 'Occupational pensions and the search for security', in H. Pemberton, P. Thane and N. Whiteside (eds), *Britain's Pension Crisis: History and Policy* (pp. 125–39), Oxford: Oxford University Press.

Index